Java™ Coding Guidelines

The SEI Series in Software Engineering

Software Engineering Institute of Carnegie Mellon University and Addison-Wesley

 Software Engineering Institute | **Carnegie Mellon**

    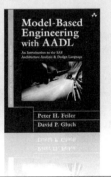

Visit **informit.com/sei** for a complete list of available publications.

The SEI Series in Software Engineering is a collaborative undertaking of the Carnegie Mellon Software Engineering Institute (SEI) and Addison-Wesley to develop and publish books on software engineering and related topics. The common goal of the SEI and Addison-Wesley is to provide the most current information on these topics in a form that is easily usable by practitioners and students.

Titles in the series describe frameworks, tools, methods, and technologies designed to help organizations, teams, and individuals improve their technical or management capabilities. Some books describe processes and practices for developing higher-quality software, acquiring programs for complex systems, or delivering services more effectively. Other books focus on software and system architecture and product-line development. Still others, from the SEI's CERT Program, describe technologies and practices needed to manage software and network security risk. These and all titles in the series address critical problems in software engineering for which practical solutions are available.

Make sure to connect with us!
informit.com/socialconnect

Addison Wesley | **informIT** | **Safari** Books Online

Java™ Coding Guidelines

75 Recommendations for Reliable and Secure Programs

Fred Long
Dhruv Mohindra
Robert C. Seacord
Dean F. Sutherland
David Svoboda

▲▼Addison-Wesley

Upper Saddle River, NJ • Boston • Indianapolis • San Francisco
New York • Toronto • Montreal • London • Munich • Paris • Madrid
Capetown • Sydney • Tokyo • Singapore • Mexico City

Software Engineering Institute | **Carnegie Mellon**

The SEI Series in Software Engineering

Many of the designations used by manufacturers and sellers to distinguish their products are claimed as trademarks. Where those designations appear in this book, and the publisher was aware of a trademark claim, the designations have been printed with initial capital letters or in all capitals.

CMM, CMMI, Capability Maturity Model, Capability Maturity Modeling, Carnegie Mellon, CERT, and CERT Coordination Center are registered in the U.S. Patent and Trademark Office by Carnegie Mellon University.

ATAM; Architecture Tradeoff Analysis Method; CMM Integration; COTS Usage-Risk Evaluation; CURE; EPIC; Evolutionary Process for Integrating COTS Based Systems; Framework for Software Product Line Practice; IDEAL; Interim Profile; OAR; OCTAVE; Operationally Critical Threat, Asset, and Vulnerability Evaluation; Options Analysis for Reengineering; Personal Software Process; PLTP; Product Line Technical Probe; PSP; SCAMPI; SCAMPI Lead Appraiser; SCAMPI Lead Assessor; SCE; SEI; SEPG; Team Software Process; and TSP are service marks of Carnegie Mellon University.

The authors and publisher have taken care in the preparation of this book, but make no expressed or implied warranty of any kind and assume no responsibility for errors or omissions. No liability is assumed for incidental or consequential damages in connection with or arising out of the use of the information or programs contained herein.

The publisher offers excellent discounts on this book when ordered in quantity for bulk purchases or special sales, which may include electronic versions and/or custom covers and content particular to your business, training goals, marketing focus, and branding interests. For more information, please contact:

U.S. Corporate and Government Sales
(800) 382-3419
corpsales@pearsontechgroup.com

For sales outside the United States, please contact:

International Sales
international@pearsoned.com

Visit us on the Web: informit.com/aw

Library of Congress Cataloging-in-Publication Data

Long, Fred, 1947-
    Java coding guidelines : 75 recommendations for reliable and secure programs / Fred Long, Dhruv Mohindra, Robert C. Seacord, Dean F. Sutherland, David Svoboda.
       pages   cm.—(The SEI series in software engineering)
    Includes bibliographical references and index.
    ISBN 978-0-321-93315-7 (pbk. : alk. paper)
1. Java (Computer program language) 2. Computer programming. I. Title.
QA76.73.J38L66 2014
005.2'762—dc23
                                                                                                      2013021384

ISBN-13:   978-0-321-93315-7
ISBN-10:   0-321-93315-X
Text printed in the United States on recycled paper at RR Donnelley in Crawfordsville, Indiana.
First printing, August 2013

Contents

Foreword

James A. Gosling

This set of *Java*™ *Coding Guidelines,* a follow-on to the earlier *The CERT® Oracle® Secure Coding Standard for Java*™, is invaluable. This book could almost be retitled *Reliable Java*™ *Coding Guidelines.* One of the things that has struck me over the years is the interplay between reliability and security. There are all sorts of explicit security tools—cryptography, authentication, and others—but most break-ins are exploitations of bugs: coding that was badly done or that was insufficiently defensive. Building a reliable system is, in many ways, equivalent to building a secure system. The work you do in reliability pays off in security, and vice versa.

This book highlights the fact that security is not a feature; it is an attitude toward taking due care at every point. It should be a continuous part of every software engineer's design thought process. It is organized around a list of guidelines. The meat of the book is the subtlety behind them. For example, "Store passwords using a hash function" appears to be a very basic and obvious point, and yet there are regular news articles about major data breaches just because some software engineer wasn't thinking. Getting it right is tricky: there are a lot of details for the devil to hide in. This book is full of excellent guidance for dealing with those details.

Preface

Java™ Coding Guidelines: 75 Recommendations for Reliable and Secure Programs provides specific advice to Java programmers. The application of these Java coding guidelines will lead to better systems that are more robust and more resistant to attack. These guidelines cover a wide range of products coded in Java for devices such as PCs, game players, mobile phones, tablets, home appliances, and automotive electronics.

Developers in any programming language should follow a set of guidelines to control the structures of their programs over and above what is specified by the programming language definition, and this is no less the case in Java.

Java programmers need more help than that provided by the Java Language Specification (JLS) [JLS 2013] to produce reliable and secure Java programs. Java contains language features and APIs that can easily be misused, and guidance is needed to avoid these pitfalls.

For a program to be *reliable*, it must work in all situations and in the face of all possible input. Inevitably, any nontrivial program will encounter a completely unexpected input or situation, and errors will occur. When such errors occur, it is important that the impact be limited, which is best achieved by localizing the error and dealing with it as soon as possible. Programmers can benefit from the experience of others in anticipating unusual input or programming situations and adopting a defensive style of programming.

Some of these guidelines may be deemed stylistic, but they are nonetheless important for readability and maintainability of the code. For Java, Oracle provides a set of code conventions [Conventions 2009] to help programmers produce a consistent programming style, and these conventions are widely adopted by Java programmers.

■ The CERT® Oracle® Secure Coding Standard for Java™

Java™ Coding Guidelines is written by the authors of The CERT® Oracle® Secure Coding Standard for Java™ [Long 2012]. That coding standard provides a set of rules for secure coding in the Java programming language. The goal of those rules is to eliminate insecure coding practices that can lead to exploitable vulnerabilities. The Secure Coding Standard establishes normative requirements for software systems. These software systems can then be evaluated for conformance to the coding standard, for example, by using the Source Code Analysis Laboratory (SCALe) [Seacord 2012]. However, there are poor Java coding practices that, despite not warranting inclusion in a secure coding standard for Java, can lead to unreliable or insecure programs. This book serves to document and warn against such coding practices.

Although not included in The CERT® Oracle® Secure Coding Standard for Java™, these guidelines should not be considered less important. Guidelines must be excluded from a coding standard when it is not possible to form a normative requirement. There are many reasons that a normative requirement cannot be formed. Perhaps the most common is that the rule depends on programmer intent. Such rules cannot be automatically enforced unless it is possible for the programmer's intent to be specified, in which case a rule could require consistency between the code and the specified intent. Forming a normative requirement also requires that a violation of that requirement represent a defect in the code. Guidelines have been excluded from the coding standard (but included in this book) in cases where compliance with the guideline is always a good idea, but violating the guideline does not always result in an error. This distinction is made because a system cannot be cited for nonconformance without a specific defect. Consequently, coding rules must be very narrowly defined. Coding guidelines can often have a more far-reaching impact on security and reliability just because they can be more broadly defined.

Many of the guidelines refer to rules in The CERT® Oracle® Secure Coding Standard for Java™. These references are of the form "IDS01-J. Normalize strings before validating them," where the first three letters of the reference identify the appropriate chapter of The CERT® Oracle® Secure Coding Standard for Java™. For example, IDS refers to Chapter 2, "Input Validation and Data Sanitization (IDS)."

The Secure Coding Standard for Java rules are also available on CERT's secure coding wiki at www.securecoding.cert.org, where they continue to evolve. The CERT® Oracle® Secure Coding Standard for Java™ provides the definition of the rules for conformance testing purposes, but the wiki may contain additional information or insights not included in the book that may help you interpret the meaning of these rules.

Cross-references to other guidelines throughout this book are given simply by the number and title of the guideline.

■ Scope

Java™ Coding Guidelines focuses on the Java SE 7 Platform environment, and includes guidelines that address the issue of secure coding using the Java SE 7 API. The Java Language Specification: Java SE 7 Edition (the JLS) [JLS 2013] prescribes the behavior of the Java programming language and serves as the primary reference for the development of these guidelines.

Traditional language standards, such as those for C and C++, include undefined, unspecified, and implementation-defined behaviors that can lead to vulnerabilities when a programmer makes incorrect assumptions about the portability of these behaviors. By contrast, the JLS more completely specifies language behaviors, because Java is designed to be a cross-platform language. Even then, certain behaviors are left to the discretion of the implementer of the Java Virtual Machine (JVM) or the Java compiler. These guidelines identify such language peculiarities, suggest solutions to help implementers address the issues, and let programmers appreciate and understand the limitations of the language and navigate around them.

Focusing only on language issues does not translate to writing reliable and secure software. Design issues in Java APIs sometimes lead to their deprecation. At other times, the APIs or the relevant documentation may be interpreted incorrectly by the programming community. These guidelines identify such problematic APIs, and highlight their correct use. Examples of commonly used faulty design patterns and idioms are also included.

The Java language, its core and extension APIs, and the JVM provide several security features, such as the security manager and access controller, cryptography, automatic memory management, strong type checking, and bytecode verification. These features provide sufficient security for most applications, but their proper use is of paramount importance. These guidelines highlight the pitfalls and caveats associated with the security architecture, and stress its correct implementation. Adherence to these guidelines safeguards trusted programs from a plethora of exploitable security bugs that can cause denial of service, information leaks, erroneous computations, and privilege escalation.

Included Libraries

Figure P–1 is a conceptual diagram of Oracle's Java SE products.

These coding guidelines address security issues primarily applicable to the `lang` and `util` base libraries as well as for "other base libraries." They avoid the inclusion of open bugs that have already been marked to be fixed or those that lack negative ramifications. A functional bug is included only if it is likely to occur with high frequency, causes considerable security or reliability concerns, or affects most Java technologies that rely on the core platform. These guidelines are not limited to secu-

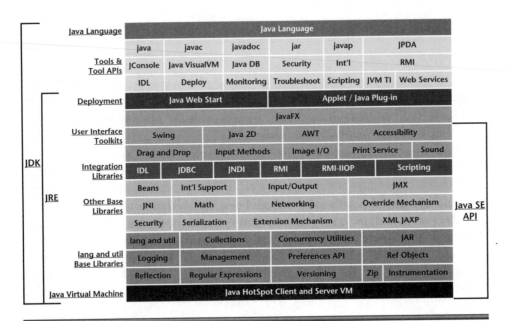

	Java Language					
Java Language	Java Language					
	java	javac	javadoc	jar	javap	JPDA
Tools & Tool APIs	JConsole	Java VisualVM	Java DB	Security	Int'l	RMI
	IDL	Deploy	Monitoring	Troubleshoot	Scripting	JVM TI · Web Services
Deployment	Java Web Start			Applet / Java Plug-in		
	JavaFX					
User Interface Toolkits	Swing		Java 2D	AWT	Accessibility	
	Drag and Drop		Input Methods	Image I/O	Print Service	Sound
Integration Libraries	IDL	JDBC	JNDI	RMI	RMI-IIOP	Scripting
	Beans	Int'l Support		Input/Output	JMX	
Other Base Libraries	JNI	Math		Networking	Override Mechanism	
	Security	Serialization		Extension Mechanism	XML JAXP	
	lang and util	Collections		Concurrency Utilities	JAR	
lang and util Base Libraries	Logging	Management		Preferences API	Ref Objects	
	Reflection	Regular Expressions		Versioning	Zip · Instrumentation	
Java Virtual Machine	Java HotSpot Client and Server VM					

JDK / JRE (left bracket) · Java SE API (right bracket)

Figure P–1. Conceptual diagram of Oracle's Java SE products. (From Oracle Java SE Documentation, http://docs.oracle.com/javase/7/docs/. Copyright © 1995, 2010, Oracle and/or its affiliates. All rights reserved.)

rity issues specific to the core API, but also include important reliability and security concerns pertaining to the standard extension APIs (`javax` package).

Demonstrating the full range of security features that Java offers requires studying interaction of code with other components and frameworks. Occasionally, the coding guidelines use examples from popular web and application frameworks such as Spring and Struts and technologies such as Java Server Pages (JSP) to highlight a security vulnerability that cannot be examined in isolation. Only when the standard API provides no option to mitigate a vulnerability are third-party libraries and solutions suggested.

Issues Not Addressed

A number of issues are not addressed by this secure coding standard.

Content

These coding guidelines apply broadly to all platforms; concerns specific to only one Java-based platform are beyond the scope of these guidelines. For example, guidelines that are applicable to Android, Java Micro Edition (ME), or Java Enterprise Edition (EE) alone and not to Java Standard Edition (SE) are typically excluded. In Java SE, APIs that deal with the user interface (user interface toolkits) or the web interface for providing features such as sound, graphical rendering, user account access control, session management, authentication, and authorization are beyond the scope of these guidelines. Nevertheless, the guidelines discuss networked Java systems in light of the risks associated with improper input validation and injection flaws and suggest appropriate mitigation strategies. These guidelines assume that the functional specification of the product correctly identifies and prevents higher-level design and architectural vulnerabilities.

Coding Style

Coding style issues are subjective; it has proven impossible to develop a consensus on appropriate style guidelines. Consequently, *Java™ Coding Guidelines* generally avoids requiring enforcement of any particular coding style. Instead, we suggest that the user define style guidelines and apply those guidelines consistently. The easiest way to consistently apply a coding style is with the use of a code formatting tool. Many integrated development environments (IDEs) provide such capabilities.

Tools

Many of these guidelines are not amenable to automatic detection or correction. In some cases, tool vendors may choose to implement checkers to identify violations of these guidelines. As a federally funded research and development center (FFRDC), the Software Engineering Institute (SEI) is not in a position to recommend particular vendors or tools for this purpose.

Controversial Guidelines

In general, *Java™ Coding Guidelines* tries to avoid the inclusion of controversial guidelines that lack a broad consensus.

Audience

Java™ Coding Guidelines is primarily intended for developers of Java language programs. Although these guidelines focus on the Java SE 7 Platform environment, they should also be informative (although incomplete) for Java developers working with Java ME or Java EE and other versions of the Java language.

While primarily designed for building reliable and secure systems, these guidelines are also useful for achieving other quality attributes such as safety, dependability, robustness, availability, and maintainability.

These guidelines may also be used by

- Developers of analyzer tools who wish to diagnose insecure or nonconforming Java language programs
- Software-development managers, software acquirers, or other software-development and acquisition specialists to establish a proscriptive set of secure coding standards
- Educators as a primary or secondary text for Java programming courses

Contents and Organization

Java™ Coding Guidelines consists of 75 guidelines organized around the following principles.

- Chapter 1, "Security," presents guidelines for ensuring the security of Java applications.

- Chapter 2, "Defensive Programming," contains guidelines for defensive programming so that the programmer can write code that protects itself from unexpected circumstances.

- Chapter 3, "Reliability," gives advice for improving the reliability and security of Java applications.

- Chapter 4, "Program Understandability," provides advice about making programs more readable and understandable.

- Chapter 5, "Programmer Misconceptions," exposes situations where Java language and programming concepts are often misunderstood.

Appendix A, "Android," describes the applicability of the guidelines in this book to developing Java apps for the Android platform. The book also contains a glossary of common terms and a list of references.

The guidelines have a consistent structure. The title and the introductory paragraphs define the essence of the guideline. This is typically followed by one or more pairs of noncompliant code examples and corresponding compliant solutions. Each guideline concludes with an applicability section and bibliographical references specific to that guideline.

Acknowledgments

This book was only made possible through a broad community effort. First, we would like to thank those who contributed guidelines to this book, including Ron Bandes, Jose Sandoval Chaverri, Ryan Hall, Fei He, Ryan Hofler, Sam Kaplan, Michael Kross, Christopher Leonavicius, Bocong Liu, Bastian Marquis, Aniket Mokashi, Jonathan Paulson, Michael Rosenman, Tamir Sen, John Truelove, and Matthew Wiethoff.

The following people also contributed to this work, and their efforts are greatly appreciated: James Ahlborn, Neelkamal Gaharwar, Ankur Goyal, Tim Halloran, Sujay Jain, Pranjal Jumde, Justin Loo, Yitzhak Mandelbaum, Todd Nowacki, Vishal Patel, Justin Pincar, Abhishek Ramani, Brendon Saulsbury, Kirk Sayre, Glenn Stroz, Yozo Toda, and Shishir Kumar Yadav. We would also like to thank Hiroshi Kumagai and JPCERT for their work on the Android appendix.

We would also like to thank the following reviewers: Thomas Hawtin, Dan Plakosh, and Steve Scholnick.

We would also like to thank SEI and CERT managers who encouraged and supported our efforts: Archie Andrews, Rich Pethia, Greg Shannon, and Bill Wilson.

Thanks also to our editor Peter Gordon and his team at Addison-Wesley: Kim Boedigheimer, Jennifer Bortel, John Fuller, Stephane Nakib, and Julie Nahil. Thanks also to project editor Anna Popick and copy editor Melinda Rankin.

We thank the remainder of the CERT team for their support and assistance, without which this book could not have been completed. And last but not least, we would like to thank our in-house editor, Carol J. Lallier, who helped make this work possible.

About the Authors

 **Fred Long** is a senior lecturer in the Department of Computer Science at Aberystwyth University in the United Kingdom. He lectures on formal methods; Java, C++, and C programming; and programming-related security issues. He is chairman of the British Computer Society's mid-Wales branch. Fred has been a visiting scientist at the Software Engineering Institute since 1992. Recently, his research has involved the investigation of vulnerabilities in Java. Fred is a coauthor of *The CERT® Oracle® Secure Coding Standard for Java™* (Addison-Wesley, 2012).

 **Dhruv Mohindra** is a technical lead in the security practices group that is part of the CTO's office at Persistent Systems Limited, India, where he provides information security consulting solutions across various technology verticals such as cloud, collaboration, banking and finance, telecommunications, enterprise, mobility, life sciences, and health care. He regularly consults for senior management and development teams of Fortune 500 companies, small and medium-sized enterprises, and start-ups on information security best practices and embedding security in the software-development life cycle.

Dhruv has worked for CERT at the Software Engineering Institute and continues to collaborate to improve the state of security awareness in the programming community. Dhruv obtained his M.S. in information security policy and management from Carnegie Mellon University. He holds an undergraduate degree in computer engineering from Pune University, India. Dhruv is also a coauthor of *The CERT® Oracle® Secure Coding Standard for Java™* (Addison-Wesley, 2012).

Robert C. Seacord is the secure coding technical manager in the CERT Division of Carnegie Mellon's Software Engineering Institute (SEI) in Pittsburgh, Pennsylvania. Robert is also a professor in the School of Computer Science and the Information Networking Institute at Carnegie Mellon University. He is the author of *The CERT® C Secure Coding Standard* (Addison-Wesley, 2009) and coauthor of *Building Systems from Commercial Components* (Addison-Wesley, 2002), *Modernizing Legacy Systems* (Addison-Wesley, 2003), *The CERT® Oracle® Secure Coding Standard for Java™* (Addison-Wesley, 2012), and *Secure Coding in C and C++, Second Edition* (Addison-Wesley, 2013). He has also published more than sixty papers on software security, component-based software engineering, web-based system design, legacy-system modernization, component repositories and search engines, and user interface design and development. Robert has been teaching *Secure Coding in C and C++* to private industry, academia, and government since 2005. He started programming professionally for IBM in 1982, working in communications and operating system software, processor development, and software engineering. Robert also has worked at the X Consortium, where he developed and maintained code for the Common Desktop Environment and the X Window System. He represents CMU at the ISO/IEC JTC1/SC22/WG14 international standardization working group for the C programming language.

Dean F. Sutherland is a senior software security engineer at CERT. Dean received his Ph.D. in software engineering from Carnegie Mellon in 2008. Before his return to academia, he spent 14 years working as a professional software engineer at Tartan, Inc. He spent the last six of those years as a senior member of the technical staff and a technical lead for compiler backend technology. He was the primary active member of the corporate R&D group, was a key instigator of the design and deployment of a new software-development process for Tartan, led R&D projects, and provided both technical and project leadership for the 12-person compiler backend group. Dean is a coauthor of *The CERT® Oracle® Secure Coding Standard for Java™* (Addison-Wesley, 2012).

**David Svoboda** is a software security engineer at CERT/ SEI and a coauthor of *The CERT® Oracle® Secure Coding Standard for Java™*. He also maintains the CERT secure coding standard web sites for Java, as well as C, C++, and Perl. David has been the primary developer on a diverse set of software-development projects at Carnegie Mellon since 1991, ranging from hierarchical chip modeling and social organization simulation to automated machine translation (AMT). His KANTOO AMT software, developed in 1996, is still in production use at Caterpillar. He has more than thirteen years of Java development experience, starting with Java 2, and his Java projects include Tomcat servlets and Eclipse plug-ins. He has taught *Secure Coding in C and C++* all over the world to various groups in the military, government, and banking industries. David is also an active participant in the ISO/IEC JTC1/SC22/WG14 working group for the C programming language and the ISO/IEC JTC1/SC22/WG21 working group for C++.

Chapter 1

Security

The Java programming language and runtime system were designed with security in mind. For example, pointer manipulation is implicit and hidden from the programmer, and any attempt to reference a null pointer results in an exception being thrown. Similarly, an exception results from any attempt to access an array or a string outside of its bounds. Java is a strongly typed language, and all implicit type conversions are well defined and platform independent, as are the arithmetic types and conversions. The Java Virtual Machine (JVM) has a built-in bytecode verifier to ensure that the bytecode being run conforms to the Java Language Specification: Java SE 7 Edition (JLS) so that all the checks defined in the language are in place and cannot be circumvented.

The Java class loader mechanism identifies classes as they are loaded into the JVM, and can distinguish between trusted system classes and other classes that may not be trusted. Classes from external sources can be given privileges by digitally signing them; these digital signatures can also be examined by the class loader, and contribute to the class's identification. Java also provides an extensible fine-grained security mechanism that enables the programmer to control access to resources such as system information, files, sockets, and any other security-sensitive resources that the programmer wishes to use. This security mechanism can require that a runtime security manager be in place to enforce a security policy. A security manager and its security policy are usually specified by command-line arguments, but they may be installed programmatically, provided that such an action is not already disallowed by an existing security policy. Privileges to access resources may be extended to nonsystem Java classes by relying on the identification provided by the class loader mechanism.

Enterprise Java applications are susceptible to attacks because they accept untrusted input and interact with complex subsystems. Injection attacks (such as cross-site scripting [XSS], XPath, and LDAP injection) are possible when the components susceptible to these attacks are used in the application. An effective mitigation strategy is to whitelist input, and encode or escape output before it is processed for rendering.

This chapter contains guidelines that are concerned specifically with ensuring the security of Java-based applications. Guidelines dealing with the following security nuances are articulated.

1. Dealing with sensitive data

2. Avoiding common injection attacks

3. Language features that can be misused to compromise security

4. Details of Java's fine-grained security mechanism

■ 1. Limit the lifetime of sensitive data

Sensitive data in memory can be vulnerable to compromise. An adversary who can execute code on the same system as an application may be able to access such data if the application

■ Uses objects to store sensitive data whose contents are not cleared or garbage-collected after use

■ Has memory pages that can be swapped out to disk as required by the operating system (for example, to perform memory management tasks or to support hibernation)

■ Holds sensitive data in a buffer (such as `BufferedReader`) that retains copies of the data in the OS cache or in memory

■ Bases its control flow on reflection that allows countermeasures to circumvent the limiting of the lifetime of sensitive variables

■ Reveals sensitive data in debugging messages, log files, environment variables, or through thread and core dumps

Sensitive data leaks become more likely if the memory containing the data is not cleared after using the data. To limit the risk of exposure, programs must minimize the lifetime of sensitive data.

Complete mitigation (that is, foolproof protection of data in memory) requires support from the underlying operating system and Java Virtual Machine. For example, if swapping sensitive data out to disk is an issue, a secure operating system that disables swapping and hibernation is required.

Noncompliant Code Example

This noncompliant code example reads user name and password information from the console and stores the password as a String object. The credentials remain exposed until the garbage collector reclaims the memory associated with this String.

```java
class Password {
  public static void main (String args[]) throws IOException {
    Console c = System.console();
    if (c == null) {
      System.err.println("No console.");
      System.exit(1);
    }

    String username = c.readLine("Enter your user name: ");
    String password = c.readLine("Enter your password: ");

    if (!verify(username, password)) {
      throw new SecurityException("Invalid Credentials");
    }

    // ...
  }

  // Dummy verify method, always returns true
  private static final boolean verify(String username,
      String password) {
    return true;
  }
}
```

Compliant Solution

This compliant solution uses the Console.readPassword() method to obtain the password from the console.

```java
class Password {
  public static void main (String args[]) throws IOException {
    Console c = System.console();

    if (c == null) {
      System.err.println("No console.");
      System.exit(1);
    }

    String username = c.readLine("Enter your user name: ");
    char[] password = c.readPassword("Enter your password: ");
```

```
    if (!verify(username, password)) {
      throw new SecurityException("Invalid Credentials");
    }

    // Clear the password
    Arrays.fill(password, ' ');
  }

  // Dummy verify method, always returns true
  private static final boolean verify(String username,
      char[] password) {
    return true;
  }
}
```

The `Console.readPassword()` method allows the password to be returned as a sequence of characters rather than as a `String` object. Consequently, the programmer can clear the password from the array immediately after use. This method also disables echoing of the password to the console.

Noncompliant Code Example

This noncompliant code example uses a `BufferedReader` to wrap an `InputStream-Reader` object so that sensitive data can be read from a file:

```
void readData() throws IOException{
  BufferedReader br = new BufferedReader(new InputStreamReader(
    new FileInputStream("file")));
  // Read from the file
  String data = br.readLine();
}
```

The `BufferedReader.readLine()` method returns the sensitive data as a `String` object, which can persist long after the data is no longer needed. The `BufferedReader` `.read(char[], int, int)` method can read and populate a `char` array. However, it requires the programmer to manually clear the sensitive data in the array after use. Alternatively, even if the `BufferedReader` were to wrap a `FileReader` object, it would suffer from the same pitfalls.

Compliant Solution

This compliant solution uses a directly allocated NIO (new I/O) buffer to read sensitive data from the file. The data can be cleared immediately after use and is not cached or buffered in multiple locations. It exists only in the system memory.

```
void readData(){
  ByteBuffer buffer = ByteBuffer.allocateDirect(16 * 1024);
  try (FileChannel rdr =
       (new FileInputStream("file")).getChannel()) {
    while (rdr.read(buffer) > 0) {
      // Do something with the buffer
      buffer.clear();
    }
  } catch (Throwable e) {
    // Handle error
  }
}
```

Note that manual clearing of the buffer data is mandatory because direct buffers are not garbage collected.

Applicability

Failure to limit the lifetime of sensitive data can lead to information leaks.

Bibliography

[API 2013]	Class ByteBuffer
[Oracle 2013b]	"Reading ASCII Passwords from an InputStream Example" from the Java Cryptography Architecture [JCA] Reference Guide
[Tutorials 2013]	I/O from the Command Line

■ 2. Do not store unencrypted sensitive information on the client side

When building an application that uses a client–server model, storing sensitive information, such as user credentials, on the client side may result in its unauthorized disclosure if the client is vulnerable to attack.

For web applications, the most common mitigation to this problem is to provide the client with a cookie and store the sensitive information on the server. Cookies are created by a web server, and are stored for a period of time on the client. When the client reconnects to the server, it provides the cookie, which identifies the client to the server, and the server then provides the sensitive information.

Cookies do not protect sensitive information against cross-site scripting (XSS) attacks. An attacker who is able to obtain a cookie either through an XSS attack, or directly by attacking the client, can obtain the sensitive information from the server using the cookie. This risk is timeboxed if the server invalidates the session after a limited time has elapsed, such as 15 minutes.

A cookie is typically a short string. If it contains sensitive information, that information should be encrypted. Sensitive information includes user names, passwords, credit card numbers, social security numbers, and any other personally identifiable information about the user. For more details about managing passwords, see Guideline 13, "Store passwords using a hash function." For more information about securing the memory that holds sensitive information, see Guideline 1, "Limit the lifetime of sensitive data."

Noncompliant Code Example

In this noncompliant code example, the login servlet stores the user name and password in the cookie to identify the user for subsequent requests:

```java
protected void doPost(HttpServletRequest request,
    HttpServletResponse response) {

  // Validate input (omitted)

  String username = request.getParameter("username");
  char[] password =
    request.getParameter("password").toCharArray();
  boolean rememberMe =
    Boolean.valueOf(request.getParameter("rememberme"));

  LoginService loginService = new LoginServiceImpl();

  if (rememberMe) {
    if (request.getCookies()[0] != null &&
      request.getCookies()[0].getValue() != null) {
      String[] value =
        request.getCookies()[0].getValue().split(";");

      if (!loginService.isUserValid(value[0],
          value[1].toCharArray())) {
        // Set error and return
      } else {
        // Forward to welcome page
      }
    } else {
      boolean validated =
        loginService.isUserValid(username, password);
```

```
   if (validated) {
     Cookie loginCookie = new Cookie("rememberme", username +
                    ";" + new String(password));
     response.addCookie(loginCookie);
     // ... forward to welcome page
   } else {
     // Set error and return
   }
 }
} else {
  // No remember-me functionality selected
  // Proceed with regular authentication;
  // if it fails set error and return
}

Arrays.fill(password, ' ');
}
```

However, the attempt to implement the remember-me functionality is insecure because an attacker with access to the client machine can obtain this information directly on the client. This code also violates Guideline 13, "Store passwords using a hash function."

Compliant Solution (Session)

This compliant solution implements the remember-me functionality by storing the user name and a secure random string in the cookie. It also maintains state in the session using HttpSession:

```
protected void doPost(HttpServletRequest request,
  HttpServletResponse response) {

  // Validate input (omitted)

  String username = request.getParameter("username");
  char[] password =
    request.getParameter("password").toCharArray();
  boolean rememberMe =
    Boolean.valueOf(request.getParameter("rememberme"));
  LoginService loginService = new LoginServiceImpl();
  boolean validated = false;
  if (rememberMe) {
    if (request.getCookies()[0] != null &&
      request.getCookies()[0].getValue() != null) {
```

```
    String[] value =
      request.getCookies()[0].getValue().split(";");

    if (value.length != 2) {
      // Set error and return
    }

    if (!loginService.mappingExists(value[0], value[1])) {
      // (username, random) pair is checked
      // Set error and return
    }
  } else {
    validated = loginService.isUserValid(username, password);

    if (!validated) {
      // Set error and return
    }
  }

  String newRandom = loginService.getRandomString();
  // Reset the random every time
  loginService.mapUserForRememberMe(username, newRandom);
  HttpSession session = request.getSession();
  session.invalidate();
  session = request.getSession(true);
  // Set session timeout to 15 minutes
  session.setMaxInactiveInterval(60 * 15);
  // Store user attribute and a random attribute
  // in session scope
  session.setAttribute("user", loginService.getUsername());
  Cookie loginCookie =
    new Cookie("rememberme", username + ";" + newRandom);
  response.addCookie(loginCookie);
  //... forward to welcome page
} else { // No remember-me functionality selected
  //... authenticate using isUserValid(),
  // and if failed, set error
}
Arrays.fill(password, ' ');
}
```

The server maintains a mapping between user names and secure random strings. When a user selects "Remember me," the doPost() method checks whether the supplied cookie contains a valid user name and random string pair. If the mapping contains a matching pair, the server authenticates the user and forwards him or her to the welcome page. If not, the server returns an error to the client. If the user selects

"Remember me" but the client fails to supply a valid cookie, the server requires the user to authenticate using his or her credentials. If the authentication is successful, the server issues a new cookie with remember-me characteristics.

This solution avoids session-fixation attacks by invalidating the current session and creating a new session. It also reduces the window during which an attacker could perform a session-hijacking attack by setting the session timeout to 15 minutes between client accesses.

Applicability

Storing unencrypted sensitive information on the client makes this information available to anyone who can attack the client.

Bibliography

[Oracle 2011c]	Package `javax.servlet.http`
[OWASP 2009]	Session Fixation in Java
[OWASP 2011]	Cross-Site Scripting (XSS)
[W3C 2003]	The World Wide Web Security FAQ

■ 3. Provide sensitive mutable classes with unmodifiable wrappers

Immutability of fields prevents inadvertent modification as well as malicious tampering so that defensive copying while accepting input or returning values is unnecessary. However, some sensitive classes cannot be immutable. Fortunately, read-only access to mutable classes can be granted to untrusted code using unmodifiable wrappers. For example, the `Collection` classes include a set of wrappers that allow clients to observe an unmodifiable view of a `Collection` object.

Noncompliant Code Example

This noncompliant code example consists of class `Mutable`, which allows the internal array object to be modified:

```
class Mutable {
  private int[] array = new int[10];

  public int[] getArray() {
    return array;
  }
```

```
  public void setArray(int[] i) {
    array = i;
  }
}

//...
private Mutable mutable = new Mutable();
public Mutable getMutable() {return mutable;}
```

An untrusted invoker may call the mutator method `setArray()`, and violate the object's immutability property. Invoking the getter method `getArray()` also allows modification of the private internal state of the class. This class also violates *The CERT® Oracle® Secure Coding Standard for Java™* [Long 2012], "OBJ05-J. Defensively copy private mutable class members before returning their references."

Noncompliant Code Example

This noncompliant code example extends the `Mutable` class with a `MutableProtector` subclass:

```
class MutableProtector extends Mutable {
  @Override
  public int[] getArray() {
    return super.getArray().clone();
  }
}
// ...
private Mutable mutable = new MutableProtector();
// May be safely invoked by untrusted caller having read ability
public Mutable getMutable() {return mutable;}
```

In this class, invoking the getter method `getArray()` does not allow modification of the private internal state of the class, in accordance with "OBJ05-J. Defensively copy private mutable class members before returning their references" [Long 2012]. However, an untrusted invoker may call the method `setArray()` and modify the `Mutable` object.

Compliant Solution

In general, sensitive classes can be transformed into safe-view objects by providing appropriate wrappers for all methods defined by the core interface, including the mutator methods. The wrappers for the mutator methods must throw an `UnsupportedOperationException` so that clients cannot perform operations that affect the immutability property of the object.

This compliant solution adds a setArray() method that overrides the Mutable .setArray() method and prevents mutation of the Mutable object:

```
class MutableProtector extends Mutable {
  @Override
  public int[] getArray() {
    return super.getArray().clone();
  }

  @Override
  public void setArray(int[] i) {
    throw new UnsupportedOperationException();
  }
}

// ...
private Mutable mutable = new MutableProtector();
// May be safely invoked by untrusted caller having read ability
public Mutable getMutable() {return mutable; }
```

The MutableProtector wrapper class overrides the getArray() method and clones the array. Although the calling code gets a copy of the mutable object's array, the original array remains unchanged and inaccessible. The overriding setArray() method throws an exception if the caller attempts to use this method on the returned object. This object can be passed to untrusted code when read access to the data is permissible.

Applicability

Failure to provide an unmodifiable, safe view of a sensitive mutable object to untrusted code can lead to malicious tampering and corruption of the object.

Bibliography

[Long 2012]   OBJ05-J. Defensively copy private mutable class members before returning their references

[Tutorials 2013]   Unmodifiable Wrappers

■ 4. Ensure that security-sensitive methods are called with validated arguments

Application code that calls security-sensitive methods must validate the arguments being passed to the methods. In particular, null values may be interpreted as benign by certain security-sensitive methods but may override default settings.

Although security-sensitive methods should be coded defensively, the client code must validate arguments that the method might otherwise accept as valid. Failure to do so can result in privilege escalation and execution of arbitrary code.

Noncompliant Code Example

This noncompliant code example shows the two-argument doPrivileged() method that takes an access control context as the second argument. This code restores privileges from a previously saved context.

```
AccessController.doPrivileged(
  new PrivilegedAction<Void>() {
    public Void run() {
      // ...
    }
  }, accessControlContext);
```

When passed a null access control context, the two-argument doPrivileged() method fails to reduce the current privileges to those of the previously saved context. Consequently, this code can grant excess privileges when the accessControlContext argument is null. Programmers who intend to call AccessController.doPrivileged() with a null access control context should explicitly pass the null constant or use the one-argument version of AccessController.doPrivileged().

Compliant Solution

This compliant solution prevents granting of excess privileges by ensuring that accessControlContext is non-null:

```
if (accessControlContext == null) {
  throw new SecurityException("Missing AccessControlContext");
}
AccessController.doPrivileged(
  new PrivilegedAction<Void>() {
    public Void run() {
      // ...
    }
  }, accessControlContext);
```

Applicability

Security-sensitive methods must be thoroughly understood and their parameters validated to prevent corner cases with unexpected argument values (such as null arguments). If unexpected argument values are passed to security-sensitive methods, arbitrary code execution becomes possible, and privilege escalation becomes likely.

Bibliography

[API 2013]   `AccessController.doPrivileged(), System.setSecurityManager()`

■ 5. Prevent arbitrary file upload

Java applications, including web applications, that accept file uploads must ensure that an attacker cannot upload or transfer malicious files. If a restricted file containing code is executed by the target system, it can compromise application-layer defenses. For example, an application that permits HTML files to be uploaded could allow malicious code to be executed—an attacker can submit a valid HTML file with a cross-site scripting (XSS) payload that will execute in the absence of an output-escaping routine. For this reason, many applications restrict the type of files that can be uploaded.

It may also be possible to upload files with dangerous extensions such as `.exe` and `.sh` that could cause arbitrary code execution on server-side applications. An application that restricts only the Content-Type field in the HTTP header could be vulnerable to such an attack.

To support file upload, a typical Java Server Pages (JSP) page consists of code such as the following:

```
<s:form action="doUpload" method="POST"
   enctype="multipart/form-data">
 <s:file name="uploadFile" label="Choose File" size="40" />
 <s:submit value="Upload" name="submit" />
</s:form>
```

Many Java enterprise frameworks provide configuration settings intended to be used as a defense against arbitrary file upload. Unfortunately, most of them fail to provide adequate protection. Mitigation of this vulnerability involves checking file size, content type, and file contents, among other metadata attributes.

Noncompliant Code Example

This noncompliant code example shows XML code from the upload action of a Struts 2 application. The interceptor code is responsible for allowing file uploads.

```
<action name="doUpload" class="com.example.UploadAction">
  <interceptor-ref name="fileUpload">
    <param name="maximumSize"> 10240 </param>
    <param name="allowedTypes">
      text/plain,image/JPEG,text/html
    </param>
  </interceptor-ref>
</action>
```

The code for file upload appears in the `UploadAction` class:

```
public class UploadAction extends ActionSupport {
  private File uploadedFile;
  // setter and getter for uploadedFile

  public String execute() {
    try {
      // File path and file name are hardcoded for illustration
      File fileToCreate = new File("filepath", "filename");
      // Copy temporary file content to this file
      FileUtils.copyFile(uploadedFile, fileToCreate);
      return "SUCCESS";
    } catch (Throwable e) {
      addActionError(e.getMessage());
      return "ERROR";
    }
  }
}
```

The value of the parameter type `maximumSize` ensures that a particular `Action` cannot receive a very large file. The `allowedTypes` parameter defines the type of files that are accepted. However, this approach fails to ensure that the uploaded file conforms to the security requirements because interceptor checks can be trivially bypassed. If an attacker were to use a proxy tool to change the content type in the raw HTTP request in transit, the framework would fail to prevent the file's upload. Consequently, an attacker could upload a malicious file that has a **.exe** extension, for example.

Compliant Solution

The file upload must succeed only when the content type matches the actual content of the file. For example, a file with an image header must contain only an image and must not contain executable code. This compliant solution uses the Apache Tika library [Apache 2013] to detect and extract metadata and structured text

content from documents using existing parser libraries. The checkMetaData()
method must be called before invoking code in execute() that is responsible for
uploading the file.

```java
public class UploadAction extends ActionSupport {
  private File uploadedFile;
  // setter and getter for uploadedFile

  public String execute() {
    try {
      // File path and file name are hardcoded for illustration
      File fileToCreate = new File("filepath", "filename");

      boolean textPlain = checkMetaData(uploadedFile,
        "text/plain");
      boolean img = checkMetaData(uploadedFile, "image/JPEG");
      boolean textHtml = checkMetaData(uploadedFile,
        "text/html");

      if (!textPlain || !img || !textHtml) {
        return "ERROR";
      }

      // Copy temporary file content to this file
      FileUtils.copyFile(uploadedFile, fileToCreate);
      return "SUCCESS";
    } catch (Throwable e) {
      addActionError(e.getMessage());
      return "ERROR";
    }
  }

  public static boolean checkMetaData(
    File f, String getContentType) {
    try (InputStream is = new FileInputStream(f)) {
      ContentHandler contenthandler = new BodyContentHandler();
      Metadata metadata = new Metadata();
      metadata.set(Metadata.RESOURCE_NAME_KEY, f.getName());
      Parser parser = new AutoDetectParser();
      try {
        parser.parse(is, contenthandler,
                  metadata, new ParseContext());
      } catch (SAXException | TikaException e) {
        // Handle error
        return false;
      }
```

```
        if (metadata.get(Metadata.CONTENT_TYPE).equalsIgnoreCase(
            getContentType)) {
          return true;
        } else {
          return false;
        }
      } catch (IOException e) {
        // Handle error
        return false;
      }
    }
  }
```

The `AutoDetectParser` selects the best available parser on the basis of the content type of the file to be parsed.

Applicability

An arbitrary file upload vulnerability could result in privilege escalation and the execution of arbitrary code.

Bibliography

[Apache 2013]   Apache Tika: A Content Analysis Toolkit

■ 6. Properly encode or escape output

Proper input sanitization can prevent insertion of malicious data into a subsystem such as a database. However, different subsystems require different types of sanitization. Fortunately, it is usually obvious which subsystems will eventually receive which inputs, and consequently what type of sanitization is required.

Several subsystems exist for the purpose of outputting data. An HTML renderer is one common subsystem for displaying output. Data sent to an output subsystem may appear to originate from a trusted source. However, it is dangerous to assume that output sanitization is unnecessary, because such data may indirectly originate from an *untrusted* source and may include malicious content. Failure to properly sanitize data passed to an output subsystem can allow several types of attacks. For example, HTML renderers are prone to HTML injection and cross-site scripting (XSS) attacks [OWASP 2011]. Output sanitization to prevent such attacks is as vital as input sanitization.

As with input validation, data should be normalized before sanitizing it for malicious characters. Properly encode all output characters other than those known to be safe to avoid vulnerabilities caused by data that bypasses validation. See *The CERT® Oracle® Secure Coding Standard for Java™* [Long 2012], "IDS01-J. Normalize strings before validating them," for more information.

Noncompliant Code Example

This noncompliant code example uses the model–view–controller (MVC) concept of the Java EE–based Spring Framework to display data to the user without encoding or escaping it. Because the data is sent to a web browser, the code is subject to both HTML injection and XSS attacks.

```
@RequestMapping("/getnotifications.htm")
public ModelAndView getNotifications(
  HttpServletRequest request, HttpServletResponse response) {
  ModelAndView mv = new ModelAndView();
  try {
    UserInfo userDetails = getUserInfo();
    List<Map<String,Object>> list =
      new ArrayList<Map<String, Object>>();
    List<Notification> notificationList =
      NotificationService.getNotificationsForUserId(
        userDetails.getPersonId());

    for (Notification notification: notificationList) {
      Map<String,Object> map = new HashMap<String, Object>();
      map.put("id", notification.getId());
      map.put("message", notification.getMessage());
      list.add(map);
    }

    mv.addObject("Notifications", list);
  } catch (Throwable t) {
    // Log to file and handle
  }

  return mv;
}
```

Compliant Solution

This compliant solution defines a ValidateOutput class that normalizes the output to a known character set, performs output sanitization using a whitelist, and encodes any unspecified data values to enforce a double-checking mechanism. Note that the required whitelisting patterns will vary according to the specific needs of different fields [OWASP 2013].

```java
public class ValidateOutput {
  // Allows only alphanumeric characters and spaces
  private static final Pattern pattern =
    Pattern.compile("^[a-zA-Z0-9\\s]{0,20}$");

  // Validates and encodes the input field based on a whitelist
  public String validate(String name, String input)
      throws ValidationException {
    String canonical = normalize(input);

    if (!pattern.matcher(canonical).matches()) {
      throw new ValidationException("Improper format in " +
                                    name + " field");
    }

    // Performs output encoding for nonvalid characters
    canonical = HTMLEntityEncode(canonical);
    return canonical;
  }

  // Normalizes to known instances
  private String normalize(String input) {
    String canonical =
      java.text.Normalizer.normalize(input,
        Normalizer.Form.NFKC);
    return canonical;
  }

  // Encodes nonvalid data
  private static String HTMLEntityEncode(String input) {
    StringBuffer sb = new StringBuffer();

    for (int i = 0; i < input.length(); i++) {
      char ch = input.charAt(i);
      if (Character.isLetterOrDigit(ch) ||
          Character.isWhitespace(ch)) {
        sb.append(ch);
      } else {
        sb.append("&#" + (int)ch + ";");
      }
    }
    return sb.toString();
  }
}
```

```
// ...

@RequestMapping("/getnotifications.htm")
public ModelAndView getNotifications(HttpServletRequest request,
   HttpServletResponse response) {
 ValidateOutput vo = new ValidateOutput();

 ModelAndView mv = new ModelAndView();
 try {
   UserInfo userDetails = getUserInfo();
   List<Map<String,Object>> list =
     new ArrayList<Map<String,Object>>();
   List<Notification> notificationList =
     NotificationService.getNotificationsForUserId(
       serDetails.getPersonId());

   for (Notification notification: notificationList) {
     Map<String,Object> map = new HashMap<String,Object>();
     map.put("id", vo.validate("id" ,notification.getId()));
     map.put("message",
       vo.validate("message", notification.getMessage()));
     list.add(map);
   }

   mv.addObject("Notifications", list);
 }
 catch (Throwable t) {
   // Log to file and handle
 }

 return mv;
}
```

Output encoding and escaping is mandatory when accepting dangerous characters such as double quotes and angle braces. Even when input is whitelisted to disallow such characters, output escaping is recommended because it provides a second
level of defense. Note that the exact escape sequence can vary depending on where
the output is embedded. For example, untrusted output may occur in an HTML value
attribute, CSS, URL, or script; the output encoding routine will be different in each
case. It is also impossible to securely use untrusted data in some contexts. Consult the
OWASP XSS (Cross-Site Scripting) Prevention Cheat Sheet for more information on
preventing XSS attacks (www.owasp.org/index.php/XSS_Prevention_Cheat_Sheet).

Applicability

Failure to encode or escape output before it is displayed or passed across a trust boundary can result in the execution of arbitrary code.

Related Vulnerabilities

The Apache GERONIMO-1474 vulnerability, reported in January 2006, allowed attackers to submit URLs containing JavaScript. The Web Access Log Viewer failed to sanitize the data it forwarded to the administrator console, thereby enabling a classic XSS attack.

Bibliography

[Long 2012]	IDS01-J. Normalize strings before validating them
[OWASP 2011]	Cross-Site Scripting (XSS)
[OWASP 2013]	How to Add Validation Logic to `HttpServletRequest` XSS (Cross-Site Scripting) Prevention Cheat Sheet

■ 7. Prevent code injection

Code injection can occur when untrusted input is injected into dynamically constructed code. One obvious source of potential vulnerabilities is the use of JavaScript from Java code. The `javax.script` package consists of interfaces and classes that define Java scripting engines and a framework for the use of those interfaces and classes in Java code. Misuse of the `javax.script` API permits an attacker to execute arbitrary code on the target system.

This guideline is a specific instance of *The CERT® Oracle® Secure Coding Standard for Java™* [Long 2012], "IDS00-J. Sanitize untrusted data passed across a trust boundary."

Noncompliant Code Example

This noncompliant code example incorporates untrusted user input into a JavaScript statement that is responsible for printing the input:

```java
private static void evalScript(String firstName)
    throws ScriptException {
  ScriptEngineManager manager = new ScriptEngineManager();
  ScriptEngine engine = manager.getEngineByName("javascript");
  engine.eval("print('"+ firstName + "')");
}
```

An attacker can enter a specially crafted argument in an attempt to inject malicious JavaScript. This example shows a malicious string that contains JavaScript code that can create or overwrite an existing file on a vulnerable system.

```
dummy\');
var bw = new JavaImporter(java.io.BufferedWriter);
var fw = new JavaImporter(java.io.FileWriter);
with(fw) with(bw) {
  bwr = new BufferedWriter(new FileWriter(\"config.cfg\"));
  bwr.write(\"some text\"); bwr.close();
}
// ;
```

The script in this example prints "dummy" and then writes "some text" to a configuration file called config.cfg. An actual exploit can execute arbitrary code.

Compliant Solution (Whitelisting)

The best defense against code injection vulnerabilities is to prevent the inclusion of executable user input in code. User input used in dynamic code must be sanitized, for example, to ensure that it contains only valid, whitelisted characters. Santization is best performed immediately after the data has been input, using methods from the data abstraction used to store and process the data. Refer to "IDS00-J. Sanitize untrusted data passed across a trust boundary" [Long 2012] for more details. If special characters must be permitted in the name, they must be normalized before comparison with their equivalent forms for the purpose of input validation. This compliant solution uses whitelisting to prevent unsanitized input from being interpreted by the scripting engine.

```
private static void evalScript(String firstName)
   throws ScriptException {
  // Allow only alphanumeric and underscore chars in firstName
  // (modify if firstName may also include special characters)
  if (!firstName.matches("[\\w]*")) {
    // String does not match whitelisted characters
    throw new IllegalArgumentException();
  }

  ScriptEngineManager manager = new ScriptEngineManager();
  ScriptEngine engine = manager.getEngineByName("javascript");
  engine.eval("print('"+ firstName + "')");
}
```

Compliant Solution (Secure Sandbox)

An alternative approach is to create a secure sandbox using a security manager (see Guideline 20, "Create a secure sandbox using a security manager"). The application should prevent the script from executing arbitrary commands, such as querying the local file system. The two-argument form of doPrivileged() can be used to lower privileges when the application must operate with higher privileges, but the scripting engine must not. The RestrictedAccessControlContext reduces the permissions granted in the default policy file to those of the newly created protection domain. The effective permissions are the intersection of the permissions of the newly created protection domain and the systemwide security policy. Refer to Guideline 16, "Avoid granting excess privileges," for more details on the two-argument form of doPrivileged().

This compliant solution illustrates the use of an AccessControlContext in the two-argument form of doPrivileged().

```
class ACC {
  private static class RestrictedAccessControlContext {
    private static final AccessControlContext INSTANCE;

    static {
      INSTANCE =
        new AccessControlContext(
          new ProtectionDomain[] {
            new ProtectionDomain(null, null) // No permissions
          });
    }
  }

  private static void evalScript(final String firstName)
      throws ScriptException {
    ScriptEngineManager manager = new ScriptEngineManager();
    final ScriptEngine engine =
      manager.getEngineByName("javascript");
    // Restrict permission using the two-argument
    // form of doPrivileged()
    try {
      AccessController.doPrivileged(
        new PrivilegedExceptionAction<Object>() {

          public Object run() throws ScriptException {
            engine.eval("print('" + firstName + "')");
            return null;
          }
        },
        // From nested class
        RestrictedAccessControlContext.INSTANCE);
```

```
    } catch (PrivilegedActionException pae) {
      // Handle error
    }
  }
}
```

This approach can be combined with whitelisting for additional security.

Applicability

Failure to prevent code injection can result in the execution of arbitrary code.

Bibliography

[API 2013]	Package `javax.script`
[Long 2012]	IDS00-J. Sanitize untrusted data passed across a trust boundary
[OWASP 2013]	Code Injection in Java

■ 8. Prevent XPath injection

Extensible Markup Language (XML) can be used for data storage in a manner similar to a relational database. Data is frequently retrieved from such an XML document using XPaths. *XPath injection* can occur when data supplied to an XPath retrieval routine to retrieve data from an XML document is used without proper sanitization. This attack is similar to SQL injection or XML injection (see *The CERT® Oracle® Secure Coding Standard for Java™* [Long 2012], "IDS00-J. Sanitize untrusted data passed across a trust boundary"). An attacker can enter valid SQL or XML constructs in the data fields of the query in use. In typical attacks, the conditional field of the query resolves to a tautology or otherwise gives the attacker access to privileged information.

This guideline is a specific example of the broadly scoped Guideline 7, "Prevent code injection."

XML Path Injection Example

Consider the following XML schema.

```
<users>
  <user>
    <username>Utah</username>
    <password>e90205372a3b89e2</password>
  </user>
  <user>
```

```
     <username>Bohdi</username>
     <password>6c16b22029df4ec6</password>
  </user>
  <user>
     <username>Busey</username>
     <password>ad39b3c2a4dabc98</password>
  </user>
</users>
```

The passwords are hashed in compliance with Guideline 13, "Store passwords using a hash function." MD5 hashes are shown here for illustrative purposes; in practice, you should use a safer algorithm such as SHA-256.

Untrusted code may attempt to retrieve user details from this file with an XPath statement constructed dynamically from user input.

```
//users/user[username/text()='&LOGIN&' and
  password/text()='&PASSWORD&' ]
```

If an attacker knows that Utah is a valid user name, he or she can specify an input such as

```
Utah' or '1'='1
```

This yields the following query string.

```
//users/user[username/text()='Utah' or '1'='1'
  and password/text()='xxxx']
```

Because the '1'='1' is automatically true, the password is never validated. Consequently, the attacker is inappropriately authenticated as user Utah without knowing Utah's password.

Noncompliant Code Example

This noncompliant code example reads a user name and password from the user and uses them to construct the query string. The password is passed as a char array and then hashed. This example is vulnerable to the attack described earlier. If the attack string described earlier is passed to evaluate(), the method call returns the corresponding node in the XML file, causing the doLogin() method to return true and bypass any authorization.

```
private boolean doLogin(String userName, char[] password)
        throws ParserConfigurationException, SAXException,
            IOException, XPathExpressionException {
```

```
DocumentBuilderFactory domFactory =
  DocumentBuilderFactory.newInstance();
domFactory.setNamespaceAware(true);
DocumentBuilder builder = domFactory.newDocumentBuilder();
Document doc = builder.parse("users.xml");
String pwd = hashPassword( password);

XPathFactory factory = XPathFactory.newInstance();
XPath xpath = factory.newXPath();
XPathExpression expr =
  xpath.compile("//users/user[username/text()='" +
    userName + "' and password/text()='" + pwd + "' ]");
Object result = expr.evaluate(doc, XPathConstants.NODESET);
NodeList nodes = (NodeList) result;

// Print first names to the console
for (int i = 0; i < nodes.getLength(); i++) {
  Node node =
    nodes.item(i).getChildNodes().item(1).
      getChildNodes().item(0);
  System.out.println(
    "Authenticated: " + node.getNodeValue()
  );
}

return (nodes.getLength() >= 1);
}
```

Compliant Solution (XQuery)

XPath injection can be prevented by adopting defenses similar to those used to prevent SQL injection.

- Treat all user input as untrusted, and perform appropriate sanitization.
- When sanitizing user input, verify the correctness of the data type, length, format, and content. For example, use a regular expression that checks for XML tags and special characters in user input. This practice corresponds to input sanitization. See Guideline 7, "Prevent code injection," for additional details.
- In a client–server application, perform validation at both the client and the server sides.
- Extensively test applications that supply, propagate, or accept user input.

An effective technique for preventing the related issue of SQL injection is parameterization. Parameterization ensures that user-specified data is passed to an API as a parameter such that the data is never interpreted as executable content. Unfortunately, Java SE currently lacks an analogous interface for XPath queries. However, an XPath analog to SQL parameterization can be emulated by using an interface such as XQuery that supports specifying a query statement in a separate file supplied at runtime.

Input File: login.xq

```
declare variable $userName as xs:string external;
declare variable $password as xs:string external;
//users/user[@userName=$userName and @password=$password]
```

This compliant solution uses a query specified in a text file by reading the file in the required format and then inserting values for the user name and password in a Map. The XQuery library constructs the XML query from these inputs.

```
private boolean doLogin(String userName, String pwd)
    throws ParserConfigurationException, SAXException,
           IOException, XPathExpressionException {

  DocumentBuilderFactory domFactory =
    DocumentBuilderFactory.newInstance();
  domFactory.setNamespaceAware(true);
  DocumentBuilder builder = domFactory.newDocumentBuilder();
  Document doc = builder.parse("users.xml");

  XQuery xquery =
    new XQueryFactory().createXQuery(new File("login.xq"));
  Map queryVars = new HashMap();
  queryVars.put("userName", userName);
  queryVars.put("password", pwd);
  NodeList nodes =
    xquery.execute(doc, null, queryVars).toNodes();

  // Print first names to the console
  for (int i = 0; i < nodes.getLength(); i++) {
    Node node =
      nodes.item(i).getChildNodes().item(1).
        getChildNodes().item(0);
    System.out.println(node.getNodeValue());
  }
```

```
    return (nodes.getLength() >= 1);
}
```

Using this method, the data specified in the `userName` and `password` fields cannot be interpreted as executable content at runtime.

Applicability

Failure to validate user input may result in information disclosure and execution of unprivileged code.

According to OWASP [OWASP 2013],

[Prevention of XPath injection] requires the following characters to be removed (that is, prohibited) or properly escaped.

- < > / ' = " to prevent straight parameter injection.
- XPath queries should not contain any meta characters (such as ' = * ? // or similar).
- XSLT expansions should not contain any user input, or if they do, [you should] comprehensively test the existence of the file, and ensure that the files are within the bounds set by the Java 2 Security Policy.

Bibliography

[Fortify 2013]   "Input Validation and Representation: XML Injection"

[Long 2012]   IDS00-J. Sanitize untrusted data passed across a trust boundary

[OWASP 2013]   Testing for XPath Injection

[Sen 2007]   Avoid the Dangers of XPath Injection

[Oracle 2011b]   Ensure Data Security

■ 9. Prevent LDAP injection

The Lightweight Directory Access Protocol (LDAP) allows an application to remotely perform operations such as searching and modifying records in directories. LDAP injection results from inadequate input sanitization and validation, and allows malicious users to glean restricted information using the directory service.

A whitelist can be used to restrict input to a list of valid characters. Characters and character sequences that must be excluded from whitelists—including Java Naming and Directory Interface (JNDI) metacharacters and LDAP special characters—are listed in Table 1–1.

Table 1–1.   Characters and sequences to exclude from whitelists

Character	Name
' and "	Single and double quote
/ and \	Forward slash and backslash
\ \	Double slashes*
space	Space character at beginning or end of string
#	Hash character at the beginning of the string
< and >	Angle brackets
, and ;	Comma and semicolon
+ and *	Addition and multiplication operators
(and)	Round braces
\u0000	Unicode NULL character

*This is a character sequence

LDAP Injection Example

Consider an LDAP Data Interchange Format (LDIF) file that contains records in the following format:

```
dn: dc=example,dc=com
objectclass: dcobject
objectClass: organization
o: Some Name
dc: example

dn: ou=People,dc=example,dc=com
ou: People
objectClass: dcobject
objectClass: organizationalUnit
dc: example

dn: cn=Manager,ou=People,dc=example,dc=com
cn: Manager
sn: John Watson
# Several objectClass definitions here (omitted)
userPassword: secret1
mail: john@holmesassociates.com

dn: cn=Senior Manager,ou=People,dc=example,dc=com
cn: Senior Manager
sn: Sherlock Holmes
# Several objectClass definitions here (omitted)
userPassword: secret2
mail: sherlock@holmesassociates.com
```

A search for a valid user name and password often takes the form

`(&(sn=<USERSN>)(userPassword=<USERPASSWORD>))`

However, an attacker could bypass authentication by using S* for the USERSN field and * for the USERPASSWORD field. Such input would yield every record whose USERSN field began with S.

An authentication routine that permitted LDAP injection would allow unauthorized users to log in. Likewise, a search routine would allow an attacker to discover part or all of the data in the directory.

Noncompliant Code Example

This noncompliant code example allows a caller of the method searchRecord() to search for a record in the directory using the LDAP protocol. The string filter is used to filter the result set for those entries that match a user name and password supplied by the caller.

```
// String userSN = "S*"; // Invalid
// String userPassword = "*"; // Invalid
public class LDAPInjection {
  private void searchRecord(String userSN, String userPassword)
      throws NamingException {
    Hashtable<String, String> env =
    new Hashtable<String, String>();
    env.put(Context.INITIAL_CONTEXT_FACTORY,
            "com.sun.jndi.ldap.LdapCtxFactory");
    try {
      DirContext dctx = new InitialDirContext(env);

      SearchControls sc = new SearchControls();
      String[] attributeFilter = {"cn", "mail"};
      sc.setReturningAttributes(attributeFilter);
      sc.setSearchScope(SearchControls.SUBTREE_SCOPE);
      String base = "dc=example,dc=com";

      // The following resolves to (&(sn=S*)(userPassword=*))
      String filter = "(&(sn=" + userSN + ")(userPassword=" +
                      userPassword + "))";
      NamingEnumeration<?> results =
        dctx.search(base, filter, sc);
      while (results.hasMore()) {
        SearchResult sr = (SearchResult) results.next();
        Attributes attrs = (Attributes) sr.getAttributes();
        Attribute attr = (Attribute) attrs.get("cn");
```

```
        System.out.println(attr);
        attr = (Attribute) attrs.get("mail");
        System.out.println(attr);
      }
      dctx.close();
    } catch (NamingException e) {
      // Forward to handler
    }
  }
}
```

When a malicious user enters specially crafted input, as outlined previously, this elementary authentication scheme fails to confine the output of the search query to the information for which the user has access privileges.

Compliant Solution

This compliant solution uses a whitelist to sanitize user input so that the `filter` string contains only valid characters. In this code, `userSN` may contain only letters and spaces, whereas a password may contain only alphanumeric characters.

```
// String userSN = "Sherlock Holmes"; // Valid
// String userPassword = "secret2";   // Valid

// ... beginning of LDAPInjection.searchRecord() ...
sc.setSearchScope(SearchControls.SUBTREE_SCOPE);
String base = "dc=example,dc=com";

if (!userSN.matches("[\\w\\s]*") ||
    !userPassword.matches("[\\w]*")) {
  throw new IllegalArgumentException("Invalid input");
}

String filter = "(&(sn = " + userSN + ")(userPassword=" +
                userPassword + "))";

// ... remainder of LDAPInjection.searchRecord() ...
```

When a database field such as a password must include special characters, it is critical to ensure that the authentic data is stored in sanitized form in the database and also that any user input is normalized before the validation or comparison takes place. Using characters that have special meanings in JNDI and LDAP in the absence of a comprehensive normalization and whitelisting-based routine is discouraged.

Special characters must be transformed to sanitized, safe values before they are added to the whitelist expression against which input will be validated. Likewise, normalization of user input should occur before the validation step.

Applicability

Failure to sanitize untrusted input can result in information disclosure and privilege escalation.

Bibliography

[OWASP 2013]   Preventing LDAP Injection in Java

■ 10. Do not use the clone() method to copy untrusted method parameters

Making defensive copies of mutable method parameters mitigates against a variety of security vulnerabilities; see *The CERT® Oracle® Secure Coding Standard for Java™* [Long 2012], "OBJ06-J. Defensively copy mutable inputs and mutable internal components," for additional information. However, inappropriate use of the clone() method can allow an attacker to exploit vulnerabilities by providing arguments that appear normal but subsequently return unexpected values. Such objects may consequently bypass validation and security checks. When such a class might be passed as an argument to a method, treat the argument as untrusted, and do not use the clone() method provided by the class. Also, do not use the clone() method of non-final classes to make defensive copies.

This guideline is a specific instance of Guideline 15, "Do not rely on methods that can be overridden by untrusted code."

Noncompliant Code Example

This noncompliant code example defines a validateValue() method that validates a time value:

```
private Boolean validateValue(long time) {
  // Perform validation
   return true; // If the time is valid
}

private void storeDateInDB(java.util.Date date)
    throws SQLException {
```

```
  final java.util.Date copy = (java.util.Date)date.clone();
  if (validateValue(copy.getTime())) {
    Connection con =
      DriverManager.getConnection(
        "jdbc:microsoft:sqlserver://<HOST>:1433",
        "<UID>", "<PWD>"
      );
    PreparedStatement pstmt =
      con.prepareStatement("UPDATE ACCESSDB SET TIME = ?");
    pstmt.setLong(1, copy.getTime());
    // ...
  }
}
```

The `storeDateInDB()` method accepts an untrusted date argument and attempts to make a defensive copy using its `clone()` method. This allows an attacker to take control of the program by creating a malicious date class that extends `Date`. If the attacker's code runs with the same privileges as `storeDateInDB()`, the attacker merely embeds malicious code inside their `clone()` method:

```
class MaliciousDate extends java.util.Date {
  @Override
  public MaliciousDate clone() {
    // malicious code goes here
  }
}
```

If, however, the attacker can only provide a malicious date with lessened privileges, the attacker can bypass validation but still confound the remainder of the program. Consider this example:

```
public class MaliciousDate extends java.util.Date {
  private static int count = 0;

  @Override
  public long getTime() {
    java.util.Date d = new java.util.Date();
    return (count++ == 1) ? d.getTime() : d.getTime() - 1000;
  }
}
```

This malicious date will appear to be a benign date object the first time that getTime() is invoked. This allows it to bypass validation in the storeDateInDB() method. However, the time that is actually stored in the database will be incorrect.

Compliant Solution

This compliant solution avoids using the clone() method. Instead, it creates a new java.util.Date object that is subsequently used for access control checks and insertion into the database.

```
private void storeDateInDB(java.util.Date date)
  throws SQLException {
 final java.util.Date copy = new java.util.Date(date.getTime());
 if (validateValue(copy.getTime())) {
  Connection con =
   DriverManager.getConnection(
    "jdbc:microsoft:sqlserver://<HOST>:1433",
    "<UID>", "<PWD>"
   );
  PreparedStatement pstmt =
   con.prepareStatement("UPDATE ACCESSDB SET TIME = ?");
  pstmt.setLong(1, copy.getTime());
  // ...
 }
}
```

Noncompliant Code Example (CVE-2012-0507)

This noncompliant code example shows a constructor of the Java core class AtomicReferenceArray present in the Java 1.7.0 update 2:

```
public AtomicReferenceArray(E[] array) {
  // Visibility guaranteed by final field guarantees
  this.array = array.clone();
}
```

This code was subsequently invoked by the Flashback exploit that infected 600,000 Macintosh computers in April 2012.[1]

---

1. "Exploiting Java Vulnerability CVE-2012-0507 Using Metasploit" is shared by user BreakTheSec on Slideshare.net (July 14, 2012); see www.slideshare.net/BreakTheSec/exploiting-java-vulnerability.

Compliant Solution (CVE-2012-0507)

In Java 1.7.0 update 3, the constructor was modified to use the `Arrays.copyOf()` method instead of the `clone()` method as follows:

```
public AtomicReferenceArray(E[] array) {
    // Visibility guaranteed by final field guarantees
    this.array = Arrays.copyOf(
      array, array.length, Object[].class);
}
```

Applicability

Using the `clone()` method to copy untrusted arguments affords attackers the opportunity to execute arbitrary code.

Bibliography

[Long 2012]   OBJ06-J. Defensively copy mutable inputs and mutable internal components

[Sterbenz 2006]   Secure Coding Antipatterns: Avoiding Vulnerabilities

■ 11. Do not use `Object.equals()` to compare cryptographic keys

The method `java.lang.Object.equals()`, by default, is unable to compare composite objects such as cryptographic keys. Most `Key` classes fail to provide an `equals()` implementation that overrides `Object.equals()`. In such cases, the components of the composite object must be compared individually to ensure correctness.

Noncompliant Code Example

This noncompliant code example compares two keys using the `equals()` method. The keys may compare as unequal even when they represent the same value.

```
private static boolean keysEqual(Key key1, Key key2) {
  if (key1.equals(key2)) {
    return true;
  }
  return false;
}
```

Compliant Solution

This compliant solution uses the `equals()` method as a first test, and then compares the encoded version of the keys to facilitate provider-independent behavior. It checks whether an `RSAPrivateKey` and an `RSAPrivateCrtKey` represent equivalent private keys [Oracle 2011b].

```
private static boolean keysEqual(Key key1, Key key2) {
  if (key1.equals(key2)) {
    return true;
  }

  if (Arrays.equals(key1.getEncoded(), key2.getEncoded())) {
    return true;
  }

  // More code for different types of keys here
  // For example, the following code can check whether
  // an RSAPrivateKey and an RSAPrivateCrtKey are equal
  if ((key1 instanceof RSAPrivateKey) &&
      (key2 instanceof RSAPrivateKey)) {

    if ((((RSAKey) key1).getModulus().equals(
            ((RSAKey) key2).getModulus())) &&
        (((RSAPrivateKey) key1).getPrivateExponent().equals(
            ((RSAPrivateKey) key2).getPrivateExponent()))) {
      return true;
    }
  }
  return false;
}
```

Automated Detection

Using `Object.equals()` to compare cryptographic keys may yield unexpected results.

Bibliography

[API 2013]   `java.lang.Object.equals()`, `Object.equals()`

[Oracle 2011b]   Determining If Two Keys Are Equal (JCA Reference Guide)

■ 12. Do not use insecure or weak cryptographic algorithms

Security-intensive applications *must* avoid use of insecure or weak cryptographic primitives. The computational capacity of modern computers permits circumvention of such cryptography via brute-force attacks. For example, the Data Encryption Standard (DES) encryption algorithm is considered highly insecure; messages encrypted using DES have been decrypted by brute force within a single day by machines such as the Electronic Frontier Foundation's (EFF) Deep Crack.

Noncompliant Code Example

This noncompliant code example encrypts a String input using a weak cryptographic algorithm (DES):

```
SecretKey key = KeyGenerator.getInstance("DES").generateKey();
Cipher cipher = Cipher.getInstance("DES");
cipher.init(Cipher.ENCRYPT_MODE, key);

// Encode bytes as UTF8; strToBeEncrypted contains
// the input string that is to be encrypted
byte[] encoded = strToBeEncrypted.getBytes("UTF8");

// Perform encryption
byte[] encrypted = cipher.doFinal(encoded);
```

Compliant Solution

This compliant solution uses the more secure Advanced Encryption Standard (AES) algorithm to perform the encryption.

```
Cipher cipher = Cipher.getInstance("AES");
KeyGenerator kgen = KeyGenerator.getInstance("AES");
kgen.init(128); // 192 and 256 bits may be unavailable

SecretKey skey = kgen.generateKey();
byte[] raw = skey.getEncoded();

SecretKeySpec skeySpec = new SecretKeySpec(raw, "AES");
cipher.init(Cipher.ENCRYPT_MODE, skeySpec);

// Encode bytes as UTF8; strToBeEncrypted contains the
// input string that is to be encrypted
byte[] encoded = strToBeEncrypted.getBytes("UTF8");
```

```
// Perform encryption
byte[] encrypted = cipher.doFinal(encoded);
```

Applicability

Use of mathematically and computationally insecure cryptographic algorithms can result in the disclosure of sensitive information.

Weak cryptographic algorithms can be disabled in Java SE 7; see the Java™ PKI Programmer's Guide, Appendix D, "Disabling Cryptographic Algorithms" [Oracle 2011a].

Weak cryptographic algorithms may be used in scenarios that specifically call for a breakable cipher. For example, the ROT13 cipher is commonly used on bulletin boards and web sites when the purpose of encryption is to protect people from information, rather than to protect information from people.

Bibliography

[Oracle 2011a]   Appendix D, "Disabling Cryptographic Algorithms"

[Oracle 2013b]   Java Cryptography Architecture (JCA) Reference Guide

■ 13. Store passwords using a hash function

Programs that store passwords as cleartext (unencrypted text data) risk exposure of those passwords in a variety of ways. Although programs generally receive passwords from users as cleartext, they should ensure that the passwords are not stored as cleartext.

An acceptable technique for limiting the exposure of passwords is the use of *hash functions*, which allow programs to indirectly compare an input password to the original password string without storing a cleartext or decryptable version of the password. This approach minimizes the exposure of the password without presenting any practical disadvantages.

Cryptographic Hash Functions

The value produced by a hash function is the *hash value* or *message digest*. Hash functions are computationally feasible functions whose inverses are computationally infeasible. In practice, a password can be encoded to a hash value, but decoding remains infeasible. The equality of the passwords can be tested through the equality of their hash values.

A good practice is to always append a *salt* to the password being hashed. A salt is a unique (often sequential) or randomly generated piece of data that is stored along with the hash value. The use of a salt helps prevent brute-force attacks against the hash value, provided that the salt is long enough to generate sufficient entropy (shorter salt values cannot significantly slow down a brute-force attack). Each password should have its own salt associated with it. If a single salt were used for more than one password, two users would be able to see whether their passwords are the same.

The choice of hash function and salt length presents a trade-off between security and performance. Increasing the effort required for effective brute-force attacks by choosing a stronger hash function can also increase the time required to validate a password. Increasing the length of the salt makes brute-force attacks more difficult but requires additional storage space.

Java's `MessageDigest` class provides implementations of various cryptographic hash functions. Avoid defective functions such as the Message-Digest Algorithm (MD5). Hash functions such as Secure Hash Algorithm (SHA)-1 and SHA-2 are maintained by the National Security Agency, and are currently considered safe. In practice, many applications use SHA-256 because this hash function has reasonable performance while still being considered secure.

Noncompliant Code Example

This noncompliant code example encrypts and decrypts the password stored in `password.bin` using a symmetric key algorithm.

```
public final class Password {
  private void setPassword(byte[] pass) throws Exception {
    // Arbitrary encryption scheme
    bytes[] encrypted = encrypt(pass);
    clearArray(pass);
    // Encrypted password to password.bin
    saveBytes(encrypted,"password.bin");
    clearArray(encrypted);
  }

  boolean checkPassword(byte[] pass) throws Exception {
    // Load the encrypted password
    byte[] encrypted = loadBytes("password.bin");
    byte[] decrypted = decrypt(encrypted);
    boolean arraysEqual = Arrays.equal(decrypted, pass);
    clearArray(decrypted);
    clearArray(pass);
```

```
    return arraysEqual;
  }

  private void clearArray(byte[] a) {
    for (int i = 0; i < a.length; i++) {
      a[i] = 0;
    }
  }
}
```

An attacker could potentially decrypt this file to discover the password, particularly when the attacker has knowledge of the key and encryption scheme used by the program. Passwords should be protected even from system administrators and privileged users. Consequently, using encryption is only partly effective in mitigating password disclosure threats.

Noncompliant Code Example

This noncompliant code example uses the SHA-256 hash function through the MessageDigest class to compare hash values instead of cleartext strings, but it uses a String to store the password:

```
import java.security.MessageDigest;
import java.security.NoSuchAlgorithmException;

public final class Password {
  private void setPassword(String pass) throws Exception {
    byte[] salt = generateSalt(12);
    MessageDigest msgDigest = MessageDigest.getInstance("SHA-256");
    // Encode the string and salt
    byte[] hashVal = msgDigest.digest((pass+salt).getBytes());
    saveBytes(salt, "salt.bin");
    // Save the hash value to password.bin
    saveBytes(hashVal,"password.bin");
  }

  boolean checkPassword(String pass) throws Exception {
    byte[] salt = loadBytes("salt.bin");
    MessageDigest msgDigest = MessageDigest.getInstance("SHA-256");
    // Encode the string and salt
    byte[] hashVal1 = msgDigest.digest((pass+salt).getBytes());
    // Load the hash value stored in password.bin
```

```
    byte[] hashVal2 = loadBytes("password.bin");
    return Arrays.equals(hashVal1, hashVal2);
  }

  private byte[] generateSalt(int n) {
    // Generate a random byte array of length n
  }
}
```

Even when an attacker knows that the program stores passwords using SHA-256 and a 12-byte salt, he or she will be unable to retrieve the actual password from password.bin and salt.bin.

Although this approach solves the decryption problem from the previous noncompliant code example, this program may inadvertently store the passwords as cleartext in memory. Java String objects are immutable, and can be copied and internally stored by the Java Virtual Machine. Consequently, Java lacks a mechanism to securely erase a password once it has been stored in a String. See Guideline 1, "Limit the lifetime of sensitive data," for more information.

Compliant Solution

This compliant solution addresses the problems from the previous noncompliant code example by using a byte array to store the password:

```
import java.security.MessageDigest;
import java.security.NoSuchAlgorithmException;

public final class Password {

  private void setPassword(byte[] pass) throws Exception {
    byte[] salt = generateSalt(12);
    byte[] input = appendArrays(pass, salt);
    MessageDigest msgDigest = MessageDigest.getInstance("SHA-256");
    // Encode the string and salt
    byte[] hashVal = msgDigest.digest(input);
    clearArray(pass);
    clearArray(input);
    saveBytes(salt, "salt.bin");
    // Save the hash value to password.bin
    saveBytes(hashVal,"password.bin");
```

```
      clearArray(salt);
      clearArray(hashVal);
    }

    boolean checkPassword(byte[] pass) throws Exception {
      byte[] salt = loadBytes("salt.bin");
      byte[] input = appendArrays(pass, salt);
      MessageDigest msgDigest = MessageDigest.getInstance("SHA-256");
      // Encode the string and salt
      byte[] hashVal1 = msgDigest.digest(input);
      clearArray(pass);
      clearArray(input);
      // Load the hash value stored in password.bin
      byte[] hashVal2 = loadBytes("password.bin");
      boolean arraysEqual = Arrays.equals(hashVal1, hashVal2);
      clearArray(hashVal1);
      clearArray(hashVal2);
      return arraysEqual;
    }

    private byte[] generateSalt(int n) {
      // Generate a random byte array of length n
    }

    private byte[] appendArrays(byte[] a, byte[] b) {
      // Return a new array of a[] appended to b[]
    }

    private void clearArray(byte[] a) {
      for (int i = 0; i < a.length; i++) {
        a[i] = 0;
      }
    }
  }
```

In both the setPassword() and checkPassword() methods, the cleartext representation of the password is erased immediately after it is converted into a hash value. Consequently, attackers must work harder to retrieve the cleartext password after the erasure. Providing guaranteed erasure is extremely challenging, is likely to be platform specific, and may even be impossible because of copying garbage collectors, dynamic paging, and other platform features that operate below the level of the Java language.

Applicability

Passwords stored without a secure hash can be exposed to malicious users. Violations of this guideline generally have a clear exploit associated with them.

Applications such as password managers may need to retrieve the original password to enter it into a third-party application. This is permitted even though it violates this guideline. The password manager is accessed by a single user, and always has the user's permission to store his or her passwords and to display those passwords on command. Consequently, the limiting factor to safety and security is the user's competence rather than the program's operation.

Bibliography

[API 2013]   Class `MessageDigest`
                     Class `String`

[Hirondelle 2013]   Passwords Never Clear in Text

[OWASP 2012]   "Why Add Salt?"

[Paar 2010]   Chapter 11, "Hash Functions"

■ 14. Ensure that SecureRandom is properly seeded

Random number generation depends on a source of entropy such as signals, devices, or hardware inputs. Secure random number generation is also addressed by *The CERT® Oracle® Secure Coding Standard for Java*™ [Long 2012], "MSC02-J. Generate strong random numbers."

The `java.security.SecureRandom` class is widely used for generating cryptographically strong random numbers. According to the `java.security` file present in the Java Runtime Environment's `lib/security` folder [API 2013]:

> Select the source of seed data for `SecureRandom`. By default an attempt is made to use the entropy gathering device specified by the `securerandom.source` property. If an exception occurs when accessing the URL then the traditional system/thread activity algorithm is used.
>
> On Solaris and Linux systems, if `file:/dev/urandom` is specified and it exists, a special SecureRandom implementation is activated by default. This "NativePRNG" reads random bytes directly from `/dev/urandom`. On Windows systems, the URLs `file:/dev/random` and `file:/dev/urandom` enables use of the Microsoft CryptoAPI seed functionality.

An adversary should not be able to determine the original seed given several samples of random numbers. If this restriction is violated, all future random numbers may be successfully predicted by the adversary.

Noncompliant Code Example

This noncompliant code example constructs a secure random number generator that is seeded with the specified seed bytes.

```
SecureRandom random = new SecureRandom(
    String.valueOf(new Date().getTime()).getBytes()
);
```

This constructor searches a registry of security providers and returns the first provider that supports secure random number generation. If no such provider exists, an implementation-specific default is selected. Furthermore, the default system-provided seed is overridden by a seed provided by the programmer. Using the current system time as the seed is predictable, and can result in the generation of random numbers with insufficient entropy.

Compliant Solution

Prefer the no-argument constructor of SecureRandom that uses the system-specified seed value to generate a 128-byte-long random number.

```
byte[] randomBytes = new byte[128];
SecureRandom random = new SecureRandom();
random.nextBytes(randomBytes);
```

It is also good practice to specify the exact random number generator and provider for better portability.

Applicability

Insufficiently secure random numbers enable attackers to gain specific information about the context in which they are used.

Insecure random numbers are useful in some contexts that do not require security. These are addressed in the exceptions to "MSC02-J. Generate strong random numbers" [Long 2012].

Bibliography

[API 2013]   SecureRandom

[Sethi 2009]   Proper Use of Java's SecureRandom

[Long 2012]   MSC02-J. Generate strong random numbers

■ 15. Do not rely on methods that can be overridden by untrusted code

Untrusted code can misuse APIs provided by trusted code to override methods such as `Object.equals()`, `Object.hashCode()`, and `Thread.run()`. These methods are valuable targets because they are commonly used behind the scenes and may interact with components in a way that is not easily discernible.

By providing overridden implementations, an attacker can use untrusted code to glean sensitive information, run arbitrary code, or launch a denial of service attack.

See Guideline 10, "Do not use the `clone()` method to copy untrusted method parameters," for more specific details regarding overriding the `Object.clone()` method.

Noncompliant Code Example (hashCode)

This noncompliant code example shows a `LicenseManager` class that maintains a `licenseMap`. The map stores a `LicenseType` and license value pair.

```java
public class LicenseManager {
  Map<LicenseType, String> licenseMap =
    new HashMap<LicenseType, String>();

  public LicenseManager() {
    LicenseType type = new LicenseType();
    type.setType("demo-license-key");
    licenseMap.put(type, "ABC-DEF-PQR-XYZ");
  }
  public Object getLicenseKey(LicenseType licenseType) {
    return licenseMap.get(licenseType);
  }
  public void setLicenseKey(LicenseType licenseType,
                            String licenseKey) {
    licenseMap.put(licenseType, licenseKey);
  }
}

class LicenseType {
  private String type;
  public String getType() {
    return type;
  }
  public void setType(String type) {
    this.type = type;
  }
```

```
    @Override
    public int hashCode() {
      int res = 17;
      res = res * 31 + type == null ? 0 : type.hashCode();
      return res;
    }
    @Override
    public boolean equals(Object arg) {
      if (arg == null || !(arg instanceof LicenseType)) {
        return false;
      }
      if (type.equals(((LicenseType) arg).getType())) {
        return true;
      }
      return false;
    }
}
```

The constructor for `LicenseManager` initializes `licenseMap` with a demo license key that must remain secret. The license key is hard-coded for illustrative purposes; it should ideally be read from an external configuration file that stores an encrypted version of the key. The `LicenseType` class provides overridden implementations of `equals()` and `hashCode()` methods.

This implementation is vulnerable to an attacker who extends the `LicenseType` class and overrides the `equals()` and `hashCode()` methods:

```
public class CraftedLicenseType extends LicenseType {
  private static int guessedHashCode = 0;
  @Override
  public int hashCode() {
    // Returns a new hashCode to test every time get() is called
    guessedHashCode++;
    return guessedHashCode;
  }
  @Override
  public boolean equals(Object arg) {
    // Always returns true
    return true;
  }
}
```

The following is the malicious client program.

```
public class DemoClient {
  public static void main(String[] args) {
    LicenseManager licenseManager = new LicenseManager();
    for (int i = 0; i <= Integer.MAX_VALUE; i++) {
      Object guessed =
        licenseManager.getLicenseKey(new CraftedLicenseType());
      if (guessed != null) {
        // prints ABC-DEF-PQR-XYZ
        System.out.println(guessed);
      }
    }
  }
}
```

The client program runs through the sequence of all possible hash codes using CraftedLicenseType until it successfully matches the hash code of the demo license key object stored in the LicenseManager class. Consequently, the attacker can discover the sensitive data present within the licenseMap in only a few minutes. The attack operates by discovering at least one hash collision with respect to the key of the map.

Compliant Solution (IdentityHashMap)

This compliant solution uses an IdentityHashMap rather than a HashMap to store the license information:

```
public class LicenseManager {
  Map<LicenseType, String> licenseMap =
    new IdentityHashMap<LicenseType, String>();

  // ...
}
```

According to the Java API class IdentityHashMap documentation [API 2006],

This class implements the Map interface with a hash table, using reference-equality in place of object-equality when comparing keys (and values). In other words, in an IdentityHashMap, two keys k1 and k2 are considered equal if and only if (k1==k2). (In normal Map implementations (like HashMap) two keys k1 and k2 are considered equal if and only if (k1==null ? k2==null : k1.equals(k2)).)

Consequently, the overridden methods cannot expose internal class details. The client program can continue to add license keys, and can even retrieve the added key–value pairs, as demonstrated by the following client code.

```
public class DemoClient {
  public static void main(String[] args) {
    LicenseManager licenseManager = new LicenseManager();
    LicenseType type = new LicenseType();
    type.setType("custom-license-key");
    licenseManager.setLicenseKey(type, "CUS-TOM-LIC-KEY");
    Object licenseKeyValue = licenseManager.getLicenseKey(type);
    // Prints CUS-TOM-LIC-KEY
    System.out.println(licenseKeyValue);
  }
}
```

Compliant Solution (final Class)

This compliant solution declares the LicenseType class final so that its methods cannot be overridden:

```
final class LicenseType {
  // ...
}
```

Noncompliant Code Example

This noncompliant code example consists of a Widget class and a LayoutManager class containing a set of widgets:

```
public class Widget {
  private int noOfComponents;

  public Widget(int noOfComponents) {
    this.noOfComponents = noOfComponents;
  }
  public int getNoOfComponents() {
    return noOfComponents;
  }
  public final void setNoOfComponents(int noOfComponents) {
    this.noOfComponents = noOfComponents;
  }
  public boolean equals(Object o) {
    if (o == null || !(o instanceof Widget)) {
      return false;
    }
    Widget widget = (Widget) o;
    return this.noOfComponents == widget.getNoOfComponents();
  }
```

```
  @Override
  public int hashCode() {
    int res = 31;
    res = res * 17 + noOfComponents;
    return res;
  }
}
public class LayoutManager {
  private Set<Widget> layouts = new HashSet<Widget>();
  public void addWidget(Widget widget) {
    if (!layouts.contains(widget)) {
      layouts.add(widget);
    }
  }
  public int getLayoutSize() {
    return layouts.size();
  }
}
```

An attacker can extend the Widget class as a Navigator widget, and override the hashCode() method:

```
public class Navigator extends Widget {
  public Navigator(int noOfComponents) {
    super(noOfComponents);
  }
  @Override
  public int hashCode() {
    int res = 31;
    res = res * 17;
    return res;
  }
}
```

The client code follows:

```
Widget nav = new Navigator(1);
Widget widget = new Widget(1);
LayoutManager manager = new LayoutManager();
manager.addWidget(nav);
manager.addWidget(widget);
System.out.println(manager.getLayoutSize()); // Prints 2
```

The set `layouts` is expected to contain just one item because the number of components for both the navigator and the widget being added is 1. However, the `getLayoutSize()` method returns 2.

The reason for this discrepancy is that the `hashCode()` method of `Widget` is used only once when the widget is added to the set. When the navigator is added, the `hashCode()` method provided by the `Navigator` class is used. Consequently, the set contains two different object instances.

Compliant Solution (`final class`)

This compliant solution declares the `Widget` class final so that its methods cannot be overridden:

```
public final class Widget {
  // ...
}
```

Noncompliant Code Example (`run()`)

In this noncompliant code example, class `Worker` and its subclass `SubWorker` each contain a `startThread()` method intended to start a thread.

```
public class Worker implements Runnable {
  Worker() { }
  public void startThread(String name) {
    new Thread(this, name).start();
  }
  @Override
  public void run() {
    System.out.println("Parent");
  }
}

public class SubWorker extends Worker {
  @Override
  public void startThread(String name) {
    super.startThread(name);
    new Thread(this, name).start();
  }
  @Override
  public void run() {
    System.out.println("Child");
  }
}
```

If a client runs the following code:

```
Worker w = new SubWorker();
w.startThread("thread");
```

the client may expect Parent and Child to be printed. However, Child is printed twice because the overridden method run() is invoked both times that a new thread is started.

Compliant Solution

This compliant solution modifies the SubWorker class and removes the call to super.startThread():

```
public class SubWorker extends Worker {
  @Override
  public void startThread(String name) {
    new Thread(this, name).start();
  }
  // ...
}
```

The client code is also modified to start the parent and child threads separately. This program produces the expected output:

```
Worker w1 = new Worker();
w1.startThread("parent-thread");
Worker w2 = new SubWorker();
w2.startThread("child-thread");
```

Bibliography

[API 2013]   Class IdentityHashMap

[Hawtin 2006]   [drlvm][kernel_classes] ThreadLocal vulnerability

■ 16. Avoid granting excess privileges

A Java security policy grants permissions to code to allow access to specific system resources. A *code source* (an object of type CodeSource), to which a permission is granted, consists of the code location (URL) and a reference to the certificate(s)

containing the public key(s) corresponding to the private key(s) used to digitally sign the code. Reference to the certificate(s) is pertinent only if the code was digitally signed. A *protection domain* encompasses a CodeSource and the permissions granted to code from that CodeSource, as determined by the security policy currently in effect. Consequently, classes signed by the same key and originating from the same URL are placed in the same protection domain. A class belongs to one and only one protection domain. Classes that have the same permissions but are from different code sources belong to different domains.

Each Java class runs in its appropriate domain, as determined by its code source. For any code running under a security manager to perform a secured action such as reading or writing a file, the code must be granted permission to perform that particular action. Privileged code can access privileged resources on behalf of an unprivileged caller by using the AccessController.doPrivileged() method. This is necessary, for example, when a system utility needs to open a font file on behalf of the user to display a document, but the application lacks permission to do so. To perform this action, the system utility uses its full privileges for obtaining the fonts, ignoring the privileges of the caller. Privileged code runs with all the privileges of the protection domain associated with the code source. These privileges often exceed those required to perform the privileged operation. Ideally, code should be granted only the minimum set of privileges required to complete its operation.

Guideline 19, "Define custom security permissions for fine-grained security," describes another approach to eliminating excess privileges.

Noncompliant Code Example

This noncompliant code example shows a library method that allows callers to perform a privileged operation (reading a file) using the wrapper method performActionOnFile():

```java
private FileInputStream openFile() {
  final FileInputStream f[] = { null };

  AccessController.doPrivileged(new PrivilegedAction() {
    public Object run() {
      try {
        f[0] = new FileInputStream("file");
      } catch(FileNotFoundException fnf) {
        // Forward to handler
      }
      return null;
    }
  });
```

```
    return f[0];
  }

  // Wrapper method
  public void performActionOnFile() {
    try (FileInputStream f = openFile()){
      // Perform operation
    } catch (Throwable t) {
      // Handle exception
    }
  }
}
```

In this example, the trusted code grants privileges beyond those required to read a file, even though read access to the file was the only permission needed by the doPrivileged() block. Consequently, this code violates the principle of least privilege by providing the code block with superfluous privileges.

Compliant Solution

The two-argument form of doPrivileged() accepts an AccessControlContext object from the caller and restricts the privileges of the contained code to the intersection of the privileges of the protection domain and those of the context passed as the second argument. Consequently, a caller that wishes to grant only permission to read the file can provide a context that has only file-reading permissions.

An AccessControlContext that grants the appropriate file-reading permissions can be created as an inner class:

```
private FileInputStream openFile(AccessControlContext context) {
  if (context == null) {
    throw new SecurityException("Missing AccessControlContext");
  }

  final FileInputStream f[] = { null };
  AccessController.doPrivileged(
    new PrivilegedAction() {
      public Object run() {
        try {
          f[0] = new FileInputStream("file");
        } catch (FileNotFoundException fnf) {
          // Forward to handler
        }
        return null;
      }
    },
```

```
      // Restrict the privileges by passing the context argument
      context);
    return f[0];
  }

  private static class FileAccessControlContext {
    public static final AccessControlContext INSTANCE;
    static {
      Permission perm = new java.io.FilePermission("file", "read");
      PermissionCollection perms = perm.newPermissionCollection();
      perms.add(perm);
      INSTANCE = new AccessControlContext(new ProtectionDomain[] {
        new ProtectionDomain(null, perms)});
    }
  }

  // Wrapper method
  public void performActionOnFile() {
    try (final FileInputStream f =
      // Grant only open-for-reading privileges
      openFile(FileAccessControlContext.INSTANCE)){
      // Perform action
    } catch (Throwable t) {
      // Handle exception
    }
  }
}
```

Callers that lack permission to create an appropriate AccessControlContext can request one using AccessController.getContext() to create the instance.

Applicability

Failure to follow the principle of least privilege can result in untrusted, unprivileged code performing unintended privileged operations. However, carefully restricting privileges adds complexity. This added complexity and the associated reduction of maintainability must be traded off against any security improvement.

Bibliography

[API 2013]   Class AccessController

[Oracle 2013a]   API for Privileged Blocks

■ 17. Minimize privileged code

Programs must comply with the principle of least privilege not only by providing privileged blocks with the minimum permissions required for correct operation (see Guideline 16, "Avoid granting excess privileges"), but also by ensuring that privileged code contains *only* those operations that require increased privileges. Superfluous code contained within a privileged block must operate with the privileges of that block, increasing the attack surface.

Noncompliant Code Example

This noncompliant code example contains a changePassword() method that attempts to open a password file within a doPrivileged block and performs operations using that file. The doPrivileged block also contains a superfluous System .loadLibrary() call that loads the authentication library.

```
public void changePassword(String currentPassword,
                           String newPassword) {
  final FileInputStream f[] = { null };

  AccessController.doPrivileged(new PrivilegedAction() {
    public Object run() {
      try {
        String passwordFile = System.getProperty("user.dir") +
          File.separator + "PasswordFileName";
        f[0] = new FileInputStream(passwordFile);
        // Check whether oldPassword matches the one in the file
        // If not, throw an exception
        System.loadLibrary("authentication");
      } catch (FileNotFoundException cnf) {
        // Forward to handler
      }
      return null;
    }
  }); // End of doPrivileged()
}
```

This example violates the principle of least privilege because an unprivileged caller could also cause the authentication library to be loaded. An unprivileged caller cannot invoke the System.loadLibrary() method directly, because this could expose native methods to the unprivileged code [SCG 2010]. Furthermore, the System.loadLibrary() method checks only the privileges of its immediate caller, so it should be used only with great care. For more information, see Guideline 18, "Do not expose methods that use reduced-security checks to untrusted code."

Compliant Solution

This compliant solution moves the call to `System.loadLibrary()` outside the `doPrivileged()` block. Doing so allows unprivileged code to perform preliminary password-reset checks using the file, but prevents it from loading the authentication library.

```java
public void changePassword(String currentPassword,
    String newPassword) {
  final FileInputStream f[] = { null };

  AccessController.doPrivileged(new PrivilegedAction() {
    public Object run() {
      try {
        String passwordFile = System.getProperty("user.dir") +
          File.separator + "PasswordFileName";
        f[0] = new FileInputStream(passwordFile);
        // Check whether oldPassword matches the one in the file
        // If not, throw an exception
      } catch (FileNotFoundException cnf) {
        // Forward to handler
      }
      return null;
    }
  }); // End of doPrivileged()

  System.loadLibrary("authentication");
}
```

The `loadLibrary()` invocation could also occur before preliminary password reset checks are performed; in this example, it is deferred for performance reasons.

Applicability

Minimizing privileged code reduces the attack surface of an application and simplifies the task of auditing privileged code.

Bibliography

[API 2013]   Class `AccessController`

■ 18. Do not expose methods that use reduced-security checks to untrusted code

Most methods lack security manager checks because they do not provide access to sensitive parts of the system, such as the file system. Most methods that do provide security manager checks verify that every class and method in the call stack is authorized before they proceed. This security model allows restricted programs, such as Java applets, to have full access to the core Java library. It also prevents a sensitive method from acting on behalf of a malicious method that hides behind trusted methods in the call stack.

However, certain methods use a reduced-security check that checks only that the calling method is authorized rather than checking every method in the call stack. Any code that invokes these methods must guarantee that they cannot be invoked on behalf of untrusted code. These methods are listed in Table 1–2.

Because the `java.lang.reflect.Field.setAccessible()` and `getAccessible()` methods are used to instruct the Java Virtual Machine (JVM) to override the language access checks, they perform standard (and more restrictive) security manager checks, and consequently lack the vulnerability described by this guideline. Nevertheless, these methods should also be used with extreme caution. The remaining `set*` and `get*` field reflection methods perform only the language access checks and are consequently vulnerable.

Class Loaders

Class loaders allow a Java application to be dynamically extended at runtime by loading additional classes. For each class that is loaded, the JVM tracks the class loader that was used to load the class. When a loaded class first refers to another class, the virtual machine requests that the referenced class be loaded by the same class loader that was used to load the referencing class. Java's class loader

Table 1–2.   Methods that check the calling method only

`java.lang.Class.newInstance`
`java.lang.reflect.Constructor.newInstance`
`java.lang.reflect.Field.get*`
`java.lang.reflect.Field.set*`
`java.lang.reflect.Method.invoke`
`java.util.concurrent.atomic.AtomicIntegerFieldUpdater.newUpdater`
`java.util.concurrent.atomic.AtomicLongFieldUpdater.newUpdater`
`java.util.concurrent.atomic.AtomicReferenceFieldUpdater.newUpdater`

architecture controls interaction between code loaded from different sources by allowing the use of different class loaders. This separation of class loaders is fundamental to the separation of code: it prevents malicious code from gaining access to and subverting trusted code.

Several methods which are charged with loading classes delegate their work to the class loader of the class of the method that called them. The security checks associated with loading classes are performed by the class loaders. Consequently, any method that invokes one of these class loading methods must guarantee that these methods cannot act on behalf of untrusted code. These methods are listed in Table 1–3.

With the exception of the `loadLibrary()` and `load()` methods, the tabulated methods do not perform any security manager checks; they delegate security checks to the appropriate class loader.

In practice, the trusted code's class loader frequently allows these methods to be invoked, whereas the untrusted code's class loader may lack these privileges. However, when the untrusted code's class loader delegates to the trusted code's class loader, the untrusted code gains visibility to the trusted code. In the absence of such a delegation relationship, the class loaders would ensure namespace separation; consequently, the untrusted code would be unable to observe members or to invoke methods belonging to the trusted code.

The class loader delegation model is fundamental to many Java implementations and frameworks. Avoid exposing the methods listed in Tables 1–2 and 1–3 to untrusted code. Consider, for example, an attack scenario where untrusted code is attempting to

Table 1–3. Methods that use the calling method's class loader

`java.lang.Class.forName`
`java.lang.Package.getPackage`
`java.lang.Package.getPackages`
`java.lang.Runtime.load`
`java.lang.Runtime.loadLibrary`
`java.lang.System.load`
`java.lang.System.loadLibrary`
`java.sql.DriverManager.getConnection`
`java.sql.DriverManager.getDriver`
`java.sql.DriverManager.getDrivers`
`java.sql.DriverManager.deregisterDriver`
`java.util.ResourceBundle.getBundle`

load a privileged class. If its class loader lacks permission to load the requested privileged class on its own, but the class loader is permitted to delegate the class loading to a trusted class's class loader, privilege escalation can occur. Furthermore, if the trusted code accepts tainted inputs, the trusted code's class loader could be persuaded to load privileged, malicious classes on behalf of the untrusted code.

Classes that have the same defining class loader will exist in the same namespace, but they can have different privileges depending on the security policy. Security vulnerabilities can arise when privileged code coexists with unprivileged code (or less privileged code) that was loaded by the same class loader. In this case, the less privileged code can freely access members of the privileged code according to the privileged code's declared accessibility. When the privileged code uses any of the tabulated APIs, it bypasses security manager checks (with the exception of `loadLibrary()` and `load()`).

This guideline is similar to *The CERT® Oracle® Secure Coding Standard for Java*™ [Long 2012], "SEC03-J. Do not load trusted classes after allowing untrusted code to load arbitrary classes." Many examples also violate "SEC00-J. Do not allow privileged blocks to leak sensitive information across a trust boundary."

Noncompliant Code Example

In this noncompliant code example, a call to `System.loadLibrary()` is embedded in a `doPrivileged` block.

```
public void load(String libName) {
  AccessController.doPrivileged(new PrivilegedAction() {
    public Object run() {
      System.loadLibrary(libName);
      return null;
    }
  });
}
```

This code is insecure because it could be used to load a library on behalf of untrusted code. In essence, the untrusted code's class loader may be able to use this code to load a library even though it lacks sufficient permissions to do so directly. After loading the library, the untrusted code can call native methods from the library, if those methods are accessible, because the `doPrivileged` block prevents any security manager checks from being applied to callers further up the execution stack.

Nonnative library code can also be susceptible to related security flaws. Suppose there exists a library that contains a vulnerability that is not directly exposed, perhaps because it lies in an unused method. Loading this library may not directly expose a vulnerability. However, an attacker could then load an additional library that exploits the first library's vulnerability. Moreover, nonnative libraries often use doPrivileged blocks, making them attractive targets.

Compliant Solution

This compliant solution hard codes the name of the library to prevent the possibility of tainted values. It also reduces the accessibility of the load() method from public to private. Consequently, untrusted callers are prohibited from loading the awt library.

```
private void load() {
  AccessController.doPrivileged(new PrivilegedAction() {
    public Object run() {
      System.loadLibrary("awt");
      return null;
    }
  });
}
```

Noncompliant Code Example

This noncompliant code example returns an instance of java.sql.Connection from trusted code to untrusted code.

```
public Connection getConnection(String url, String username,
    String password) {
  // ...
  return DriverManager.getConnection(url, username, password);
}
```

Untrusted code that lacks the permissions required to create a SQL connection can bypass these restrictions by using the acquired instance directly. The getConnection() method is unsafe because it uses the url argument to indicate a class to be loaded; this class serves as the database driver.

Compliant Solution

This compliant solution prevents malicious users from supplying their own URL to the database connection, thereby limiting their ability to load untrusted drivers.

```
private String url = // Hardwired value

public Connection getConnection(String username,
    String password) {
  // ...
  return DriverManager.getConnection(this.url,
    username, password);
}
```

Noncompliant Code Example (CERT Vulnerability 636312)

CERT Vulnerability Note VU#636312 describes a vulnerability in Java 1.7.0 update 6 that was widely exploited in August 2012. The exploit actually used two vulnerabilities; the other one is described in *The CERT® Oracle® Secure Coding Standard for Java™* [Long 2012], "SEC05-J. Do not use reflection to increase accessibility of classes, methods, or fields."

The exploit runs as a Java applet. The applet class loader ensures that an applet cannot directly invoke methods of classes present in the com.sun.* package. A normal security manager check ensures that specific actions are allowed or denied depending on the privileges of all of the caller methods on the call stack (the privileges are associated with the code source that encompasses the class).

The first goal of the exploit code was to access the private sun.awt.SunToolkit class. However, invoking class.forName() directly on the name of this class would cause a SecurityException to be thrown. Consequently, the exploit code used the following method to access any class, bypassing the security manager:

```
private Class GetClass(String paramString)
    throws Throwable {
  Object arrayOfObject[] = new Object[1];
  arrayOfObject[0] = paramString;
  Expression localExpression =
    new Expression(Class.class, "forName", arrayOfObject);
  localExpression.execute();
  return (Class)localExpression.getValue();
}
```

The java.beans.Expression.execute() method delegates its work to the following method:

```
private Object invokeInternal() throws Exception {
  Object target = getTarget();
  String methodName = getMethodName();
```

```
    if (target == null || methodName == null) {
      throw new NullPointerException(
        (target == null ? "target" : "methodName") +
        " should not be null");
    }

    Object[] arguments = getArguments();
    if (arguments == null) {
      arguments = emptyArray;
    }
    // Class.forName() won't load classes outside
    // of core from a class inside core, so it
    // is handled as a special case.
    if (target == Class.class && methodName.equals("forName")) {
      return ClassFinder.resolveClass((String)arguments[0],
                            this.loader);
    }

  // ...
```

The `com.sun.beans.finder.ClassFinder.resolveClass()` method delegates its work to its `findClass()` method:

```
public static Class<?> findClass(String name)
    throws ClassNotFoundException {
  try {
    ClassLoader loader =
      Thread.currentThread().getContextClassLoader();
    if (loader == null) {
      loader = ClassLoader.getSystemClassLoader();
    }
    if (loader != null) {
      return Class.forName(name, false, loader);
    }
  } catch (ClassNotFoundException exception) {
    // Use current class loader instead
  } catch (SecurityException exception) {
    // Use current class loader instead
  }
  return Class.forName(name);
}
```

Although this method is called in the context of an applet, it uses `Class.forName()` to obtain the requested class. `Class.forName()` delegates the search to the calling method's class loader. In this case, the calling class (`com.sun.beans.finder.ClassFinder`) is part of core Java, so the trusted class loader is used in place of the more restrictive applet class loader, and the trusted class loader loads the class, unaware that it is acting on behalf of malicious code.

Compliant Solution (CVE-2012-4681)

Oracle mitigated this vulnerability in Java 1.7.0 update 7 by patching the com.sun .beans.finder.ClassFinder.findClass() method. The checkPackageAccess() method checks the entire call stack to ensure that Class.forName(), in this instance only, fetches classes only on behalf of trusted methods.

```
public static Class<?> findClass(String name)
    throws ClassNotFoundException {
  checkPackageAccess(name);
  try {
    ClassLoader loader =
      Thread.currentThread().getContextClassLoader();
    if (loader == null) {
      // Can be null in IE (see 6204697)
      loader = ClassLoader.getSystemClassLoader();
    }
    if (loader != null) {
      return Class.forName(name, false, loader);
    }

  } catch (ClassNotFoundException exception) {
    // Use current class loader instead
  } catch (SecurityException exception) {
    // Use current class loader instead
  }
  return Class.forName(name);
}
```

Noncompliant Code Example (CVE-2013-0422)

Java 1.7.0 update 10 was widely exploited in January 2013 because of several vulnerabilities. One such vulnerability in the com.sun.jmx.mbeanserver.MBeanInstantiator class granted unprivileged code the ability to access any class regardless of the current security policy or accessibility rules. The MBeanInstantiator.findClass() method could be invoked with any string and would attempt to return the Class object named after the string. This method delegated its work to the MBeanInstantiator.loadClass() method, whose source code is shown here:

```
/**
 * Load a class with the specified loader, or with this object
 * class loader if the specified loader is null.
 **/
```

```
static Class<?> loadClass(String className, ClassLoader loader)
    throws ReflectionException {
  Class<?> theClass;
  if (className == null) {
    throw new RuntimeOperationsException(
      new IllegalArgumentException(
        "The class name cannot be null"),
        "Exception occurred during object instantiation");
  } try {
    if (loader == null) {
      loader = MBeanInstantiator.class.getClassLoader();
    }
    if (loader != null) {
      theClass = Class.forName(className, false, loader);
    } else {
      theClass = Class.forName(className);
    }
  } catch (ClassNotFoundException e) {
    throw new ReflectionException(
      e, "The MBean class could not be loaded");
  }
  return theClass;
}
```

This method delegates the task of dynamically loading the specified class to the Class.forName() method, which delegates the work to its calling method's class loader. Because the calling method is MBeanInstantiator.loadClass(), the core class loader is used, which provides no security checks.

Compliant Solution (CVE-2013-0422)

Oracle mitigated this vulnerability in Java 1.7.0 update 11 by adding an access check to the MBeanInstantiator.loadClass() method. This access check ensures that the caller is permitted to access the class being sought:

```
// ...
  if (className == null) {
    throw new RuntimeOperationsException(
      new IllegalArgumentException(
        "The class name cannot be null"),
        "Exception occurred during object instantiation");
  }
  ReflectUtil.checkPackageAccess(className);
  try {
    if (loader == null)
// ...
```

Applicability

Allowing untrusted code to invoke methods with reduced-security checks can result in privilege escalation. Likewise, allowing untrusted code to perform actions using the immediate caller's class loader may allow the untrusted code to execute with the same privileges as the immediate caller.

Methods that avoid using the immediate caller's class loader instance fall outside the scope of this guideline. For example, the three-argument `java.lang.Class` `.forName()` method requires an explicit argument that specifies the class loader instance to use.

```
public static Class forName(String name, boolean initialize,
        ClassLoader loader) throws ClassNotFoundException
```

Do not use the immediate caller's class loader as the third argument when instances must be returned to untrusted code.

Bibliography

[API 2013]	Class `ClassLoader`
[Chan 1998]	`java.lang.reflect AccessibleObject`
[Guillardoy 2012]	Java 0Day Analysis (CVE-2012-4681)
[Long 2012]	SEC00-J. Do not allow privileged blocks to leak sensitive information across a trust boundary
	SEC03-J. Do not load trusted classes after allowing untrusted code to load arbitrary classes
	SEC05-J. Do not use reflection to increase accessibility of classes, methods, or fields
[Manion 2013]	"Anatomy of Java Exploits"
[Oracle 2013d]	Oracle Security Alert for CVE-2013-0422

■ 19. Define custom security permissions for fine-grained security

The default `SecurityManager` checks whether the caller of a particular method has sufficient permissions to proceed with an action. An action is defined in Java's security architecture as a level of access, and requires certain permissions before it can be performed. For example, the actions for `java.io.FilePermission` are *read, write, execute,* and *delete* [API 2013]. The "Permission Descriptions and Risks" guide [Oracle 2011d] enumerates the default permissions and the risks associated with granting these permissions to Java code.

Sometimes, stronger restrictions than those provided by the default security manager are necessary. Failure to provide custom permissions when no corresponding default permissions exist can lead to privilege escalation vulnerabilities that enable untrusted callers to execute restricted operations or actions.

This guideline addresses the problem of excess privileges. See Guideline 16, "Avoid granting excess privileges," for another approach to solving this problem.

Noncompliant Code Example

This noncompliant code example contains a privileged block that is used to perform two sensitive operations: loading a library and setting the default exception handler.

```
class LoadLibrary {
  private void loadLibrary() {
    AccessController.doPrivileged(
      new PrivilegedAction() {
        public Object run() {
          // Privileged code
          System.loadLibrary("myLib.so");
          // Perform some sensitive operation like
          // setting the default exception handler
          MyExceptionReporter.setExceptionReporter(reporter);
          return null;
        }
    });
  }
}
```

When used, the default security manager forbids the loading of the library unless the `RuntimePermission loadLibrary.myLib` is granted in the policy file. However, the security manager does not automatically guard a caller from performing the second sensitive operation of setting the default exception handler because the permission for this operation is nondefault and, consequently, unavailable. This security weakness can be exploited, for example, by programming and installing an exception handler that reveals information that a legitimate handler would filter out.

Compliant Solution

This compliant solution defines a custom permission `ExceptionReporterPermission` with the target `exc.reporter` to prohibit illegitimate callers from setting the default exception handler. This can be achieved by subclassing `BasicPermission`, which allows *binary*-style permissions (either allow or disallow). The compliant solution then uses a security manager to check whether the caller has the requisite permission to set the handler. The code throws a `SecurityException` if the check fails. The custom permission class `ExceptionReporterPermission` is also defined with the two required constructors.

```java
class LoadLibrary {
  private void loadLibrary() {
    AccessController.doPrivileged(
      new PrivilegedAction() {
        public Object run() {
          // Privileged code
          System.loadLibrary("myLib.so");

          // Perform some sensitive operation like
          // setting the default exception handler
          MyExceptionReporter.setExceptionReporter(reporter);
          return null;
        }
      });
  }
}

final class MyExceptionReporter extends ExceptionReporter {
  public void setExceptionReporter(ExceptionReporter reporter) {
    SecurityManager sm = System.getSecurityManager();
    if(sm != null) {
      sm.checkPermission(
        new ExceptionReporterPermission("exc.reporter"));
    }

    // Proceed to set the exception reporter
  }
  // ... Other methods of MyExceptionReporter
}

final class ExceptionReporterPermission extends BasicPermission {
  public ExceptionReporterPermission(String permName) {
    super(permName);
  }

  // Even though the actions parameter is ignored,
  // this constructor has to be defined
  public ExceptionReporterPermission(String permName,
                                     String actions) {
    super(permName, actions);
  }
}
```

The policy file needs to grant two permissions: `ExceptionReporterPermission` `exc.reporter` and `RuntimePermission` `loadlibrary.myLib`. The following policy file assumes that the preceding sources reside in the `c:\package` directory on a Windows-based system.

```
grant codeBase "file:/c:/package" {
  // For *nix, file:${user.home}/package/
  permission ExceptionReporterPermission "exc.reporter";
  permission java.lang.RuntimePermission "loadLibrary.myLib";
};
```

By default, permissions cannot be defined to support actions using `Basic-Permission`, but the actions can be freely implemented in the subclass `Exception-ReporterPermission` if required. `BasicPermission` is abstract even though it contains no abstract methods; it defines all the methods that it extends from the `Permission` class. The custom-defined subclass of the `BasicPermission` class must define two constructors to call the most appropriate (one- or two-argument) superclass constructor (because the superclass lacks a default constructor). The two-argument constructor also accepts an action, even though a basic permission does not use it. This behavior is required for constructing permission objects from the policy file. Note that the custom-defined subclass of the `BasicPermission` class is declared to be `final`.

Applicability

Running Java code without defining custom permissions where default permissions are inapplicable can leave an application open to privilege escalation vulnerabilities.

Bibliography

[API 2013]	Class `FilePermission`
	Class `SecurityManager`
[Oaks 2001]	"Permissions" subsection of Chapter 5, "The Access Controller,"
[Oracle 2011d]	Permissions in the Java™ SE 6 Development Kit (JDK)
[Oracle 2013c]	Java Platform Standard Edition 7 Documentation
[Policy 2010]	"Permission Descriptions and Risks"

■ 20. Create a secure sandbox using a security manager

According to the Java API Class `SecurityManager` documentation [API 2013],

> The security manager is a class that allows applications to implement a security policy. It allows an application to determine, before performing a possibly unsafe or

sensitive operation, what the operation is and whether it is being attempted in a security context that allows the operation to be performed. The application can allow or disallow the operation.

A security manager may be associated with any Java code.

The applet security manager denies applets all but the most essential privileges. It is designed to protect against inadvertent system modification, information leakage, and user impersonation. The use of security managers is not limited to client-side protection. Web servers, such as Tomcat and WebSphere, use this facility to isolate trojan servlets and malicious Java Server Pages (JSP) as well as to protect sensitive system resources from inadvertent access.

Java applications that run from the command line can set a default or custom security manager using a command-line flag. Alternatively, it is possible to install a security manager programmatically. Installing a security manager programmatically helps create a default sandbox that allows or denies sensitive actions on the basis of the security policy in effect.

From Java 2 SE Platform onward, `SecurityManager` is a nonabstract class. As a result, there is no explicit requirement to override its methods. To create and use a security manager programmatically, the code must have the runtime permissions `createSecurityManager` (to instantiate `SecurityManager`) and `setSecurityManager` (to install it). These permissions are checked only if a security manager is already installed. This is useful for situations in which a default security manager is in place, such as on a virtual host, and individual hosts must be denied the requisite permissions for overriding the default security manager with a custom one.

The security manager is closely tied to the `AccessController` class. The former is used as a hub for access control, whereas the latter provides the actual implementation of the access control algorithm. The security manager supports

■ Providing backward compatibility: Legacy code often contains custom implementations of the security manager class because it was originally abstract.

■ Defining custom policies: Subclassing the security manager permits definition of custom security policies (for example, multilevel, coarse, or fine grain).

Regarding the implementation and use of custom security managers as opposed to default ones, the Java security architecture specification [SecuritySpec 2010] states:

> We encourage the use of `AccessController` in application code, while customization of a security manager (via subclassing) should be the last resort and should be done with extreme care. Moreover, a customized security manager, such as one that always checks the time of the day before invoking standard security checks, could and should utilize the algorithm provided by `AccessController` whenever appropriate.

Many of the Java SE APIs perform security manager checks by default before performing sensitive operations. For example, the constructor of class `java.io`

`.FileInputStream` throws a `SecurityException` if the caller does not have the permission to read a file. Because `SecurityException` is a subclass of `RuntimeException`, the declarations of some API methods (for example, those of the `java.io.FileReader` class) may lack a `throws` clause that lists the `SecurityException`. Avoid depending on the presence or absence of security manager checks that are not specified in the API method's documentation.

Noncompliant Code Example (Command-Line Installation)

This noncompliant code example fails to install any security manager from the command line. Consequently, the program runs with all permissions enabled; that is, there is no security manager to prevent any nefarious actions the program might perform.

```
java LocalJavaApp
```

Compliant Solution (Default Policy File)

Any Java program can attempt to install a `SecurityManager` programmatically, although the currently active security manager may forbid this operation. Applications designed to run locally can specify a default security manager by use of a flag on the command line at invocation.

The command-line option is preferred when applications must be prohibited from installing custom security managers programmatically, and are required to abide by the default security policy under all circumstances. This compliant solution installs the default security manager using the appropriate command-line flags. The security policy file grants permissions to the application for its intended actions.

```
java -Djava.security.manager -Djava.security.policy=policyURL \
    LocalJavaApp
```

The command-line flag can specify a custom security manager whose policies are enforced globally. Use the `-Djava.security.manager` flag, as follows:

```
java -Djava.security.manager=my.security.CustomManager ...
```

If the current security policy enforced by the current security manager forbids replacements (by omitting the `RuntimePermission("setSecurityManager")`), any attempt to invoke `setSecurityManager()` will throw a `SecurityException`.

The default security policy file `java.policy`—found in the `/path/to/java.home/lib/security` directory on UNIX-like systems and its equivalent on Microsoft Windows systems—grants a few permissions (reading system properties, binding to unprivileged ports, and so forth). A user-specific policy file may also be located in the user's home directory. The union of these policy files specifies the permissions granted to a program. The `java.security` file can specify which policy files are used. If either of the systemwide `java.policy` or `java.security` files is deleted, no permissions are granted to the executing Java program.

Compliant Solution (Custom Policy File)

Use double equals (==) instead of the single equals (=) when overriding the global Java security policy file with a custom policy file:

```
java -Djava.security.manager \
     -Djava.security.policy==policyURL \
     LocalJavaApp
```

Compliant Solution (Additional Policy Files)

The `appletviewer` automatically installs a security manager with the standard policy file. To specify additional policy files, use the `-J` flag.

```
appletviewer -J-Djava.security.manager \
             -J-Djava.security.policy==policyURL LocalJavaApp
```

Note that the policy file specified in the argument is ignored when the `policy` `.allowSystemProperty` property in the security properties file (`java.security`) is set to `false`; the default value of this property is `true`. Default Policy Implementation and Policy File Syntax [Policy 2010] discusses in depth the issues and syntax for writing policy files.

Noncompliant Code Example (Programmatic Installation)

A `SecurityManager` can also be activated using the static `System.setSecurityManager()` method. Only one `SecurityManager` may be active at a time. This method replaces the currently active `SecurityManager` with the `SecurityManager` provided in its argument, or no `SecurityManager` if its argument is `null`.

This noncompliant code example deactivates any current `SecurityManager` but does not install another `SecurityManager` in its place. Consequently, subsequent code will run with all permissions enabled; there will be no restrictions on any nefarious action the program might perform.

```
try {
  System.setSecurityManager(null);
} catch (SecurityException se) {
  // Cannot set security manager, log to file
}
```

An active SecurityManager that enforces a sensible security policy will prevent the system from deactivating it, causing this code to throw a SecurityException.

Compliant Solution (Default Security Manager)

This compliant solution instantiates and sets the default security manager.

```
try {
  System.setSecurityManager(new SecurityManager());
} catch (SecurityException se) {
  // Cannot set security manager, log appropriately
}
```

Compliant Solution (Custom Security Manager)

This compliant solution demonstrates how to instantiate a custom Security-Manager class called CustomSecurityManager by invoking its constructor with a password; this custom security manager is then installed as the active security manager.

```
char password[] = /* initialize */
try {
  System.setSecurityManager(
    new CustomSecurityManager("password here")
  );
} catch (SecurityException se) {
  // Cannot set security manager, log appropriately
}
```

After this code executes, APIs that perform security checks will use the custom security manager. As noted earlier, custom security managers should be installed only when the default security manager lacks the required functionality.

Applicability

Java security fundamentally depends on the existence of a security manager. In its absence, sensitive actions can execute without restriction.

Programmatic detection of the presence or absence of a SecurityManager at runtime is straightforward. Static analysis can address the presence or absence of code that would attempt to install a SecurityManager if the code were executed. Checking whether the SecurityManager is installed early enough, whether it specifies the desired properties, or whether it is guaranteed to be installed may be possible in some special cases, but is generally undecidable.

Invocation of the `setSecurityManager()` method may be omitted in controlled environments in which it is known that a global-default security manager is *always* installed from the command line. This is difficult to enforce, and can result in vulnerabilities if the environment is incorrectly configured.

Bibliography

[API 2013]	Class `SecurityManager`
	Class `AccessControlContext`
	Class `AccessController`
[Gong 2003]	§6.1, "Security Manager"
[Pistoia 2004]	§7.4, "The Security Manager"
[Policy 2010]	Default Policy Implementation and Policy File Syntax
[SecuritySpec 2010]	§6.2, "`SecurityManager` versus `AccessController`"

■ 21. Do not let untrusted code misuse privileges of callback methods

Callbacks provide a means to register a method to be invoked (or *called back*) when an interesting event occurs. Java uses callbacks for applet and servlet life-cycle events, AWT and Swing event notifications such as button clicks, asynchronous reads and writes to storage, and even in `Runnable.run()` wherein a new thread automatically executes the specified `run()` method.

In Java, callbacks are typically implemented using interfaces. The general structure of a callback is as follows:

```
public interface CallBack {
  void callMethod();
}

class CallBackImpl implements CallBack {
  public void callMethod() {
    System.out.println("CallBack invoked");
  }
}

class CallBackAction {
  private CallBack callback;
```

```
   public CallBackAction(CallBack callback) {
     this.callback = callback;
   }

   public void perform() {
     callback.callMethod();
   }
 }

class Client {
  public static void main(String[] args) {
    CallBackAction action =
      new CallBackAction(new CallBackImpl());
    // ...
    action.perform(); // Prints "CallBack invoked"
  }
}
```

Callback methods are often invoked without changes in privileges, which means that they may be executed in a context that has more privileges than the context in which they are declared. If these callback methods accept data from untrusted code, privilege escalation may occur.

According to Oracle's secure coding guidelines [SCG 2010],

> Callback methods are generally invoked from the system with full permissions. It seems reasonable to expect that malicious code needs to be on the stack in order to perform an operation, but that is not the case. Malicious code may set up objects that bridge the callback to a security checked operation. For instance, a file chooser dialog box that can manipulate the filesystem from user actions, may have events posted from malicious code. Alternatively, malicious code can disguise a file chooser as something benign while redirecting user events.

This guideline is an instance of Guideline 17, "Minimize privileged code," and is related to *The CERT® Oracle® Secure Coding Standard for Java*™ [Long 2012], "SEC01-J. Do not allow tainted variables in privileged blocks."

Noncompliant Code Example

This noncompliant code example uses a UserLookupCallBack class that implements the CallBack interface to look up a user's name given the user's ID. This lookup code assumes that this information lives in the /etc/passwd file, which requires elevated privileges to open. Consequently, the Client class invokes all callbacks with elevated privileges (within a doPrivileged block).

```java
public interface CallBack {
  void callMethod();
}

class UserLookupCallBack implements CallBack {
  private int uid;
  private String name;

  public UserLookupCallBack(int uid) {
    this.uid = uid;
  }

  public String getName() {
    return name;
  }

  public void callMethod() {
    try (InputStream fis = new FileInputStream("/etc/passwd")) {
      // Look up uid & assign to name
    } catch (IOException x) {
      name = null;
    }
  }
}

final class CallBackAction {
  private CallBack callback;

  public CallBackAction(CallBack callback) {
    this.callback = callback;
  }

  public void perform() {
    AccessController.doPrivileged(new PrivilegedAction<Void>() {
      public Void run() {
        callback.callMethod();
        return null;
      }
    });
  }
}
```

This code could be safely used by a client, as follows:

```java
public static void main(String[] args) {
  int uid = Integer.parseInt(args[0]);
```

```
CallBack callBack = new UserLookupCallBack(uid);
CallBackAction action = new CallBackAction(callBack);

// ...
action.perform(); // Looks up user name
System.out.println("User " + uid + " is named " +
                   callBack.getName());
}
```

However, an attacker can use `CallBackAction` to execute malicious code with elevated privileges by registering a `MaliciousCallBack` instance:

```
class MaliciousCallBack implements CallBack {
  public void callMethod() {
    // Code here gets executed with elevated privileges
  }
}

// Client code
public static void main(String[] args) {
  CallBack callBack = new MaliciousCallBack();
  CallBackAction action = new CallBackAction(callBack);
  action.perform(); // Executes malicious code
}
```

Compliant Solution (Callback-Local `doPrivileged` Block)

According to Oracle's secure coding guidelines [SCG 2010],

> By convention, instances of `PrivilegedAction` and `PrivilegedExceptionAction` may be made available to untrusted code, but `doPrivileged` must not be invoked with caller-provided actions.

This compliant solution moves the invocation of `doPrivileged()` out of the `CallBackAction` code and into the callback itself.

```
public interface CallBack {
  void callMethod();
}

class UserLookupCallBack implements CallBack {
  private int uid;
  private String name;
```

```
  public UserLookupCallBack(int uid) {
    this.uid = uid;
  }

  public String getName() {
    return name;
  }

  public final void callMethod() {
    AccessController.doPrivileged(new PrivilegedAction<Void>() {
      public Void run() {
        try (InputStream fis =
          new FileInputStream("/etc/passwd")) {
          // Look up userid and assign to
          // UserLookupCallBack.this.name
        } catch (IOException x) {
          UserLookupCallBack.this.name = null;
        }
        return null;
      }
    });
  }
}

final class CallBackAction {
  private CallBack callback;

  public CallBackAction(CallBack callback) {
    this.callback = callback;
  }

  public void perform() {
    callback.callMethod();
  }
}
```

This code behaves the same as before, but an attacker can no longer execute malicious callback code with elevated privileges. Even though an attacker can pass a malicious callback instance using the constructor of class CallBackAction, the code is not executed with elevated privileges because the malicious instance must contain a doPrivileged block that cannot have the same privileges as trusted code. Additionally, class CallBackAction cannot be subclassed to override the perform() method as it is declared final.

Compliant Solution (Declare Callback Final)

This compliant solution declares the `UserLookupCallBack` class `final` to prevent overriding of `callMethod()`.

```
final class UserLookupCallBack implements CallBack {
  // ...
}

// Remaining code is unchanged
```

Applicability

Exposing sensitive methods through callbacks can result in misuse of privileges and arbitrary code execution.

Bibliography

[API 2013]   `AccessController.doPrivileged()`

[Long 2012]   SEC01-J. Do not allow tainted variables in privileged blocks

[SCG 2010]   Guideline 9-2: Beware of callback methods

                  Guideline 9-3: Safely invoke `java.security.AccessCon-troller.doPrivileged`

Defensive Programming

Defensive programming is carefully guarded programming that helps you to construct reliable software by designing each component to protect itself as much as possible: for example, by checking that undocumented assumptions remain valid [Goodliffe 2007]. The guidelines in this chapter address areas of the Java language that can help to constrain the effect of an error or help to recover from an error.

Java language mechanisms should be used to limit the scope, lifetime, and accessibility of program resources. Also, Java annotations can be used to document the program, aiding readability and maintenance. Java programmers should be aware of implicit behaviors and avoid unwarranted assumptions about how the system behaves.

A good overall principle for defensive programming is simplicity. A complicated system is difficult to understand, difficult to maintain, and difficult to get right in the first place. If a construct turns out to be complicated to implement, consider redesigning or refactoring it to reduce the complexity.

Finally, the program should be designed to be as robust as possible. Wherever possible, the program should help the Java runtime system by limiting the resources it uses and by releasing acquired resources when they are no longer needed. Again, this can often be achieved by limiting the lifetime and accessibility of objects and other programming constructs. Not all eventualities can be anticipated, so a strategy should be developed to provide a graceful exit of last resort.

■ 22. Minimize the scope of variables

Scope minimization helps developers avoid common programming errors, improves code readability by connecting the declaration and actual use of a variable, and improves maintainability because unused variables are more easily detected and removed. It may also allow objects to be recovered by the garbage collector more quickly, and it prevents violations of Guideline 37, "Do not shadow or obscure identifiers in subscopes."

Noncompliant Code Example

This noncompliant code example shows a variable that is declared outside the for loop.

```
public class Scope {
  public static void main(String[] args) {
    int i = 0;
    for (i = 0; i < 10; i++) {
      // Do operations
    }
  }
}
```

This code is noncompliant because, even though variable i is not intentionally used outside the for loop, it is declared in method scope. One of the few scenarios where variable i needs to be declared in method scope is when the loop contains a break statement, and the value of i must be inspected after conclusion of the loop.

Compliant Solution

Minimize the scope of variables where possible. For example, declare loop indices within the for statement:

```
public class Scope {
  public static void main(String[] args) {
    for (int i = 0; i < 10; i++) { // Contains declaration
      // Do operations
    }
  }
}
```

Noncompliant Code Example

This noncompliant code example shows a variable count that is declared outside the counter() method, although the variable is not used outside the counter() method.

```
public class Foo {
  private int count;
  private static final int MAX_COUNT = 10;

  public void counter() {
    count = 0;
    while (condition()) {
      /* ... */
      if (count++ > MAX_COUNT) {
        return;
      }
    }
  }

  private boolean condition() {/* ... */}
  // No other method references count
  // but several other methods reference MAX_COUNT
}
```

The reusability of the method is reduced because if the method were copied to another class, then the count variable would also need to be redefined in the new context. Furthermore, the analyzability of the counter method would be reduced, as whole program data flow analysis would be necessary to determine possible values for count.

Compliant Solution

In this compliant solution, the count field is declared local to the counter() method:

```
public class Foo {
  private static final int MAX_COUNT = 10;

  public void counter() {
    int count = 0;
    while (condition()) {
      /* ... */
      if (count++ > MAX_COUNT) {
        return;
      }
    }
  }
}
```

```
    private boolean condition() {/* ... */}
    // No other method references count
    // but several other methods reference MAX_COUNT
}
```

Applicability

Detecting local variables that are declared in a larger scope than is required by the code as written is straightforward and can eliminate the possibility of false positives.

Detecting multiple for statements that use the same index variable is straightforward; it produces false positives only in the unusual case where the value of the index variable is intended to persist between loops.

Bibliography

[Bloch 2001]   Item 29, "Minimize the Scope of Local Variables"

[JLS 2013]   §14.4, "Local Variable Declaration Statements"

■ 23. Minimize the scope of the @SuppressWarnings annotation

When the compiler detects potential type-safety issues arising from mixing raw types with generic code, it issues *unchecked warnings*, including *unchecked cast warnings, unchecked method invocation warnings, unchecked generic array creation warnings*, and *unchecked conversion warnings* [Bloch 2008]. It is permissible to use the @SuppressWarnings("unchecked") annotation to suppress unchecked warnings when, and only when, the warning-emitting code is guaranteed to be type safe. A common use case is mixing legacy code with new client code. The perils of ignoring unchecked warnings are discussed extensively in *The CERT® Oracle® Secure Coding Standard for Java™* [Long 2012], "OBJ03-J. Do not mix generic with nongeneric raw types in new code."

According to the Java API Annotation Type SuppressWarnings documentation [API 2013],

> As a matter of style, programmers should always use this annotation on the most deeply nested element where it is effective. If you want to suppress a warning in a particular method, you should annotate that method rather than its class.

The @SuppressWarnings annotation can be used in the declaration of variables and methods as well as an entire class. It is, however, important to narrow its scope so that only those warnings that occur in the narrower scope are suppressed.

Noncompliant Code Example

In this noncompliant code example, the @SuppressWarnings annotation's scope encompasses the whole class:

```
@SuppressWarnings("unchecked")
class Legacy {
  Set s = new HashSet();
  public final void doLogic(int a, char c) {
    s.add(a);
    s.add(c); // Type-unsafe operation, ignored
  }
}
```

This code is dangerous because all unchecked warnings within the class are suppressed. Oversights of this nature can result in a ClassCastException at runtime.

Compliant Solution

Limit the scope of the @SuppressWarnings annotation to the nearest code that generates a warning. In this case, it may be used in the declaration for the Set:

```
class Legacy {
  @SuppressWarnings("unchecked")
  Set s = new HashSet();
  public final void doLogic(int a, char c) {
    s.add(a); // Produces unchecked warning
    s.add(c); // Produces unchecked warning
  }
}
```

Noncompliant Code Example (ArrayList)

This noncompliant code example is from an old implementation of java.util.ArrayList:

```
@SuppressWarnings("unchecked")
public <T> T[] toArray(T[] a) {
  if (a.length < size) {
    // Produces unchecked warning
    return (T[]) Arrays.copyOf(elements, size, a.getClass());
  }
  // ...
}
```

When the class is compiled, it emits an unchecked cast warning:

```
// Unchecked cast warning
ArrayList.java:305: warning: [unchecked] unchecked cast found :
  Object[], required: T[]
return (T[]) Arrays.copyOf(elements, size, a.getClass());
```

This warning cannot be suppressed for just the `return` statement because it is not a declaration [JLS 2013]. As a result, the programmer suppresses warnings for the entire method. This can cause issues when functionality that performs type-unsafe operations is added to the method at a later date [Bloch 2008].

Compliant Solution (`ArrayList`)

When it is impossible to use the `@SuppressWarnings` annotation in an appropriate scope, as in the preceding noncompliant code example, declare a new variable to hold the return value and adorn it with the `@SuppressWarnings` annotation.

```
// ...
@SuppressWarnings("unchecked")
T[] result = (T[]) Arrays.copyOf(elements, size, a.getClass());
return result;
// ...
```

Applicability

Failure to reduce the scope of the `@SuppressWarnings` annotation can lead to runtime exceptions and break type-safety guarantees.

This rule cannot be statically enforced in full generality; however, static analysis can be used for some special cases.

Bibliography

[API 2013]   Annotation Type `SuppressWarnings`

[Bloch 2008]   Item 24, "Eliminate Unchecked Warnings"

[Long 2012]   OBJ03-J. Do not mix generic with nongeneric raw types in new code

■ 24. Minimize the accessibility of classes and their members

Classes and class members (classes, interfaces, fields, and methods) are access-controlled in Java. Access is indicated by an access modifier (`public`, `protected`, or `private`) or by the absence of an access modifier (the default access, also called *package-private access*).

Table 2–1. Access control rules

Access Specifier	Class	Package	Subclass	World
private	x			
None	x	x	x*	
protected	x	x	x**	
public	x	x	x	x

*Subclasses within the same package can also access members that lack access specifiers (default or package-private visibility). An additional requirement for access is that the subclasses must be loaded by the class loader that loaded the class containing the package-private members. Subclasses in a different package cannot access such package-private members.

**To reference a protected member, the accessing code must be contained in either the class that defines the protected member or in a subclass of that defining class. Subclass access is permitted without regard to the package location of the subclass.

Table 2–1 presents a simplified view of the access control rules. An *x* indicates that the particular access is permitted from within that domain. For example, an *x* in the class column means that the class member is accessible to code present within the same class in which it is declared. Similarly, the package column indicates that the member is accessible from any class (or subclass) defined in the same package, provided that the class (or subclass) is loaded by the class loader that loaded the class containing the member. The same class loader condition applies only to package-private member access.

Classes and class members must be given the minimum possible access so that malicious code has the least opportunity to compromise security. As far as possible, classes should avoid exposing methods that contain (or invoke) sensitive code through interfaces; interfaces allow only publicly accessible methods, and such methods are part of the public application programming interface (API) of the class. (Note that this is the opposite of Joshua Bloch's recommendation to prefer interfaces for APIs [Bloch 2008, Item 16].) One exception to this is implementing an *unmodifiable* interface that exposes a public immutable view of a mutable object. (See *The CERT® Oracle® Secure Coding Standard for Java™* [Long 2012], "OBJ04-J. Provide mutable classes with copy functionality to safely allow passing instances to untrusted code.") Note that even if a nonfinal class's visibility is default, it can be susceptible to misuse if it contains public methods. Methods that perform all necessary security checks and sanitize all inputs may be exposed through interfaces.

Protected accessibility is invalid for non-nested classes, but nested classes may be declared protected. Fields of nonfinal public classes should rarely be declared protected; untrusted code in another package can subclass the class, and access the member. Furthermore, protected members are part of the API of the class, and consequently require continued support. When this rule is followed, declaring fields as protected is unnecessary. "OBJ01-J. Declare data members as private and provide accessible wrapper methods" [Long 2012] recommends declaring fields as private.

If a class, interface, method, or field is part of a published API, such as a web service endpoint, it may be declared public. Other classes and members should be declared either package-private or private. For example, non-security-critical classes are encouraged to provide public static factories to implement instance control with a private constructor.

Noncompliant Code Example (Public Class)

This noncompliant code example defines a class that is internal to a system and not part of any public API. Nonetheless, this class is declared public.

```java
public final class Point {
  private final int x;
  private final int y;

  public Point(int x, int y) {
    this.x = x;
    this.y = y;
  }

  public void getPoint() {
    System.out.println("(" + x + "," + y + ")");
  }
}
```

Even though this example complies with "OBJ01-J. Declare data members as private and provide accessible wrapper methods" [Long 2012], untrusted code could instantiate Point and invoke the public getPoint() method to obtain the coordinates.

Compliant Solution (Final Classes with Public Methods)

This compliant solution declares the Point class as package-private in accordance with its status as not part of any public API:

```
final class Point {
  private final int x;
  private final int y;

  Point(int x, int y) {
    this.x = x;
    this.y = y;
  }

  public void getPoint() {
    System.out.println("(" + x + "," + y + ")");
  }
}
```

A top-level class, such as `Point`, cannot be declared private. Package-private accessibility is acceptable, provided package insertion attacks are avoided. (See "ENV01-J. Place all security-sensitive code in a single JAR and sign and seal it" [Long 2012].) A package insertion attack occurs when, at runtime, any protected or package-private members of a class can be called directly by a class that is maliciously inserted into the same package. However, this attack is difficult to carry out in practice because, in addition to the requirement of infiltrating the package, the target and the untrusted class must be loaded by the same class loader. Untrusted code is typically deprived of such levels of access.

Because the class is final, the `getPoint()` method can be declared public. A public subclass that violates this rule cannot override the method and expose it to untrusted code, so its accessibility is irrelevant. For nonfinal classes, reducing the accessibility of methods to private or package-private eliminates this threat.

Compliant Solution (Nonfinal Classes with Nonpublic Methods)

This compliant solution declares the `Point` class and its `getPoint()` method as package-private, which allows the `Point` class to be nonfinal and allows `getPoint()` to be invoked by classes present within the same package and loaded by a common class loader:

```
class Point {
  private final int x;
  private final int y;

  Point(int x, int y) {
    this.x = x;
    this.y = y;
  }
```

```
    void getPoint() {
      System.out.println("(" + x + "," + y + ")");
    }
  }
```

Noncompliant Code Example (Public Class with Public Static Method)

This noncompliant code example again defines a class that is internal to a system and not part of any public API. Nonetheless, this class is declared public.

```
public final class Point {
  private static final int x = 1;
  private static final int y = 2;

  private Point(int x, int y) {}

  public static void getPoint() {
    System.out.println("(" + x + "," + y + ")");
  }
}
```

This example also complies with "OBJ01-J. Declare data members as private and provide accessible wrapper methods" [Long 2012], untrusted code could access Point and invoke the public static getPoint() to obtain the default coordinates. The attempt to implement instance control using a private constructor is futile because the public static method exposes internal class contents.

Compliant Solution (Package-Private Class)

This compliant solution reduces the accessibility of the class to package-private.

```
final class Point {
  private static final int x = 1;
  private static final int y = 2;

  private Point(int x, int y) {}

  public static void getPoint() {
    System.out.println("(" + x + "," + y + ")");
  }
}
```

Access to the `getPoint()` method is restricted to classes located within the same package. Untrusted code is prevented from invoking `getPoint()` and obtaining the coordinates.

Applicability

Granting excessive access breaks encapsulation and weakens the security of Java applications.

A system with an API designed for use (and possibly extended) by third-party code must expose the API through a public interface. The demands of such an API override this guideline.

For any given piece of code, the minimum accessibility for each class and member can be computed so as to avoid introducing compilation errors. A limitation is that the result of this computation may lack any resemblance to what the programmer intended when the code was written. For example, unused members can obviously be declared private. However, such members could be unused only because the particular body of code examined coincidentally lacks references to the members. Nevertheless, this computation can provide a useful starting point for a programmer who wishes to minimize the accessibility of classes and their members.

Bibliography

[Bloch 2008]	Item 13, "Minimize the Accessibility of Classes and Members"
	Item 16, "Prefer Interfaces to Abstract Classes"
[Campione 1996]	Access Control
[JLS 2013]	§6.6, "Access Control"
[Long 2012]	ENV01-J. Place all security-sensitive code in a single JAR and sign and seal it
	OBJ01-J. Declare data members as private and provide accessible wrapper methods
	OBJ04-J. Provide mutable classes with copy functionality to safely allow passing instances to untrusted code
[McGraw 1999]	Chapter 3, "Java Language Security Constructs"

■ 25. Document thread-safety and use annotations where applicable

The Java language annotation facility is useful for documenting design intent. Source code annotation is a mechanism for associating metadata with a program element and making it available to the compiler, analyzers, debuggers, or Java Virtual

Machine (JVM) for examination. Several annotations are available for documenting thread-safety or the lack thereof.

Obtaining Concurrency Annotations

Two sets of concurrency annotations are freely available and licensed for use in any code. The first set consists of four annotations described in *Java Concurrency in Practice* (JCIP) [Goetz 2006], which can be downloaded from http://jcip.net. The JCIP annotations are released under the Creative Commons Attribution License.

The second, larger set of concurrency annotations is available from and supported by SureLogic. These annotations are released under the Apache Software License, Version 2.0, and can be downloaded at www.surelogic.com. The annotations can be verified by the SureLogic JSure tool, and they remain useful for documenting code even when the tool is unavailable. These annotations include the JCIP annotations because they are supported by the JSure tool. (JSure also supports use of the JCIP JAR file.)

To use the annotations, download and add one or both of the aforementioned JAR files to the code's build path. The use of these annotations to document thread-safety is described in the following sections.

Documenting Intended Thread-Safety

JCIP provides three class-level annotations to describe the programmer's design intent with respect to thread-safety.

The `@ThreadSafe` annotation is applied to a class to indicate that it is *thread-safe*. This means that no sequences of accesses (reads and writes to public fields, calls to public methods) can leave the object in an inconsistent state, regardless of the interleaving of these accesses by the runtime or any external synchronization or coordination on the part of the caller.

For example, the following `Aircraft` class specifies that it is thread-safe as part of its locking policy documentation. This class protects the x and y fields using a reentrant lock.

```
@ThreadSafe
@Region("private AircraftState")
@RegionLock("StateLock is stateLock protects AircraftState")
public final class Aircraft {
  private final Lock stateLock = new ReentrantLock();
  // ...
  @InRegion("AircraftState")
  private long x, y;
  // ...
```

```
public void setPosition(long x, long y) {
  stateLock.lock();
  try {
    this.x = x;
    this.y = y;
  } finally {
    stateLock.unlock();
  }
}
// ...
}
```

The @Region and @RegionLock annotations document the locking policy upon which the promise of thread-safety is predicated.

Even when one or more @RegionLock or @GuardedBy annotations have been used to document the locking policy of a class, the @ThreadSafe annotation provides an intuitive way for reviewers to learn that the class is thread-safe.

The @Immutable annotation is applied to *immutable* classes. Immutable objects are inherently thread-safe; once they are fully constructed, they may be published via a reference and shared safely among multiple threads.

The following example shows an immutable Point class:

```
@Immutable
public final class Point {
  private final int f_x;
  private final int f_y;

  public Point(int x, int y) {
    f_x = x;
    f_y = y;
  }

  public int getX() {
    return f_x;
  }

  public int getY() {
    return f_y;
  }
}
```

According to Joshua Bloch [Bloch 2008],

> It is not necessary to document the immutability of enum types. Unless it is obvious from the return type, static factories must document the thread safety of the returned object, as demonstrated by Collections.synchronizedMap.

The @NotThreadSafe annotation is applied to classes that are not thread-safe. Many classes fail to document whether they are safe for multithreaded use. Consequently, a programmer has no easy way to determine whether the class is thread-safe. This annotation provides clear indication of the class's lack of thread-safety.

For example, most of the collection implementations provided in java.util are not thread-safe. The class java.util.ArrayList could document this as follows:

```
package java.util.ArrayList;

@NotThreadSafe
public class ArrayList<E> extends ... {
  // ...
}
```

Documenting Locking Policies

It is important to document all the locks that are being used to protect shared state. According to Brian Goetz and colleagues [Goetz 2006],

> For each mutable state variable that may be accessed by more than one thread, *all* accesses to that variable must be performed with the *same* lock held. In this case, we say that the variable is *guarded by* that lock. (p. 28)

JCIP provides the @GuardedBy annotation for this purpose, and SureLogic provides the @RegionLock annotation. The field or method to which the @GuardedBy annotation is applied can be accessed only when holding a particular lock. It may be an intrinsic lock or a dynamic lock such as java.util.concurrent.Lock.

For example, the following MovablePoint class implements a movable point that can remember its past locations using the memo array list:

```
@ThreadSafe
public final class MovablePoint {

  @GuardedBy("this")
  double xPos = 1.0;
```

```
@GuardedBy("this")
double yPos = 1.0;
@GuardedBy("itself")
static final List<MovablePoint> memo
  = new ArrayList<MovablePoint>();

public void move(double slope, double distance) {
  synchronized (this) {
    rememberPoint(this);
    xPos += (1 / slope) * distance;
    yPos += slope * distance;
  }
}

public static void rememberPoint(MovablePoint value) {
  synchronized (memo) {
    memo.add(value);
  }
}
}
```

The @GuardedBy annotations on the xPos and yPos fields indicate that access to these fields is protected by holding a lock on this. The move() method also synchronizes on this, which modifies these fields. The @GuardedBy annotation on the memo list indicates that a lock on the ArrayList object protects its contents. The rememberPoint() method also synchronizes on the memo list.

One issue with the @GuardedBy annotation is that it fails to indicate when there is a relationship between the fields of a class. This limitation can be overcome by using the SureLogic @RegionLock annotation, which declares a new region lock for the class to which this annotation is applied. This declaration creates a new named lock that associates a particular lock object with a region of the class. The region may be accessed only when the lock is held. For example, the SimpleLock locking policy indicates that synchronizing on the instance protects all of its state:

```
@RegionLock("SimpleLock is this protects Instance")
class Simple { ... }
```

Unlike @GuardedBy, the @RegionLock annotation allows the programmer to give an explicit, and hopefully meaningful, name to the locking policy.

In addition to naming the locking policy, the @Region annotation allows a name to be given to the region of the state that is being protected. That name makes it clear that the state and locking policy belong together, as demonstrated in the following example:

```
@Region("private AircraftPosition")
@RegionLock("StateLock is stateLock protects AircraftPosition")
public final class Aircraft {
  private final Lock stateLock = new ReentrantLock();

  @InRegion("AircraftPosition")
  private long x, y;

  @InRegion("AircraftPosition")
  private long altitude;
  // ...
  public void setPosition(long x, long y) {
    stateLock.lock();
    try {
      this.x = x;
      this.y = y;
    } finally {
      stateLock.unlock();
    }
  }
}
// ...
}
```

In this example, a locking policy named StateLock is used to indicate that locking on stateLock protects the named AircraftPosition region, which includes the mutable state used to represent the position of the aircraft.

Construction of Mutable Objects

Typically, object construction is considered an exception to the locking policy because objects are thread-confined when they are first created. An object is confined to the thread that uses the new operator to create its instance. After creation, the object can be published to other threads safely. However, the object is not shared until the thread that created the instance allows it to be shared. Safe publication approaches discussed in *The CERT® Oracle® Secure Coding Standard for Java™* [Long 2012], "TSM01-J. Do not let the this reference escape during object construction," can be expressed succinctly with the @Unique("return") annotation.

For example, in the following code, the @Unique("return") annotation documents that the object returned from the constructor is a unique reference:

```
@RegionLock("Lock is this protects Instance")
public final class Example {
  private int x = 1;
  private int y;

  @Unique("return")
  public Example(int y) {
    this.y = y;
  }
  // ...
}
```

Documenting Thread-Confinement Policies

Dean Sutherland and William Scherlis propose annotations that can document thread-confinement policies. Their approach allows verification of the annotations against as-written code [Sutherland 2010].

For example, the following annotations express the design intent that a program has, at most, one Abstract Window Toolkit (AWT) event dispatch thread and several compute threads, and that the compute threads are forbidden to handle AWT data structures or events:

```
@ThreadRole AWT, Compute
@IncompatibleThreadRoles AWT, Compute
@MaxRoleCount AWT 1
```

Documenting Wait–Notify Protocols

According to Goetz and colleagues [Goetz 2006],

> A state-dependent class should either fully expose (and document) its waiting and notification protocols to subclasses, or prevent subclasses from participating in them at all. (This is an extension of "design and document for inheritance, or else prohibit it" [EJ Item 15].) At the very least, designing a state-dependent class for inheritance requires exposing the condition queues and locks and documenting the condition predicates and synchronization policy; it may also require exposing the underlying state variables. (The worst thing a state-dependent class can do is expose its state to subclasses but not document its protocols for waiting and notification; this is like a class exposing its state variables but not documenting its invariants.) (p. 395)

Wait–notify protocols should be documented adequately. Currently, we are not aware of any annotations for this purpose.

Applicability

Annotating concurrent code helps document the design intent and can be used to automate the detection and prevention of race conditions and data races.

Bibliography

[Bloch 2008]   Item 70, "Document Thread Safety"

[Goetz 2006]   *Java Concurrency in Practice*

[Long 2012]   TSM01-J. Do not let the `this` reference escape during object construction

[Sutherland 2010] "Composable Thread Coloring"

■ 26. Always provide feedback about the resulting value of a method

Methods should be designed to return a value that allows the developer to learn about the current state of the object and/or the result of an operation. This advice is consistent with *The CERT® Oracle® Secure Coding Standard for Java*™ [Long 2012], "EXP00-J. Do not ignore values returned by methods." The returned value should be representative of the last known state and should be chosen keeping in mind the perceptions and mental model of the developer.

Feedback can also be provided by throwing either standard or custom exception objects derived from the `Exception` class. With this approach, the developer can still get precise information about the outcome of the method and proceed to take the necessary actions. To do so, the exception should provide a detailed account of the abnormal condition at the appropriate abstraction level.

APIs should use a combination of these approaches, both to help clients distinguish correct results from incorrect ones and to encourage careful handling of any incorrect results. In cases where there is a commonly accepted error value that cannot be misinterpreted as a valid return value for the method, that error value should be returned; and in other cases an exception should be thrown. A method must not return a value that can hold both valid return data and an error code; see Guideline 52, "Avoid in-band error indicators," for more details.

Alternatively, an object can provide a state-testing method [Bloch 2008] that checks whether the object is in a consistent state. This approach is useful only in cases where the object's state cannot be modified by external threads. This prevents a time-of-check, time-of-use (TOCTOU) race condition between invocation of the object's state-testing method and the call to a method that depends on the object's state. During this interval, the object's state could change unexpectedly or even maliciously.

Method return values and/or error codes must accurately specify the object's state at an appropriate level of abstraction. Clients must be able to rely on the value for performing critical actions.

Noncompliant Code Example

The updateNode() method in this noncompliant code example modifies a node if it can find it in a linked list and does nothing if the node is not found.

```java
public void updateNode(int id, int newValue) {
  Node current = root;
  while (current != null) {
    if (current.getId() == id) {
      current.setValue(newValue);
      break;
    }
    current = current.next;
  }
}
```

This method fails to indicate whether it modified any node. Consequently, a caller cannot determine that the method succeeded or failed silently.

Compliant Solution (Boolean)

This compliant solution returns the result of the operation as true if it modified a node and false if it did not.

```java
public boolean updateNode(int id, int newValue) {
  Node current = root;
  while (current != null) {
    if (current.getId() == id) {
      current.setValue(newValue);
      return true; // Node successfully updated
    }
    current = current.next;
  }
  return false;
}
```

Compliant Solution (Exception)

This compliant solution returns the modified Node when one is found and throws a
NodeNotFoundException when the node is not available in the list.

```
public Node updateNode(int id, int newValue)
    throws NodeNotFoundException {
  Node current = root;
  while (current != null) {
    if (current.getId() == id) {
      current.setValue(newValue);
      return current;
    }
    current = current.next;
  }
  throw new NodeNotFoundException();
}
```

Using exceptions to indicate failure can be a good design choice, but throwing
exceptions is not always appropriate. In general, a method should throw an exception only when it is expected to succeed but an unrecoverable situation occurs or
when it expects a method higher up in the call hierarchy to initiate recovery.

Compliant Solution (Null Return Value)

This compliant solution returns the updated Node so that the developer can simply
check for a null return value if the operation fails.

```
public Node updateNode(int id, int newValue) {
  Node current = root;
  while (current != null) {
    if (current.getId() == id) {
      current.setValue(newValue);
      return current;
    }
    current = current.next;
  }
  return null;
}
```

A return value that might be null is an in-band error indicator, which is discussed
more thoroughly in Guideline 52, "Avoid in-band error indicators." This design is

permitted but is considered inferior to other designs, such as those shown in the other compliant solutions in this guideline.

Applicability

Failure to provide appropriate feedback through a combination of return values, error codes, and exceptions can lead to inconsistent object state and unexpected program behavior.

Bibliography

[Bloch 2008]   Item 59. Avoid unnecessary use of checked exceptions

[Long 2012]   EXP00-J. Do not ignore values returned by methods

[Ware 2008]   *Writing Secure Java Code*

■ 27. Identify files using multiple file attributes

Many file-related security vulnerabilities result from a program accessing an unintended file object. This often happens because file names are only loosely bound to underlying file objects. File names provide no information regarding the nature of the file object itself. Furthermore, the binding of a file name to a file object is reevaluated each time the file name is used in an operation. This reevaluation can introduce a time-of-check, time-of-use (TOCTOU) race condition into an application. Objects of type `java.io.File` and of type `java.nio.file.Path` are bound to underlying file objects by the operating system only when the file is accessed.

The `java.io.File` constructors and the `java.io.File` methods `renameTo()` and `delete()` rely solely on file names for file identification. The same holds for the `java.nio.file.Path.get()` methods for creating `Path` objects and the `move()` and `delete()` methods of `java.nio.file.Files`. Use all of these methods with caution.

Fortunately, files can often be identified by other attributes in addition to the file name—for example, by comparing file creation times or modification times. Information about a file that has been created and closed can be stored and then used to validate the identity of the file if it must be reopened. Comparing multiple attributes of the file increases the likelihood that the reopened file is the same file that was previously opened.

File identification is less crucial for applications that maintain their files in secure directories where they can be accessed only by the owner of the file and (possibly) by a system administrator (see *The CERT® Oracle® Secure Coding Standard for Java™* [Long 2012], "FIO00-J. Do not operate on files in shared directories").

Noncompliant Code Example

In this noncompliant code example, the file identified by the string `filename` is opened, processed, closed, and then reopened for reading:

```
public void processFile(String filename){
  // Identify a file by its path
  Path file1 = Paths.get(filename);

  // Open the file for writing
  try (BufferedWriter bw = new BufferedWriter(new
      OutputStreamWriter(Files.newOutputStream(file1)))) {
    // Write to file...
  } catch (IOException e) {
    // Handle error
  }

  // Close the file

  /*
   * A race condition here allows an attacker to switch
   * out the file for another
   */

  // Reopen the file for reading
  Path file2 = Paths.get(filename);

  try (BufferedReader br = new BufferedReader(new
      InputStreamReader(Files.newInputStream(file2)))) {
    String line;
    while ((line = br.readLine()) != null) {
      System.out.println(line);
    }
  } catch (IOException e) {
    // Handle error
  }
}
```

Because the binding between the file name and the underlying file object is reevaluated when the `BufferedReader` is created, this code cannot guarantee that the file opened for reading is the same file that was previously opened for writing. An attacker might have replaced the original file (with a symbolic link, for example) between the first call to `close()` and the subsequent creation of the `BufferedReader`.

Noncompliant Code Example (`Files.isSameFile()`)

In this noncompliant code example, the programmer attempts to ensure that the file opened for reading is the same as the file previously opened for writing by calling the method `Files.isSameFile()`:

```java
public void processFile(String filename){
  // Identify a file by its path
  Path file1 = Paths.get(filename);

  // Open the file for writing
  try (BufferedWriter bw = new BufferedWriter(new
      OutputStreamWriter(Files.newOutputStream(file1)))) {
    // Write to file
  } catch (IOException e) {
    // Handle error
  }


  // ...
  // Reopen the file for reading
  Path file2 = Paths.get(filename);
  if (!Files.isSameFile(file1, file2)) {
    // File was tampered with, handle error
  }

  try (BufferedReader br = new BufferedReader(new
      InputStreamReader(Files.newInputStream(file2)))) {
    String line;
    while ((line = br.readLine()) != null) {
      System.out.println(line);
    }
  } catch (IOException e) {
    // Handle error
  }
}
```

Unfortunately, the Java API lacks any guarantee that the `isSameFile()` method actually checks whether the files are the same file. The Java 7 API for `isSameFile()` [API 2013] says:

> If both `Path` objects are equal then this method returns true without checking if the file exists.

That is, isSameFile() may simply check that the paths to the two files are the same and cannot detect if the file at that path had been replaced by a different file between the two open operations.

Compliant Solution (Multiple Attributes)

This compliant solution checks the creation and last-modified times of the files to increase the likelihood that the file opened for reading is the same file that was written:

```
public void processFile(String filename) throws IOException{
  // Identify a file by its path
  Path file1 = Paths.get(filename);
  BasicFileAttributes attr1 =
    Files.readAttributes(file1, BasicFileAttributes.class);
  FileTime creation1 = attr1.creationTime();
  FileTime modified1 = attr1.lastModifiedTime();

  // Open the file for writing
  try (BufferedWriter bw = new BufferedWriter(new
       OutputStreamWriter(Files.newOutputStream(file1)))) {
    // Write to file...
  } catch (IOException e) {
    // Handle error
  }

  // Reopen the file for reading
  Path file2 = Paths.get(filename);
  BasicFileAttributes attr2 =
    Files.readAttributes(file2, BasicFileAttributes.class);
  FileTime creation2 = attr2.creationTime();
  FileTime modified2 = attr2.lastModifiedTime();
  if ( (!creation1.equals(creation2)) ||
       (!modified1.equals(modified2)) ) {
    // File was tampered with, handle error
  }

  try (BufferedReader br = new BufferedReader(new
       InputStreamReader(Files.newInputStream(file2)))){
    String line;
    while ((line = br.readLine()) != null) {
      System.out.println(line);
    }
  } catch (IOException e) {
    // Handle error
  }
}
```

Although this solution is reasonably secure, a determined attacker could create a symbolic link with the same creation and last-modified times as the original file. Also, a TOCTOU race condition occurs between the time the file's attributes are first read and the time the file is first opened. Likewise, another TOCTOU condition occurs the second time the attributes are read and the file is reopened.

Compliant Solution (POSIX `fileKey` Attribute)

In environments that support the `fileKey` attribute, a more reliable approach is to check that the `fileKey` attributes of the two files are the same. The `fileKey` attribute is an object that "uniquely identifies the file" [API 2013], as shown in this compliant solution:

```java
public void processFile(String filename) throws IOException{
  // Identify a file by its path
  Path file1 = Paths.get(filename);
  BasicFileAttributes attr1 =
    Files.readAttributes(file1, BasicFileAttributes.class);
  Object key1 = attr1.fileKey();
  // Open the file for writing
  try (BufferedWriter bw =
        new BufferedWriter(
          new OutputStreamWriter(Files.newOutputStream(file1)))) {
    // Write to file
  } catch (IOException e) {
    // Handle error
  }

  // Reopen the file for reading
  Path file2 = Paths.get(filename);
  BasicFileAttributes attr2 =
    Files.readAttributes(file2, BasicFileAttributes.class);
  Object key2 = attr2.fileKey();

  if ( !key1.equals(key2) ) {
    System.out.println("File tampered with");
    // File was tampered with, handle error
  }

  try (BufferedReader br =
        new BufferedReader(
          new InputStreamReader(Files.newInputStream(file2)))) {
    String line;
    while ((line = br.readLine()) != null) {
      System.out.println(line);
    }
  } catch (IOException e) {
    // Handle error
  }
}
```

This approach will not work on all platforms. For example, on Windows 7 Enterprise Edition, all `fileKey` attributes are null.

The file key returned by the `fileKey()` method is guaranteed to be unique only if the file system and files remain static. A file system may reuse an identifier, for example, after a file is deleted. Like the previous compliant solution, there is a TOCTOU race window between the time the file's attributes are first read and the time the file is first opened. Another TOCTOU condition occurs the second time the attributes are read and the file is reopened.

Compliant Solution (RandomAccessFile)

A better approach is to avoid reopening files. The following compliant solution demonstrates use of a `RandomAccessFile`, which can be opened for both reading and writing. Because the file is only closed automatically by the `try-with-resources` statement, no race condition can occur. Note that this compliant solution and others use the `readLine()` method for illustrative purposes, but see "MSC05-J. Do not exhaust heap space" [Long 2012] for more information about possible weaknesses of this method.

```
public void processFile(String filename) throws IOException{
  // Identify a file by its path
  try (RandomAccessFile file = new
      RandomAccessFile(filename, "rw")) {

    // Write to file...

    // Go back to beginning and read contents
    file.seek(0);
    String line;
    while ((line = file.readLine()) != null) {
      System.out.println(line);
    }
  }
}
```

Noncompliant Code Example (File Size)

This noncompliant code example tries to ensure that the file it opens contains exactly 1024 bytes:

```
static long goodSize = 1024;

public void doSomethingWithFile(String filename) {
  long size = new File(filename).length();
  if (size != goodSize) {
```

```
     System.out.println("File has wrong size!");
     return;
   }

   try (BufferedReader br = new BufferedReader(new
       InputStreamReader(new FileInputStream(filename)))) {
     // ... Work with file
   } catch (IOException e) {
     // Handle error
   }
 }
```

This code is subject to a TOCTOU race condition between when the file size is checked and when the file is opened. If an attacker replaces a 1024-byte file with another file during this race window, they can cause this program to open any file, defeating the check.

Compliant Solution (File Size)

This compliant solution uses the `FileChannel.size()` method to obtain the file size. Because this method is applied to the `FileInputStream` only after the file has been opened, this solution eliminates the race window.

```
static long goodSize = 1024;

public void doSomethingWithFile(String filename) {
  try (FileInputStream in = new FileInputStream(filename);
       BufferedReader br = new BufferedReader(
                         new InputStreamReader(in))) {
    long size = in.getChannel().size();
    if (size != goodSize) {
      System.out.println("File has wrong size!");
      return;
    }

    String line;
    while ((line = br.readLine()) != null) {
      System.out.println(line);
    }
  } catch (IOException e) {
    // Handle error
  }
}
```

Applicability

Attackers frequently exploit file-related vulnerabilities to cause programs to access an unintended file. Proper file identification is necessary to prevent exploitation.

Bibliography

[API 2013]   Class `java.io.File`

                    Interface `java.nio.file.Path`

                    Class `java.nio.file.Files`

                    Interface `java.nio.file.attribute.BasicFileAttributes`

[Long 2012]   FIO00-J. Do not operate on files in shared directories

▪ 28. Do not attach significance to the ordinal associated with an enum

Java language enumeration types have an `ordinal()` method that returns the numerical position of each enumeration constant in its class declaration.

According to the Java API, Class `Enum<E extends Enum<E>>` [API 2013], `public final int ordinal()`

> returns the ordinal of the enumeration constant (its position in its enum declaration, where the initial constant is assigned an ordinal of zero). Most programmers will have no use for this method. It is designed for use by sophisticated enum-based data structures, such as `EnumSet` and `EnumMap`.

The Java Language Specification (JLS), §8.9, "Enums" [JLS 2013], does not specify the use of `ordinal()` in programs. However, attaching external significance to the `ordinal()` value of an enum constant is error prone and should be avoided for defensive programming.

Noncompliant Code Example

This noncompliant code example declares enum `Hydrocarbon` and uses its `ordinal()` method to provide the result of the `getNumberOfCarbons()` method:

```
enum Hydrocarbon {
  METHANE, ETHANE, PROPANE, BUTANE, PENTANE,
  HEXANE, HEPTANE, OCTANE, NONANE, DECANE;

  public int getNumberOfCarbons() {
    return ordinal() + 1;
  }
}
```

Although this noncompliant code example behaves as expected, its maintenance is likely to be problematic. If the enum constants were reordered, the getNumberOfCarbons() method would return incorrect values. Furthermore, adding an additional BENZENE constant to the model would break the invariant assumed by the getNumberOfCarbons() method, because benzene has six carbons, but the ordinal value six is already taken by hexane.

Compliant Solution

In this compliant solution, enum constants are explicitly associated with the corresponding integer values for the number of carbon atoms they contain:

```
enum Hydrocarbon {
  METHANE(1), ETHANE(2), PROPANE(3), BUTANE(4), PENTANE(5),
  HEXANE(6), BENZENE(6), HEPTANE(7), OCTANE(8), NONANE(9),
  DECANE(10);

  private final int numberOfCarbons;

  Hydrocarbon(int carbons) { this.numberOfCarbons = carbons; }

  public int getNumberOfCarbons() {
    return numberOfCarbons;
  }
}
```

The getNumberOfCarbons() method no longer uses the ordinal() to discover the number of carbon atoms for each value. Different enum constants may be associated with the same value, as shown for HEXANE and BENZENE. Furthermore, this solution lacks any dependence on the order of the enumeration; the getNumberOfCarbons() method would continue to work correctly even if the enumeration were reordered.

Applicability

It is acceptable to use the ordinals associated with an enumerated type when the order of the enumeration constants is standard and extra constants cannot be added. For example, the use of ordinals is permitted with the following enumerated type:

```
public enum Day { SUNDAY, MONDAY, TUESDAY, WEDNESDAY,
                  THURSDAY, FRIDAY, SATURDAY }
```

In general, the use of ordinals to derive integer values reduces the program's maintainability and can lead to errors in the program.

Bibliography

[API 2013]	Class Enum<E extends Enum<E>>
[Bloch 2008]	Item 31, "Use Instance Fields Instead of Ordinals"
[JLS 2013]	§8.9, "Enums"

■ 29. Be aware of numeric promotion behavior

Numeric promotions are used to convert the operands of a numeric operator to a common type so that an operation can be performed. When using arithmetic operators with mixed operand sizes, narrower operands are promoted to the type of the wider operand.

Promotion Rules

The JLS, §5.6, "Numeric Promotions" [JLS 2013], describes numeric promotion as the following:

1. If any of the operands is of a reference type, unboxing conversion is performed.
2. If either operand is of type `double`, the other is converted to `double`.
3. Otherwise, if either operand is of type `float`, the other is converted to `float`.
4. Otherwise, if either operand is of type `long`, the other is converted to `long`.
5. Otherwise, both operands are converted to type `int`.

Widening conversions, resulting from integer promotions, preserve the overall magnitude of the number. However, promotions in which the operands are converted from an `int` to a `float` or from a `long` to a `double` can cause a loss of precision. (See *The CERT® Oracle® Secure Coding Standard for Java™* [Long 2012], "NUM13-J. Avoid loss of precision when converting primitive integers to floating-point," for more details.)

These conversions can occur when using multiplicative operators (%, *, /), additive operators (+, -), comparison operators (<, >, <=, >=), equality operators (==, !=), and integer bitwise operators (&, |, ^).

Examples

In the following example, a is promoted to a `double` before the + operator is applied:

```
int a = some_value;
double b = some_other_value;
double c = a + b;
```

In the following program fragment, b is first converted to int so that the + operator can be applied to operands of the same type:

```
int a = some_value;
char b = some_character;

if ((a + b) > 1.1f) {
  // Do something
}
```

The result of (a+b) is then converted to a float, and the comparison operator is finally applied.

Compound Operators

Type coercion may occur when compound expressions are used with mixed operand types. Examples of compound assignment operators are +=, -=, *=, /=, &=, ^=, %=, <<=, >>=, >>>=, and |=.

According to the JLS §15.26.2, "Compound Assignment Operators" [JLS 2013],

A compound assignment expression of the form E1 op= E2 is equivalent to E1 = (T)((E1) op (E2)), where T is the type of E1, except that E1 is evaluated only once.

That is, the compound assignment expression implicitly casts the resulting computation to the type of the left-hand operand.

When the operands are different types, multiple conversions can occur. For example, when E1 is an int, and E2 is either a long, a float, or a double, then E1 is widened from type int to the type of E2 (before the "op"), followed by a narrowing conversion from the type of E2 back to type int (after the "op," but before the assignment).

Noncompliant Code Example (Multiplication)

In this noncompliant code example, a variable of type int (big) is multiplied by a value of type float (one).

```
int big = 1999999999;
float one = 1.0f;
// Binary operation, loses precision because of implicit cast
System.out.println(big * one);
```

In this case, numeric promotions require that `big` be promoted to the type `float` before the multiplication occurs, resulting in loss of precision. (See "NUM13-J. Avoid loss of precision when converting primitive integers to floating-point" [Long 2012].) This code outputs 2.0E9 rather than 1.999999999E9.

Compliant Solution (Multiplication)

This compliant solution uses the `double` type, instead of `float`, as a safer means of handling the widening primitive conversion resulting from integer promotion:

```
int big = 1999999999;
double one = 1.0d; // Double instead of float
System.out.println(big * one);
```

This solution produces the expected output of 1.999999999E9, which is the value obtained when an `int` is assigned (implicitly cast) to a `double`.

See also Guideline 60, "Convert integers to floating-point for floating-point operations," for more information about mixing integer and floating-point arithmetic.

Noncompliant Code Example (Left Shift)

This noncompliant code example shows integer promotion resulting from the use of the bitwise OR operator.

```
byte[] b = new byte[4];
int result = 0;
for (int i = 0; i < 4; i++) {
  result = (result << 8) | b[i];
}
```

Each byte array element is sign-extended to 32 bits before it is used as an operand. If it originally contained the value 0xff, it would contain 0xffffffff [FindBugs 2008]. This causes `result` to contain a value other than the concatenation of the four array elements.

Compliant Solution (Left Shift)

This compliant solution masks off the upper 24 bits of the byte array element to achieve the intended result:

```
byte[] b = new byte[4];
int result = 0;
for (int i = 0; i < 4; i++) {
  result = (result << 8) | (b[i] & 0xff);
}
```

Noncompliant Code Example (Compound Addition and Assignment)

This noncompliant code example performs a compound assignment operation.

```
int x = 2147483642; // 0x7ffffffa
x += 1.0f;           // x contains 2147483647 (0x7fffffff)
                     // after the computation
```

The compound operation involves an int value that contains too many significant bits to fit in the 23-bit mantissa of a Java float, causing the widening conversion from int to float to lose precision. The resulting value is frequently unexpected.

Compliant Solution (Compound Addition and Assignment)

For defensive programming purposes, avoid using any of the compound assignment operators on variables of type byte, short, or char. Also, refrain from using a wider operand on the right-hand side. In this compliant solution, all operands are of the Java type double.

```
double x = 2147483642; // 0x7ffffffa
x += 1.0; // x contains 2147483643.0 (0x7ffffffb.0) as expected
```

Noncompliant Code Example (Compound Bit Shift and Assignment)

This noncompliant code example uses a compound right-shift operator for shifting the value of i by one bit.

```
short i = -1;
i >>>= 1;
```

Unfortunately, the value of i remains the same. The value of i is first promoted to an int. This is a widening primitive conversion, so no data is lost. As a short, −1 is represented as `0xffff`. The conversion to `int` results in the value `0xffffffff`, which is right-shifted by 1 bit to yield `0x7fffffff`. To store the value back into the `short` variable i, Java performs an implicit narrowing conversion, discarding the 16 higher-order bits. The final result is again `0xffff`, or `-1`.

Compliant Solution (Compound Bit Shift and Assignment)

This compliant solution applies the compound assignment operator to an `int`, which does not require widening and subsequent narrowing. Consequently, i gets the value `0x7fffffff`.

```
int i = -1;
i >>>= 1;
```

Applicability

Failing to consider integer promotions when dealing with floating-point and integer operands can result in loss of precision.

Bibliography

[Bloch 2005]	Puzzle 9, "Tweedledum"
	Puzzle 31, "Ghost of Looper"
[Findbugs 2008]	"BIT: Bitwise OR of Signed Byte Value"
[JLS 2013]	§4.2.2, "Integer Operations"
	§5.6, "Numeric Promotions"
	§15.26.2, "Compound Assignment Operators"
[Long 2012]	NUM13-J. Avoid loss of precision when converting primitive integers to floating-point

■ 30. Enable compile-time type checking of variable arity parameter types

A variable arity (aka *varargs*) method is a method that can take a variable number of arguments. The method must contain at least one fixed argument. When processing a variable arity method call, the Java compiler checks the types of all arguments, and all of the variable actual arguments must match the variable formal argument type. However, compile-time type checking is ineffective when `Object` or generic parameter types are used [Bloch 2008]. The presence of initial parameters of specific types is irrelevant; the compiler will remain unable to check `Object` or generic variable parameter types. Enable strong compile-time type checking of variable arity methods by using the most specific type possible for the method parameter.

Noncompliant Code Example (Object)

This noncompliant code example sums a set of numbers using a variable arity method that uses Object as the variable arity type. Consequently, this method accepts an arbitrary mix of parameters of any object type. Legitimate uses of such declarations are rare (but see the "Applicability" section of this guideline).

```
double sum(Object... args) {
   double result = 0.0;
    for (Object arg : args) {
      if (arg instanceof Byte) {
        result += ((Byte) arg).byteValue();
      } else if (arg instanceof Short) {
        result += ((Short) arg).shortValue();
      } else if (arg instanceof Integer) {
        result += ((Integer) arg).intValue();
      } else if (arg instanceof Long) {
        result += ((Long) arg).longValue();
      } else if (arg instanceof Float) {
        result += ((Float) arg).floatValue();
      } else if (arg instanceof Double) {
        result += ((Double) arg).doubleValue();
      } else {
        throw new ClassCastException();
      }
    }
   return result;
}
```

Compliant Solution (Number)

This compliant solution defines the same method, but uses the Number type. This abstract class is general enough to encompass all numeric types, yet specific enough to exclude nonnumeric types.

```
double sum(Number... args) {
  // ...
}
```

Noncompliant Code Example (Generic Type)

This noncompliant code example declares the same variable arity method using a generic type parameter. It accepts a variable number of parameters that are all of the *same* object type; however, it may be any object type. Again, legitimate uses of such declarations are rare.

```
<T> double sum(T... args) {
  // ...
}
```

Compliant Solution (Generic Type)

This compliant solution defines the same generic method using the Number type.

```
<T extends Number> double sum(T... args) {
  // ...
}
```

Be as specific as possible when declaring parameter types; avoid Object and imprecise generic types in variable arity methods. Retrofitting old methods containing final array parameters with generically typed variable arity parameters is not always a good idea. For example, given a method that does not accept an argument of a particular type, it could be possible to override the compile-time checking—through the use of generic variable arity parameters—so that the method would compile cleanly rather than correctly, causing a runtime error [Bloch 2008].

Also, note that autoboxing prevents strong compile-time type checking of primitive types and their corresponding wrapper classes. For example, this compliant solution produces the following warning, but works as expected:

```
Java.java:10: warning: [unchecked] Possible heap pollution from
parameterized vararg type T
  <T extends Number> double sum(T... args) {
```

This particular compiler warning can be safely ignored.

Applicability

Injudicious use of variable arity parameter types prevents strong compile-time type checking, creates ambiguity, and diminishes code readability.

Variable arity signatures using `Object` and imprecise generic types are acceptable when the body of the method lacks both casts and autoboxing, and it also compiles without error. Consider the following example, which operates correctly for all object types and type-checks successfully:

```
<T> Collection<T> assembleCollection(T... args) {
  return new HashSet<T>(Arrays.asList(args));
}
```

In some circumstances, it is necessary to use a variable arity parameter of type `Object`. A good example is the method `java.util.Formatter.format(String format, Object... args)`, which can format objects of any type.

Automated detection is straightforward.

Bibliography

[Bloch 2008]	Item 42, "Use Varargs Judiciously"
[Steinberg 2008]	Using the Varargs Language Feature
[Oracle 2011b]	Varargs

■ 31. Do not apply public final to constants whose value might change in later releases

The `final` keyword can be used to specify constant values (that is, values that cannot change during program execution). However, constants that can change over the lifetime of a program should not be declared public final. The JLS [JLS 2013] allows implementations to insert the value of any public final field inline in any compilation unit that reads the field. Consequently, if the declaring class is edited so that the new version gives a different value for the field, compilation units that read the public final field could still see the old value until they are recompiled. This problem may occur, for example, when a third-party library is updated to the latest version, but the referencing code is not recompiled.

A related error can arise when a programmer declares a `static final` reference to a mutable object; see Guideline 73, "Never confuse the immutability of a reference with that of the referenced object," for additional information.

Noncompliant Code Example

In this noncompliant code example, class `Foo` in `Foo.java` declares a field whose value represents the version of the software:

```
class Foo {
  public static final int VERSION = 1;
  // ...
}
```

The field is subsequently accessed by class `Bar` from a separate compilation unit (`Bar.java`):

```
class Bar {
  public static void main(String[] args) {
    System.out.println("You are using version " + Foo.VERSION);
  }
}
```

When compiled and run, the software correctly prints

```
You are using version 1
```

But if a developer were to change the value of `VERSION` to 2 by modifying `Foo.java` and subsequently recompile `Foo.java`, while failing to recompile `Bar.java`, the software would incorrectly print

```
You are using version 1
```

Although recompiling `Bar.java` solves this problem, a better solution is available.

Compliant Solution

According to §13.4.9, "`final` Fields and Constants," of the JLS [JLS 2013],

> Other than for true mathematical constants, we recommend that source code make very sparing use of class variables that are declared `static` and `final`. If the read-only nature of `final` is required, a better choice is to declare a `private static` variable and a suitable accessor method to get its value.

In this compliant solution, the `version` field in `Foo.java` is declared `private static` and accessed by the `getVersion()` method:

```
class Foo {
  private static int version = 1;
  public static final int getVersion() {
    return version;
  }

  // ...
}
```

The Bar class in Bar.java is modified to invoke the getVersion() accessor method to retrieve the version field from Foo.java:

```
class Bar {
  public static void main(String[] args) {
    System.out.println(
      "You are using version " + Foo.getVersion()
    );
  }
}
```

In this solution, the private version value cannot be copied into the Bar class when it is compiled, consequently preventing the bug. Note that this transformation imposes little or no performance penalty because most just-in-time (JIT) code generators can inline the getVersion() method at runtime.

Applicability

Declaring a value that changes over the lifetime of the software as final may lead to unexpected results.

According to §9.3, "Field (Constant) Declarations," of the JLS [JLS 2013], "Every field declaration in the body of an interface is implicitly public, static, and final. It is permitted to redundantly specify any or all of these modifiers for such fields." Therefore, this guideline does not apply to fields defined in interfaces. Clearly, if the value of a field in an interface changes, every class that implements or uses the interface must be recompiled. See Guideline 35, "Carefully design interfaces before releasing them," for more information.

Constants declared using the enum type are permitted to violate this guideline.

Constants whose value never changes throughout the entire lifetime of the software may be declared as final. For example, the JLS recommends that mathematical constants be declared final.

Bibliography

[JLS 2013]   §4.12.4, "`final` Variables"

§8.3.1.1, "`static` Fields"

§9.3, "Field (Constant) Declarations"

§13.4.9, "`final` Fields and Constants"

■ 32. Avoid cyclic dependencies between packages

Both *The Elements of Java™ Style* [Allen 2000] and the JPL Java Coding Standard [Havelund 2009] require that the dependency structure of a package must never contain cycles; that is, it must be representable as a directed acyclic graph (DAG). Eliminating cycles between packages has several advantages.

- *Testing and maintainability.* Cyclic dependencies magnify the repercussions of changes or patches to source code. Reducing the repercussions of changes simplifies testing and improves maintainability. Inability to perform adequate testing because of cyclic dependencies is a frequent source of security vulnerabilities.

- *Reusability.* Cyclic dependencies between packages require that the packages be released and upgraded in lockstep. This requirement reduces reusability.

- *Releases and builds.* Avoiding cycles also helps to steer the development toward an environment that fosters modularization.

- *Deployment.* Avoiding cyclic dependencies between packages reduces coupling between packages. Reduced coupling reduces the frequency of runtime errors such as `ClassNotFoundError`. This, in turn, simplifies deployment.

Noncompliant Code Example

This noncompliant code example contains packages named `account` and `user` that consist of the classes `AccountHolder`, `User`, and `UserDetails`, respectively. The class `UserDetails` extends from `AccountHolder` because a user is a kind of account holder. The class `AccountHolder` depends on a non-static utility method defined in the `User` class. Likewise, `UserDetails` depends on `AccountHolder` by extending it.

```
package account;
import user.User;
public class AccountHolder {
```

```
  private User user;
  public void setUser(User newUser) {user = newUser;}

  synchronized void depositFunds(String username,
                                    double amount) {
    // Use a utility method of User to check whether
    // username exists
    if (user.exists(username)) {
      // Deposit the amount
    }
  }

  protected double getBalance(String accountNumber) {
    // Return the account balance
    return 1.0;
  }
}
package user;
import account.AccountHolder;
public class UserDetails extends AccountHolder {
  public synchronized
  double getUserBalance(String accountNumber) {
    // Use a method of AccountHolder to get the account balance
    return getBalance(accountNumber);
  }
}

public class User {
  public boolean exists(String username) {
    // Check whether user exists
    return true; // Exists
  }
}
```

Compliant Solution

The tight coupling between the classes in the two packages can be weakened by introducing an interface called BankApplication in a third package, bank. The cyclic package dependency is eliminated by ensuring that the AccountHolder does not depend on User, but instead relies on the interface by importing the bank package (and not by implementing the interface).

In this compliant solution, such functionality is achieved by adding a parameter of the interface type BankApplication to the depositFunds() method. This solution gives the AccountHolder a solid contract to bank on. Additionally, UserDetails implements the interface and provides concrete implementations of the methods while at the same time inheriting the other methods from AccountHolder.

```
package bank;
public interface BankApplication {
  void depositFunds(BankApplication ba, String username,
                    double amount);
  double getBalance(String accountNumber);
  double getUserBalance(String accountNumber);
  boolean exists(String username);
}
package account;
import bank.BankApplication;  // Import from a third package
class AccountHolder {
  private BankApplication ba;
  public void setBankApplication(BankApplication newBA) {
    ba = newBA;
  }

  public synchronized void depositFunds(BankApplication ba,
      String username, double amount) {
    // Use a utility method of UserDetails to
    // check whether username exists
    if (ba.exists(username)) {
      // Deposit the amount
    }
  }
  public double getBalance(String accountNumber) {
    // Return the account balance
    return 1.0;
  }
}

package user;
import account.AccountHolder; // One-way dependency
import bank.BankApplication;  // Import from a third package
public class UserDetails extends AccountHolder
      implements BankApplication {
  public synchronized double getUserBalance(
      String accountNumber) {
    // Use a method of AccountHolder to get the account balance
    return getBalance(accountNumber);
  }
  public boolean exists(String username) {
    // Check whether user exists
    return true;
  }
}
```

The interface BankApplication appears to contain superfluous methods such as depositFunds() and getBalance(). These methods are present so that if the subclass overrides them, the superclass retains the capability of internally invoking the subclass's methods polymorphically (for example, calling ba.getBalance() with an overridden implementation of the method in UserDetails). One consequence of this solution is that methods declared in the interface are required to be public in the classes that define them.

Applicability

Cyclic dependencies between packages can result in fragile builds. A security vulnerability in a package can easily percolate to other packages.

Bibliography

[Allen 2000]	*The Elements of Java™ Style*
[Havelund 2009]	JPL Coding Standard, Version 1.1
[Knoernschild 2002]	Chapter 1, "OO Principles and Patterns"

■ 33. Prefer user-defined exceptions over more general exception types

Because an exception is caught by its type, it is better to define exceptions for specific purposes than to use general exception types for multiple purposes. Throwing general exception types makes code hard to understand and maintain, and defeats much of the advantage of the Java exception-handling mechanism.

Noncompliant Code Example

This noncompliant code example attempts to distinguish between different exceptional behaviors by looking at the exception's message:

If doSomething() throws an exception or error whose type is a subclass of Throwable, the switch statement allows selection of a specific case to execute. For

```
try {
  doSomething();
} catch (Throwable e) {
  String msg = e.getMessage();
  switch (msg) {
    case "file not found":
```

```
      // Handle error
      break;
    case "connection timeout":
      // Handle error
      break;
    case "security violation":
      // Handle error
      break;
    default: throw e;
  }
}
```

example, if the exception message is "file not found," the appropriate action is taken in the exception-handling code.

However, any change to the exception message literals involved will break the code. For example, suppose this code is executed:

```
throw new Exception("cannot find file");
```

This exception should be handled by the first case clause, but it will instead be rethrown because the string does not match any case clause.

Furthermore, exceptions may be thrown without a message.

This noncompliant code example falls under ERR08-EX0 of *The CERT® Oracle® Secure Coding Standard for Java™* [Long 2012], "ERR08-J. Do not catch NullPointerException or any of its ancestors," because it catches general exceptions but rethrows them.

Compliant Solution

This compliant solution uses specific exception types and defines new special-purpose exception types where required.

```
public class TimeoutException extends Exception {
  TimeoutException () {
    super();
  }
  TimeoutException (String msg) {
    super(msg);
  }
}
```

```
// ...

try {
  doSomething();
} catch (FileNotFoundException e) {
  // Handle error
} catch (TimeoutException te) {
  // Handle error
} catch (SecurityException se) {
  // Handle error
}
```

Applicability

Exceptions are used to handle exceptional conditions. If an exception is not caught, the program will be terminated. An exception that is incorrectly caught or is caught at the wrong level of recovery will often cause incorrect behavior.

Bibliography

[JLS 2013]   Chapter 11, "Exceptions"

[Long 2012]   ERR08-J. Do not catch `NullPointerException` or any of its ancestors

■ 34. Try to gracefully recover from system errors

According to the JLS, §11.1.1, "The Kinds of Exceptions" [JLS 2013],

> The unchecked exceptions classes are the class `RuntimeException` and its subclasses, and the class `Error` and its subclasses. All other exception classes are checked exception classes.

Unchecked exception classes are not subject to compile-time checking because it is tedious to account for all exceptional conditions and because recovery is often difficult or impossible. However, even when recovery is impossible, the Java Virtual Machine (JVM) allows a graceful exit and a chance to at least log the error. This is made possible by using a `try-catch` block that catches `Throwable`. Also, when code must avoid leaking potentially sensitive information, catching `Throwable` is permitted. In all other cases, catching `Throwable` is not recommended because it makes handling specific exceptions difficult. Where cleanup operations such as releasing system resources can be performed, code should use a `finally` block to release the resources or a `try-with-resources` statement.

Catching Throwable is disallowed in general by *The CERT® Oracle® Secure Coding Standard for Java™* [Long 2012], "ERR08-J. Do not catch NullPointer-Exception or any of its ancestors," but it is permitted when filtering exception traces by the exception ERR08-EX0 in that rule.

Noncompliant Code Example

This noncompliant code example generates a StackOverflowError as a result of infinite recursion. It exhausts the available stack space and may result in denial of service.

```java
public class StackOverflow {
  public static void main(String[] args) {
    infiniteRun();
    // ...
  }

  private static void infiniteRun() {
    infiniteRun();
  }
}
```

Compliant Solution

This compliant solution shows a try-catch block that can be used to capture java .lang.Error or java.lang.Throwable. A log entry can be made at this point, followed by attempts to free key system resources in the finally block.

```java
public class StackOverflow {
  public static void main(String[] args) {
    try {
      infiniteRun();
    } catch (Throwable t) {
      // Forward to handler
    } finally {
      // Free cache, release resources
    }
    // ...
  }

  private static void infiniteRun() {
    infiniteRun();
  }
}
```

Note that the `Forward to handler` code must operate correctly in constrained memory conditions because the stack or heap may be nearly exhausted. In such a scenario, one useful technique is for the program to initially reserve memory specifically to be used by an out-of-memory exception handler.

Note that this solution catches `Throwable` in an attempt to handle the error; it falls under exception ERR08-EX2 in "ERR08-J. Do not catch `NullPointerException` or any of its ancestors" [Long 2012].

Applicability

Allowing a system error to abruptly terminate a Java program may result in a denial-of-service vulnerability.

In the event of actually running out of memory, it is likely that some program data will be in an inconsistent state. Consequently, it might be best to restart the process. If an attempt is made to carry on, reducing the number of threads may be an effective workaround. This measure can help in such scenarios because threads often leak memory, and their continued existence can increase the memory footprint of the program.

The methods `Thread.setUncaughtExceptionHandler()` and `ThreadGroup.uncaughtException()` can be used to help deal with an `OutOfMemoryError` in threads.

Bibliography

[JLS 2013]	§11.2, "Compile-Time Checking of Exceptions"
[Kalinovsky 2004]	Chapter 16, "Intercepting Control Flow: Intercepting System Errors"
[Long 2012]	ERR08-J. Do not catch `NullPointerException` or any of its ancestors

■ 35. Carefully design interfaces before releasing them

Interfaces are used to group all the methods that a class promises to publicly expose. The implementing classes are obliged to provide concrete implementations for all of these methods. Interfaces are a necessary ingredient of most public APIs; once released, flaws can be hard to fix without breaking any code that implements the older version. The repercussions include the following.

- Interface changes resulting from fixes can severely impair the contracts of the implementing classes. For example, a fix introduced in a later version may be accompanied by modifications to an unrelated interface that must now be implemented by the client. The client may be prevented from implementing the fix because the new interface may impose additional implementation burden on it.

- Implementers can provide default or skeletal implementations of interface methods for their clients to extend; however, such code can adversely affect the behavior of the subclasses. Conversely, when such default implementations are absent, the subclasses must provide dummy implementations. Such implementations foster an environment where comments such as "ignore this code, does nothing" occur incessantly. Such code may never even get tested.

■ If there is a security flaw in a public API (see, for example, the discussion of ThreadGroup methods in *The CERT® Oracle® Secure Coding Standard for Java™* [Long 2012], "THI01-J. Do not invoke ThreadGroup methods"), it will persist throughout the lifetime of the API, affecting the security of any application or library that uses it. Even after the security flaw is mitigated, applications and libraries may continue using the insecure version until they are also updated.

Noncompliant Code Example

In this noncompliant code example, an interface User is frozen with two methods: authenticate() and subscribe(). Sometime later, the providers release a free service that does not rely on authentication.

```
public interface User {
  boolean authenticate(String username, char[] password);
  void subscribe(int noOfDays);
  // Introduced after the class is publicly released
  void freeService();
}
```

The addition of the freeService() method, unfortunately, breaks all the client code that implements the interface. Moreover, the implementers who wish to use only freeService() have to face the onus of also providing the other two methods, which pollute the API, for reasons discussed earlier.

Noncompliant Code Example

An alternative idea is to prefer abstract classes for dealing with constant evolution, but that comes at the cost of flexibility that interfaces offer (a class may implement multiple interfaces, but extend only one class). One notable pattern is for the provider to distribute an abstract skeletal class that implements the evolving interface. The skeletal class can selectively implement a few methods, and force the extending classes to provide concrete implementations of the others. If a new method is added to the interface, the skeletal class can provide a non-abstract default implementation that the extending class can optionally override. This noncompliant code example shows such a skeletal class.

```
public interface User {
  boolean authenticate(String username, char[] password);
  void subscribe(int noOfDays);
  void freeService(); // Introduced after API is
                      // publicly released
}

abstract class SkeletalUser implements User {
  public abstract boolean authenticate(String username,
                                       char[] password);
  public abstract void subscribe(int noOfDays);
  public void freeService() {
    // Added later, provide implementation and re-release class
  }
}

class Client extends SkeletalUser {
  // Implements authenticate() and subscribe(), not freeService()
}
```

Although useful, this pattern may be insecure because a provider who is unaware of the extending class's code may choose an implementation that introduces security weaknesses in the client API.

Compliant Solution (Modularize)

A better design strategy is to anticipate the future evolution of the service. The core functionality should be implemented in the User interface; in this case, only the premium service may be required to extend from it. To make use of the new free service, an existing class may then choose to implement the new interface FreeUser, or it may just completely ignore it.

```
public interface User {
  boolean authenticate(String username, char[] password);
}

public interface PremiumUser extends User {
  void subscribe(int noOfDays);
}

public interface FreeUser {
  void freeService();
}
```

Compliant Solution (Make New Method Unusable)

Another compliant solution is to throw an exception from within the new freeSer-
vice() method defined in the implementing subclass.

```
class Client implements User {
  public void freeService() {
    throw new AbstractMethodError();
  }
}
```

Compliant Solution (Delegate Implementation to Subclasses)

Although allowable, a less flexible compliant solution is to delegate the implementation of the method to subclasses of the client's core interface-implementing class.

```
abstract class Client implements User  {
  public abstract void freeService();
  // Delegate implementation of new method to subclasses
  // Other concrete implementations
}
```

Applicability

Failing to publish stable, flaw-free interfaces can break the contracts of the implementing classes, pollute the client API, and possibly introduce security weaknesses
in the implementing classes.

Bibliography

[Bloch 2008]   Item 18, "Prefer Interfaces to Abstract Classes"

[Long 2012]   THI01-J. Do not invoke ThreadGroup methods

■ 36. Write garbage collection–friendly code

Java's garbage-collection feature provides significant benefits over non-garbage-
collected languages. The garbage collector (GC) is designed to automatically reclaim
unreachable memory, and to avoid memory leaks. Although the GC is quite adept at
performing this task, a malicious attacker can nevertheless launch a denial-of-service
(DoS) attack against the GC, such as by inducing abnormal heap memory allocation

or abnormally prolonged object retention. For example, some versions of the GC could need to halt all executing threads to keep up with incoming allocation requests that trigger increased heap management activity. System throughput rapidly diminishes in this scenario.

Real-time systems, in particular, are vulnerable to a more subtle slow-heap-exhaustion DoS attack, perpetrated by stealing CPU cycles. An attacker can perform memory allocations in a way that increases the consumption of resources (such as CPU, battery power, and memory) without triggering an OutOfMemoryError. Writing garbage collection–friendly code restricts many attack avenues.

Use Short-Lived Immutable Objects

Beginning with JDK 1.2, the generational GC has reduced memory allocation costs, in many cases to levels lower than in C or C++. Generational garbage collection reduces garbage collection costs by grouping objects into generations. The *younger generation* consists of short-lived objects. The GC performs a minor collection on the younger generation when it fills up with dead objects [Oracle 2010a]. Improved garbage collection algorithms have reduced the cost of garbage collection so that it is proportional to the number of live objects in the younger generation, rather than to the number of objects allocated since the last garbage collection.

Note that objects in the younger generation that persist for longer durations are *tenured* and are moved to the *tenured generation*. Few younger-generation objects continue to live through to the next garbage-collection cycle. The rest become ready to be collected in the impending collection cycle [Oracle 2010a].

With generational GCs, use of short-lived immutable objects is generally more efficient than use of long-lived mutable objects, such as object pools. Avoiding object pools improves the GC's efficiency. Object pools bring additional costs and risks: they can create synchronization problems and can require explicit management of deallocations, possibly creating problems with dangling pointers. Further, determining the correct amount of memory to reserve for an object pool can be difficult, especially for mission-critical code. Use of long-lived mutable objects remains appropriate when allocation of objects is particularly expensive (for example, when performing multiple joins across databases). Similarly, object pools are an appropriate design choice when the objects represent scarce resources, such as thread pools and database connections.

Avoid Large Objects

The allocation of large objects is expensive, in part because the cost to initialize their fields is proportional to their size. Additionally, frequent allocation of large objects of different sizes can cause fragmentation issues or compacting collect operations.

Do Not Explicitly Invoke the Garbage Collector

The GC can be explicitly invoked by calling the `System.gc()` method. Even though the documentation says that it "runs the garbage collector," there is no guarantee as to when or whether the GC will actually run. In fact, the call merely *suggests* that the GC should subsequently execute; the JVM is free to ignore this suggestion.

Irresponsible use of this feature can severely degrade system performance by triggering garbage collection at inopportune moments, rather than waiting until ripe periods when it is safe to garbage-collect without significant interruption of the program's execution.

In the Java Hotspot VM (default since JDK 1.2), `System.gc()` forces an explicit garbage collection. Such calls can be buried deep within libraries, so they may be difficult to trace. To ignore the call in such cases, use the flag `-XX:+DisableExplicitGC`. To avoid long pauses while performing a full garbage collection, a less demanding concurrent cycle may be invoked by specifying the flag `-XX:ExplicitGCInvokedConcurrent`.

Applicability

Misusing garbage-collection utilities can cause severe performance degradation, which can be exploited to cause a DoS attack. The Apache Geronimo and Tomcat vulnerability GERONIMO-4574, reported in March 2009, resulted from `PolicyContext` handler data objects being set in a thread and never released, causing these data objects to remain in memory longer than necessary.

When an application goes through several phases, such as an initialization and a ready phase, it could require heap compaction between phases. The `System.gc()` method may be invoked in such cases, provided a suitable uneventful period occurs between phases.

Bibliography

[API 2013]   Class `System`

[Bloch 2008]   Item 6, "Eliminate Obsolete Object References"

[Coomes 2007]   "Garbage Collection Concepts and Programming Tips"

[Goetz 2004]   Java Theory and Practice: Garbage Collection and Performance

[Lo 2005]   "Security Issues in Garbage Collection"

[Long 2012]   OBJ05-J. Defensively copy private mutable class members before returning their references

                    OBJ06-J. Defensively copy mutable inputs and mutable internal components

[Oracle 2010a]   Java SE 6 HotSpot™ Virtual Machine Garbage Collection Tuning

Chapter 3

Reliability

ISO/IEC/IEEE 24765:2010, *Systems and software engineering—Vocabulary*, defines reliability as the ability of a system or component to perform its required functions under stated conditions for a specified period of time [ISO/IEC/IEEE 24765:2010]. ISO/IEC 9126-1:2001, *Software engineering—Product quality—Part 1: Quality model*, provides a similar definition of reliability as the capability of the software product to maintain a specified level of performance when used under specified conditions [ISO/IEC 9126-1:2001].

Software reliability is an important factor affecting system reliability. It differs from hardware reliability in that it reflects design perfection, rather than manufacturing perfection. Wear or aging does not occur in software. Limitations in reliability are the results of faults in requirements, design, and implementation. Failures resulting from these faults depend on the way the software product is used and the program options selected rather than on elapsed time.

ISO/IEC/IEEE 24765:2010 defines software reliability as the probability that software will not cause the failure of a system for a specified time under specified conditions [ISO/IEC/IEEE 24765:2010]. The probability is a function not only of the inputs to and use of the system, but also of the existence of faults in the software. The inputs to the system determine whether existing faults, if any, are encountered. The high complexity of software is the major contributing factor to software reliability problems.

These guidelines deal with Java language features that can easily be misused by the unwary. The Java language allows a great deal of flexibility in the ways in which it is used, but some of these uses can lead to obscure techniques and code that is difficult to understand and maintain. By following these guidelines, programmers will produce code that is less prone to bugs and runtime failure.

This chapter includes guidelines that

1. Help reduce errors, and are consequently important for developing reliable Java code
2. Contain specific Java coding recommendations to improve software reliability

■ 37. Do not shadow or obscure identifiers in subscopes

Reuse of identifier names in subscopes leads to obscuration or shadowing. Reused identifiers in the current scope can render those defined elsewhere inaccessible. Although the Java Language Specification (JLS) [JLS 2013] clearly resolves any syntactic ambiguity arising from obscuring or shadowing, such ambiguity burdens source code maintainers and auditors, especially when code requires access to both the original named entity and the inaccessible one. The problem is exacerbated when the reused name is defined in a different package.

According to §6.4.2, "Obscuring," of the JLS [JLS 2013],

> A simple name may occur in contexts where it may potentially be interpreted as the name of a variable, a type, or a package. In these situations, the rules of §6.5 specify that a variable will be chosen in preference to a type, and that a type will be chosen in preference to a package.

This implies that a variable can *obscure* a type or a package, and a type can obscure a package name. *Shadowing*, on the other hand, refers to one variable rendering another variable inaccessible in a containing scope. One type can also shadow another type.

No identifier should obscure or shadow another identifier in a containing scope. For example, a local variable should not reuse the name of a class field or method or a class name or package name. Similarly, an inner class name should not reuse the name of an outer class or package.

Both overriding and shadowing differ from *hiding*, in which an accessible member (typically non-private) that should have been inherited by a subclass is replaced by a locally declared subclass member that assumes the same name but has a different, incompatible method signature.

Noncompliant Code Example (Field Shadowing)

This noncompliant code example reuses the name of the `val` instance field in the scope of an instance method.

```
class MyVector {
  private int val = 1;
  private void doLogic() {
    int val;
    //...
  }
}
```

The resulting behavior can be classified as shadowing; the method variable renders the class variable inaccessible within the scope of the method. For example, assigning to this.val from within the method does not affect the value of the class variable.

Compliant Solution (Field Shadowing)

This compliant solution eliminates shadowing by changing the name of the variable defined in the method scope from val to newValue:

```
class MyVector {
  private int val = 1;
  private void doLogic() {
    int newValue;
    //...
  }
}
```

Noncompliant Code Example (Variable Shadowing)

This example is noncompliant because the variable i defined in the scope of the second for loop block shadows the definition of the instance variable i defined in the MyVector class:

```
class MyVector {
  private int i = 0;
  private void doLogic() {
    for (i = 0; i < 10; i++) {/* ... */}
    for (int i = 0; i < 20; i++) {/* ... */}
  }
}
```

Compliant Solution (Variable Shadowing)

In this compliant solution, the loop counter i is only defined in the scope of each for loop block:

```
class MyVector {
  private void doLogic() {
    for (int i = 0; i < 10; i++) {/* ... */}
    for (int i = 0; i < 20; i++) {/* ... */}
  }
}
```

Applicability

Name reuse makes code more difficult to read and maintain, which can result in security weaknesses. An automated tool can easily detect the reuse of identifiers in containing scopes.

Bibliography

[Bloch 2005]   Puzzle 67, "All Strung Out"

[Bloch 2008]   Item 16, "Prefer Interfaces to Abstract Classes"

[Conventions 2009]   §6.3, "Placement"

[FindBugs 2008]   DLS, "Dead store to local variable that shadows field"

[JLS 2013]   §6.4.1, "Shadowing"

                        §6.4.2, "Obscuring"

                        §7.5.2, "Type-Import-on-Demand Declarations"

■ 38. Do not declare more than one variable per declaration

Declaring multiple variables in a single declaration could cause confusion about the types of variables and their initial values. In particular, do not declare any of the following in a single declaration:

- ■ Variables of different types
- ■ A mixture of initialized and uninitialized variables

In general, you should declare each variable on its own line with an explanatory comment regarding its role. While not required for conformance with this guideline, this practice is also recommended in the Code Conventions for the Java Programming Language, §6.1, "Number Per Line" [Conventions 2009].

This guideline applies to

- Local variable declaration statements [JLS 2013, §14.4]
- Field declarations [JLS 2013, §8.3]
- Field (constant) declarations [JLS 2013, §9.3]

Noncompliant Code Example (Initialization)

This noncompliant code example might lead a programmer or reviewer to mistakenly believe that both i and j are initialized to 1. In fact, only j is initialized, while i remains uninitialized:

```
int i, j = 1;
```

Compliant Solution (Initialization)

In this compliant solution, it is readily apparent that both i and j are initialized to 1:

```
int i = 1;  // Purpose of i...
int j = 1;  // Purpose of j...
```

Compliant Solution (Initialization)

In this compliant solution, it is readily apparent that both i and j are initialized to 1:

```
int i = 1, j = 1;
```

Declaring each variable on a separate line is the preferred method. However, multiple variables on one line are acceptable when they are trivial temporary variables such as array indices.

Noncompliant Code Example (Different Types)

In this noncompliant code example, the programmer declares multiple variables, including an array, on the same line. All instances of the type T have access to methods of the Object class. However, it is easy to forget that arrays require special treatment when some of these methods are overridden.

```
public class Example<T> {
  private T a, b, c[], d;

  public Example(T in) {
    a = in;
    b = in;
    c = (T[]) new Object[10];
    d = in;
  }
}
```

When an Object method, such as toString(), is overridden, a programmer could accidentally provide an implementation for type T that fails to consider that c is an array of T rather than a reference to an object of type T.

```
public String toString() {
  return a.toString() + b.toString() +
         c.toString() + d.toString();
}
```

However, the programmer's intent could have been to invoke toString() on each individual element of the array c.

```
// Correct functional implementation
public String toString() {
  String s = a.toString() + b.toString();
  for (int i = 0; i < c.length; i++){
    s += c[i].toString();
  }
  s += d.toString();
  return s;
}
```

Compliant Solution (Different Types)

This compliant solution places each declaration on its own line and uses the preferred notation for array declaration:

```
public class Example<T> {
  private T a;   // Purpose of a...
  private T b;   // Purpose of b...
  private T[] c; // Purpose of c[]...
  private T d;   // Purpose of d...
```

```
public Example(T in){
  a = in;
  b = in;
  c = (T[]) new Object[10];
  d = in;
  }
}
```

Applicability

Declaration of multiple variables per line can reduce code readability and lead to programmer confusion.

When more than one variable is declared in a single declaration, ensure that both the type and the initial value of each variable are self-evident.

Declarations of loop indices should be included within a for statement, even when this results in variable declarations that lack a comment about the purpose of the variable:

```
public class Example {
  void function() {
    int mx = 100; // Some max value

    for (int i = 0; i < mx; ++i ) {
      /* ... */
    }

  }
}
```

Such declarations are not required to be on a separate line, and the explanatory comment may be omitted.

Bibliography

[Conventions 2009]	§6.1, "Number Per Line"
[ESA 2005]	Rule 9, Put Single Variable Definitions in Separate Lines
[JLS 2013]	§4.3.2, "The class Object"
	§6.1, "Declarations"
	§8.3, "Field Declarations"
	§9.3, "Field (Constant) Declarations"
	§14.4, "Local Variable Declaration Statements"

■ 39. Use meaningful symbolic constants to represent literal values in program logic

Java supports the use of various types of literals, such as integers (5, 2), floating-point numbers (2.5, 6.022e+23), characters ('a', '\n'), Booleans (true, false), and strings ("Hello\n"). Extensive use of literals in a program can lead to two problems. First, the meaning of the literal is often obscured or unclear from the context. Second, changing a frequently used literal requires searching the entire program source for that literal and distinguishing the uses that must be modified from those that should remain unmodified.

Avoid these problems by declaring class variables with meaningfully named constants, setting their values to the desired literals, and referencing the constants instead of the literals throughout the program. This approach clearly indicates the meaning or intended use of each literal. Furthermore, should the constant require modification, the change is limited to the declaration; searching the code is unnecessary.

Constants should be declared as static and final. However, constants should not be declared public and final if their values might change (see Guideline 31, "Do not apply public final to constants whose value might change in later releases," for more details). For example,

```
private static final int SIZE = 25;
```

Although final can be used to specify immutable constants, there is a caveat when dealing with composite objects. See Guideline 73, "Never confuse the immutability of a reference with that of the referenced object," for more details.

Noncompliant Code Example

This noncompliant code example calculates approximate dimensions of a sphere, given its radius:

```
double area(double radius) {
  return 3.14 * radius * radius;
}

double volume(double radius) {
  return 4.19 * radius * radius * radius;
}

double greatCircleCircumference(double radius) {
  return 6.28 * radius;
}
```

The methods use the seemingly arbitrary literals 3.14, 4.19, and 6.28 to represent various scaling factors used to calculate these dimensions. A developer or maintainer reading this code would have little idea about how they were generated or what they mean and consequently would not understand the function of this code.

Noncompliant Code Example

This noncompliant code example attempts to avoid the problem by explicitly calculating the required constants:

```
double area(double radius) {
  return 3.14 * radius * radius;
}

double volume(double radius) {
  return 4.0 / 3.0 * 3.14 * radius * radius * radius;
}

double greatCircleCircumference(double radius) {
  return 2 * 3.14 * radius;
}
```

The code uses the literal 3.14 to represent the value π. Although it removes some of the ambiguity from the literals, it complicates code maintenance. If the programmer were to decide that a more precise value of π is desired, all occurrences of 3.14 in the code would have to be found and replaced.

Compliant Solution (Constants)

In this compliant solution, a constant PI is declared and initialized to 3.14. Thereafter, it is referenced in the code whenever the value of π is needed.

```
private static final double PI = 3.14;

double area(double radius) {
  return PI * radius * radius;
}

double volume(double radius) {
  return 4.0/3.0 * PI * radius * radius * radius;
}

double greatCircleCircumference(double radius) {
  return 2 * PI * radius;
}
```

This technique reduces clutter and promotes maintainability. If a more precise approximation of the value of π is required, the programmer can simply redefine the constant. The use of the literals 4.0, 3.0, and 2 does not violate this guideline, for reasons explained in the "Applicability" section of this guideline.

Compliant Solution (Predefined Constants)

Use predefined constants when they are available. The class java.lang.Math defines a large group of numeric constants, including PI and the exponential constant E.

```
double area(double radius) {
  return Math.PI * radius * radius;
}

double volume(double radius) {
  return 4.0/3.0 * Math.PI * radius * radius * radius;
}

double greatCircleCircumference(double radius) {
  return 2 * Math.PI * radius;
}
```

Noncompliant Code Example

This noncompliant code example defines a constant BUFSIZE, but then defeats the purpose of defining BUFSIZE as a constant by assuming a specific value for BUFSIZE in the following expression:

```
private static final int BUFSIZE = 512;

// ...

public void shiftBlock() {
  int nblocks = 1 + ((nbytes - 1) >> 9);  // BUFSIZE = 512 = 2^9
  // ...
}
```

The programmer has assumed that BUFSIZE is 512, and right-shifting 9 bits is the same (for positive numbers) as dividing by 512. However, if BUFSIZE changes to 1024 in the future, modifications will be difficult and error prone.

This code also fails to conform to *The CERT® Oracle® Secure Coding Standard for Java*™ [Long 2012], "NUM01-J. Do not perform bitwise and arithmetic operations on the same data." Replacing a division operation with a right shift is considered a premature optimization. Normally, the compiler will do a better job of determining when this optimization should be performed.

Compliant Solution

This compliant solution uses the identifier assigned to the constant value in the expression:

```
private static final int BUFSIZE = 512;

// ...

public void shiftBlock(int nbytes) {
  int nblocks = 1 + (nbytes - 1) / BUFSIZE;
  // ...
}
```

Applicability

Using numeric literals makes code more difficult to read, understand, and edit.

The use of symbolic constants should be restricted to cases in which they improve the readability and maintainability of the code. When the intent of the literal is obvious, or where the literal is not likely to change, using symbolic constants can impair code readability. The following code example obscures the meaning of the code by using *too many* symbolic constants.

```
private static final double FOUR = 4.0;
private static final double THREE = 3.0;

double volume(double radius) {
  return FOUR / THREE * Math.PI * radius * radius * radius;
}
```

The values 4.0 and 3.0 in the volume calculation are clearly scaling factors used to calculate the sphere's volume and are not subject to change (unlike the approximate value for π), so they can be represented exactly. There is no reason to change them to increase precision because replacing them with symbolic constants actually impairs the readability of the code.

Bibliography

[Core Java 2003]

[Long 2012]   NUM01-J. Do not perform bitwise and arithmetic operations on the
                         same data

■ 40. Properly encode relationships in constant definitions

The definitions of constant expressions should be related *exactly* when the values
they express are also related.

Noncompliant Code Example

In this noncompliant code example, OUT_STR_LEN must always be exactly two greater
than IN_STR_LEN. These definitions fail to reflect this requirement:

```
public static final int IN_STR_LEN = 18;
public static final int OUT_STR_LEN = 20;
```

Compliant Solution

In this compliant solution, the relationship between the two values is represented in
the definitions:

```
public static final int IN_STR_LEN = 18;
public static final int OUT_STR_LEN = IN_STR_LEN + 2;
```

Noncompliant Code Example

In this noncompliant code example, there appears to be an underlying relationship
between the two constants where none exists:

```
public static final int VOTING_AGE = 18;
public static final int ALCOHOL_AGE = VOTING_AGE + 3;
```

A programmer performing routine maintenance may modify the definition
for VOTING_AGE, but fail to recognize the resulting change in the definition for
ALCOHOL_AGE.

Compliant Solution

In this compliant solution, the definitions reflect the independence of the two constants:

```
public static final int VOTING_AGE = 18;
public static final int ALCOHOL_AGE = 21;
```

Bibliography

[JLS 2013]   §4.12.4, "final Variables"

■ 41. Return an empty array or collection instead of a null value for methods that return an array or collection

Some APIs intentionally return a null reference to indicate that instances are unavailable. This practice can lead to denial-of-service vulnerabilities when the client code fails to explicitly handle the null return value case. A null return value is an example of an in-band error indicator, which is discouraged by Guideline 52, "Avoid in-band error indicators." For methods that return a set of values using an array or collection, returning an empty array or collection is an excellent alternative to returning a null value, as most callers are better equipped to handle an empty set than a null value.

Noncompliant Code Example

This noncompliant code example returns a null ArrayList when the size of the Array-List is 0. The class Inventory contains a getStock() method that constructs a list of items that have 0 inventory and returns the list of items to the caller.

```
class Inventory {
  private final Hashtable<String, Integer> items;
  public Inventory() {
    items = new Hashtable<String, Integer>();
  }

  public List<String> getStock() {
    List<String> stock = new ArrayList<String>();
    Enumeration itemKeys = items.keys();
    while (itemKeys.hasMoreElements()) {
      Object value = itemKeys.nextElement();
      if ((items.get(value)) == 0) {
        stock.add((String)value);
```

```
    }
  }

    if (items.size() == 0) {
      return null;
    } else {
      return stock;
    }
  }
}

public class Client {
  public static void main(String[] args) {
    Inventory inv = new Inventory();
    List<String> items = inv.getStock();
    System.out.println(items.size());
  }
}
```

When the size of this list is 0, a null value is returned with the assumption that the client will install the necessary checks. In this code example, the client lacks any null value check, causing a NullPointerException at runtime.

Compliant Solution

Instead of returning a null value, this compliant solution simply returns the List, even when it is empty.

```
class Inventory {
  private final Hashtable<String, Integer> items;
  public Inventory() {
    items = new Hashtable<String, Integer>();
  }

  public List<String> getStock() {
    List<String> stock = new ArrayList<String>();
    Integer noOfItems; // Number of items left in the inventory
    Enumeration itemKeys = items.keys();
    while (itemKeys.hasMoreElements()) {
      Object value = itemKeys.nextElement();

      if ((noOfItems = items.get(value)) == 0) {
        stock.add((String)value);
```

```
    }
  }
  return stock; // Return list (possibly zero-length)
  }
}

public class Client {
  public static void main(String[] args) {
    Inventory inv = new Inventory();
    List<String> items = inv.getStock();
    System.out.println(items.size());
  }
}
```

The client can handle this situation effectively without being interrupted by runtime exceptions. When returning arrays rather than collections, ensure that the client avoids attempts to access individual elements of a zero-length array. This prevents an ArrayIndexOutOfBoundsException from being thrown.

Compliant Solution

This compliant solution returns an explicit empty list, which is an equivalent permissible technique.

```
public List<String> getStock() {
  List<String> stock = new ArrayList<String>();
  Integer noOfItems; // Number of items left in the inventory
  Enumeration itemKeys = items.keys();
  while (itemKeys.hasMoreElements()) {
    Object value = itemKeys.nextElement();

    if ((noOfItems = items.get(value)) == 0) {
      stock.add((String)value);
    }
  }

  if (l.isEmpty()) {
    return Collections.EMPTY_LIST; // Always zero-length
  } else {
    return stock; // Return list
  }
}

// Class Client ...
```

Applicability

Returning a null value rather than a zero-length array or collection may lead to denial-of-service vulnerabilities when the client code fails to handle null return values properly.

Automatic detection is straightforward; fixing the problem typically requires programmer intervention.

Bibliography

[Bloch 2008]   Item 43, "Return Empty Arrays or Collections, Not Nulls"

■ 42. Use exceptions only for exceptional conditions

Exceptions should be used only to denote exceptional conditions; they should not be used for ordinary control flow purposes. Catching a generic object such as `Throwable` is likely to catch unexpected errors; see *The CERT® Oracle® Secure Coding Standard for Java*™ [Long 2012] ERR08-J, "Do not catch `NullPointerException` or any of its ancestors," for examples. When a program catches a specific type of exception, it does not always know from where that exception was thrown. Using a `catch` clause to handle an exception that occurs in a distant known location is a poor solution; it is preferable to handle the error as soon as it occurs or to prevent it, if possible.

The nonlocality of `throw` statements and corresponding `catch` statements can also impede optimizers from improving code that relies on exception handling. Relying on catching exceptions for control flow also complicates debugging, because exceptions indicate a jump in control flow from the `throw` statement to the `catch` clause. Finally, exceptions need not be highly optimized as it is assumed that they are thrown only in exceptional circumstances. Throwing and catching an exception frequently has worse performance than handling the error with some other mechanism.

Noncompliant Code Example

This noncompliant code example attempts to concatenate the processed elements of the `strings` array:

```
public String processSingleString(String string) {
  // ...
  return string;
}
public String processStrings(String[] strings) {
  String result = "";
```

```
    int i = 0;
    try {
      while (true) {
        result = result.concat(processSingleString(strings[i]));
        i++;
      }
    } catch (ArrayIndexOutOfBoundsException e) {
      // Ignore, we're done
    }
    return result;
  }
```

This code uses an `ArrayIndexOutOfBoundsException` to detect the end of the array. Unfortunately, because `ArrayIndexOutOfBoundsException` is a `RuntimeException`, it could be thrown by `processSingleString()` without being declared in a throws clause. So it is possible for `processStrings()` to terminate prematurely before processing all of the strings.

Compliant Solution

This compliant solution uses a standard `for` loop to concatenate the strings.

```
public String processStrings(String[] strings) {
  String result = "";
  for (int i = 0; i < strings.length; i++) {
    result = result.concat(processSingleString(strings[i]));
  }
  return result;
}
```

This code need not catch `ArrayIndexOutOfBoundsException` because it is a runtime exception, and such exceptions indicate programmer errors, which are best resolved by fixing the defect.

Applicability

Use of exceptions for any purpose other than detecting and handling exceptional conditions complicates program analysis and debugging, degrades performance, and can increase maintenance costs.

Bibliography

[Bloch 2001]   Item 39, "Use Exceptions Only for Exceptional Conditions"

[JLS 2013]   Chapter 11, "Exceptions"

[Long 2012]   ERR08-J. Do not catch `NullPointerException` or any of its ancestors

■ 43. Use a try-with-resources statement to safely handle closeable resources

The Java Development Kit 1.7 (JDK 1.7) introduced the `try-with-resources` statement (see the JLS, §14.20.3, "try-with-resources" [JLS 2013]), which simplifies correct use of resources that implement the `java.lang.AutoCloseable` interface, including those that implement the `java.io.Closeable` interface.

Using the `try-with-resources` statement prevents problems that can arise when closing resources with an ordinary `try-catch-finally` block, such as failing to close a resource because an exception is thrown as a result of closing another resource, or masking an important exception when a resource is closed.

Use of the `try-with-resources` statement is also illustrated in *The CERT® Oracle® Secure Coding Standard for Java™* [Long 2012], "ERR05-J. Do not let checked exceptions escape from a finally block," "FIO03-J. Remove temporary files before termination," and "FIO04-J. Close resources when they are no longer needed."

Noncompliant Code Example

This noncompliant code example uses an ordinary `try-catch-finally` block in an attempt to close two resources.

```
public void processFile(String inPath, String outPath)
    throws IOException{
  BufferedReader br = null;
  BufferedWriter bw = null;
  try {
    br = new BufferedReader(new FileReader(inPath));
    bw = new BufferedWriter(new FileWriter(outPath));
    // Process the input and produce the output
  } finally {
    try {
      if (br != null) {
        br.close();
      }
```

```
    if (bw != null) {
      bw.close();
    }
  } catch (IOException x) {
    // Handle error
  }
 }
}
```

However, if an exception is thrown when the BufferedReader br is closed, then the BufferedWriter bw will not be closed.

Compliant Solution (Second `finally` Block)

This compliant solution uses a second `finally` block to guarantee that bw is properly closed even when an exception is thrown while closing br.

```
public void processFile(String inPath, String outPath)
    throws IOException {
  BufferedReader br = null;
  BufferedWriter bw = null;
  try {
    br = new BufferedReader(new FileReader(inPath));
    bw = new BufferedWriter(new FileWriter(outPath));
    // Process the input and produce the output
  } finally {
    if (br != null) {
      try {
        br.close();
      } catch (IOException x) {
        // Handle error
      } finally {
        if (bw != null) {
          try {
            bw.close();
          } catch (IOException x) {
            // Handle error
          }
        }
      }
    }
  }
}
```

Compliant Solution (try-with-resources)

This compliant solution uses a `try-with-resources` statement to manage both `br`
and `bw`:

```
public void processFile(String inPath, String outPath)
    throws IOException{
  try (BufferedReader br =
        new BufferedReader(new FileReader(inPath));
      BufferedWriter bw =
        new BufferedWriter(new FileWriter(outPath));) {
    // Process the input and produce the output
  } catch (IOException ex) {
    // Print out all exceptions, including suppressed ones
    System.err.println("thrown exception: " + ex.toString());
    Throwable[] suppressed = ex.getSuppressed();
    for (int i = 0; i < suppressed.length; i++) {
      System.err.println("suppressed exception: " +
        suppressed[i].toString());
    }
  }
}
```

This solution preserves any exceptions thrown during the processing of the
input while still guaranteeing that both `br` and `bw` are properly closed, regardless of
what exceptions occur. Finally, this code demonstrates how to access every exception that may be produced from the `try-with-resources` block.

If only one exception is thrown, during opening, processing, or closing of the
files, the exception will be printed after `"thrown exception:"`. If an exception is
thrown during processing, and a second exception is thrown while trying to close
either file, the second exception will be printed after `"thrown exception:"`, and the
first exception will be printed after `"suppressed exception:"`.

Applicability

Failing to correctly handle all failure cases when working with closeable resources
may result in some resources not being closed or in important exceptions being
masked, possibly resulting in a denial of service. Note that failure to use a `try-with-`
`resources` statement cannot be considered a security vulnerability *in and of itself*,
because it is possible to write a correctly structured group of nested `try-catch-`
`finally` blocks guarding the resources that are in use (see "ERR05-J. Do not let
checked exceptions escape from a finally block" [Long 2012]). That said, failure to
correctly handle such error cases is a common source of vulnerabilities. Use of a
try-with-resources statement mitigates this issue by guaranteeing that the resources
are managed correctly and that exceptions are never masked.

Bibliography

[JLS 2013]	§14.20.3, "`try-with-resources`"
[Long 2012]	ERR05-J. Do not let checked exceptions escape from a `finally` block
	FIO03-J. Remove temporary files before termination
	FIO04-J. Close resources when they are no longer needed
[Tutorials 2013]	The `try`-with-resources Statement

■ 44. Do not use assertions to verify the absence of runtime errors

Diagnostic tests can be incorporated into programs by using the `assert` statement. Assertions are primarily intended for use during debugging and are often turned off before code is deployed by using the `-disableassertions` (or `-da`) Java runtime switch. Consequently, assertions should be used to protect against incorrect programmer assumptions, and not for runtime error checking.

Assertions should never be used to verify the absence of runtime (as opposed to logic) errors, such as

- Invalid user input (including command-line arguments and environment variables)
- File errors (for example, errors opening, reading, or writing files)
- Network errors (including network protocol errors)
- Out-of-memory conditions (when the Java Virtual Machine cannot allocate space for a new object, and the garbage collector cannot make sufficient space available)
- System resource exhaustion (for example, out-of-file descriptors, processes, threads)
- System call errors (for example, errors executing files or locking or unlocking mutexes)
- Invalid permissions (for example, file, memory, user)

Code that protects against an I/O error, for example, cannot be implemented as an assertion because it *must* be present in the deployed executable.

Assertions are generally unsuitable for server programs or embedded systems in deployment. A failed assertion can lead to a denial-of-service (DoS) attack if triggered by a malicious user. In such situations, a soft failure mode, such as writing to a log file, is more appropriate.

Noncompliant Code Example

This noncompliant code example uses the `assert` statement to verify that input was available:

```
BufferedReader br;

// Set up the BufferedReader br

String line;

// ...

line = br.readLine();

assert line != null;
```

Because input availability depends on the user and can be exhausted at any point during program execution, a robust program must be prepared to gracefully handle and recover from the unavailability of input. However, using the `assert` statement to verify that some significant input was available is inappropriate because it might lead to an abrupt termination of the process, resulting in a denial of service.

Compliant Solution

This compliant solution demonstrates the recommended way to detect and handle unavailability of input:

```
BufferedReader br;

// Set up the BufferedReader br

String line;

// ...

line = br.readLine();

if (line == null) {
  // Handle error
}
```

Applicability

Assertions are a valuable diagnostic tool for finding and eliminating software defects that may result in vulnerabilities. The absence of assertions, however, does not mean that code is bug-free.

In general, the misuse of the `assert` statement for runtime checking rather than checking for logical errors cannot be detected automatically.

Bibliography

[JLS 2013]   §14.10, "The `assert` Statement"

■ 45. Use the same type for the second and third operands in conditional expressions

The conditional operator `?:` uses the `boolean` value of its first operand to decide which of the other two expressions will be evaluated. (See §15.25, "Conditional Operator `? :`," of the JLS [JLS 2013].)

The general form of a Java conditional expression is `operand1 ? operand2 : operand3`.

- If the value of the first operand (`operand1`) is `true`, then the second operand expression (`operand2`) is chosen.

- If the value of the first operand is `false`, then the third operand expression (`operand3`) is chosen.

The conditional operator is syntactically right-associative. For example, `a?b:c?d:e?f:g` is equivalent to `a?b:(c?d:(e?f:g))`.

The JLS rules for determining the result type of a conditional expression (see Table 3–1) are complicated; programmers could be surprised by the type conversions required for expressions they have written.

Result type determination begins from the top of the table; the compiler applies the first matching rule. The Operand 2 and Operand 3 columns refer to `operand2` and `operand3` (from the previous definition) respectively. In the table, `constant int` refers to constant expressions of type `int` (such as `'0'` or variables declared `final`).

For the final table row, S1 and S2 are the types of the second and third operands, respectively. T1 is the type that results from applying boxing conversion to S1, and T2 is the type that results from applying boxing conversion to S2. The type of the conditional expression is the result of applying capture conversion to the least upper bound of T1 and T2. See §5.1.7, "Boxing Conversion," §5.1.10, "Capture Conversion," and §15.12.2.7, "Inferring Type Arguments Based on Actual Arguments" of the JLS for additional information [JLS 2013].

The complexity of the rules that determine the result type of a conditional expression can result in unintended type conversions. Consequently, the second and third operands of each conditional expression should have identical types. This recommendation also applies to boxed primitives.

Table 3–1.   Determining the result type of a conditional expression

Rule	Operand 2	Operand 3	Resultant Type
1	Type T	Type T	Type T
2	`boolean`	`Boolean`	`boolean`
3	`Boolean`	`boolean`	`boolean`
4	`null`	reference	reference
5	reference	`null`	reference
6	`byte` or `Byte`	`short` or `Short`	`short`
7	`short` or `Short`	`byte` or `Byte`	`short`
8	`byte`, `short`, `char`, `Byte`, `Short`, `Character`	`constant int`	`byte`, `short`, `char` if value of `int` is representable
9	`constant int`	`byte`, `short`, `char`, `Byte`, `Short`, `Character`	`byte`, `short`, `char` if value of `int` is representable
10	Other numeric	Other numeric	Promoted type of the second and third operands
11	T1 = boxing conversion(S1)	T2 = boxing conversion(S2)	Apply capture conversion to the least upper bound of T1 and T2

Noncompliant Code Example

In this noncompliant code example, the programmer expects that both print statements will print the value of `alpha` as a `char`:

```
public class Expr {
  public static void main(String[] args) {
    char alpha = 'A';
    int i = 0;
    // Other code. Value of i may change
    boolean trueExp = true; // Expression that evaluates to true
    System.out.print(trueExp ? alpha : 0); // Prints A
    System.out.print(trueExp ? alpha : i); // Prints 65
  }
}
```

The first print statement prints A because the compiler applies rule 8 from the result type determination table to determine that the second and third operands of the conditional expression are, or are converted to, type char. However, the second print statement prints 65—the value of alpha as an int. The first matching rule from the table is rule 10. Consequently, the compiler promotes the value of alpha to type int.

Compliant Solution

This compliant solution uses identical types for the second and third operands of each conditional expression; the explicit casts specify the type expected by the programmer:

```
public class Expr {
  public static void main(String[] args) {
    char alpha = 'A';
    int i = 0;
    boolean trueExp = true; // Expression that evaluates to true
    System.out.print(trueExp ? alpha : 0); // Prints A
    // Deliberate narrowing cast of i; possible truncation OK
    System.out.print(trueExp ? alpha : ((char) i)); // Prints A
  }
}
```

When the value of i in the second conditional expression falls outside the range that can be represented as a char, the explicit cast will truncate its value. This usage complies with exception NUM12-EX0 of NUM12-J, "Ensure conversions of numeric types to narrower types do not result in lost or misinterpreted data" in *The CERT® Oracle® Secure Coding Standard for Java™* [Long 2012].

Noncompliant Code Example

This noncompliant code example prints 100 as the size of the HashSet rather than the expected result (some value between 0 and 50):

```
public class ShortSet {
  public static void main(String[] args) {
    HashSet<Short> s = new HashSet<Short>();
    for (short i = 0; i < 100; i++) {
      s.add(i);
      // Cast of i-1 is safe,
      // because value is always representable
      Short workingVal = (short) (i-1);
      // ... Other code may update workingVal
```

```
      s.remove(((i % 2) == 1) ? i-1 : workingVal);
    }
    System.out.println(s.size());
  }
}
```

The combination of values of types short and int in the second argument of the conditional expression (the operation i-1) causes the result to be an int, as specified by the integer promotion rules. Consequently, the Short object in the third argument is unboxed into a short, which is then promoted to an int. The result of the conditional expression is then autoboxed into an object of type Integer. Because the HashSet contains only values of type Short, the call to HashSet.remove() has no effect.

Compliant Solution

This compliant solution casts the second operand to type short, then explicitly invokes the Short.valueOf() method to create a Short instance whose value is i-1:

```
public class ShortSet {
  public static void main(String[] args) {
    HashSet<Short> s = new HashSet<Short>();
    for (short i = 0; i < 100; i++) {
      s.add(i);
      // Cast of i-1 is safe, because the
      // resulting value is always representable
      Short workingVal = (short) (i-1);
      // ... other code may update workingVal

      // Cast of i-1 is safe, because the
      // resulting value is always representable
      s.remove(((i % 2) == 1) ? Short.valueOf((short) (i-1)) :
        workingVal);
    }
    System.out.println(s.size());
  }
}
```

As a result of the cast, the second and third operands of the conditional expression both have type Short, and the remove() call has the expected result.

Writing the conditional expression as ((i % 2) == 1) ? (short) (i-1)) : workingVal also complies with this guideline because both the second and third operands in this form have type short. However, this alternative is less efficient because it forces unboxing of workingVal on each even iteration of the loop and autoboxing of the result of the conditional expression (from short to Short) on every iteration of the loop.

Applicability

When the second and third operands of a conditional expression have different types, they can be subject to unexpected type conversions.

Automated detection of condition expressions whose second and third operands are of different types is straightforward.

Bibliography

[Bloch 2005]	Puzzle 8, "Dos Equis"
[Findbugs 2008]	"Bx: Primitive Value Is Unboxed and Coerced for Ternary Operator"
[JLS 2013]	§15.25, "Conditional Operator ? :"
[Long 2012]	NUM12-J. Ensure conversions of numeric types to narrower types do not result in lost or misinterpreted data

■ 46. Do not serialize direct handles to system resources

Serialized objects can be altered outside of any Java program unless they are protected using mechanisms such as sealing and signing. (See *The CERT® Oracle® Secure Coding Standard for Java™* [Long 2012], "ENV01-J. Place all security-sensitive code in a single JAR and sign and seal it.") If an object referring to a system resource becomes serialized, and an attacker can alter the serialized form of the object, it becomes possible to modify the system resource that the serialized handle refers to. For example, an attacker may modify a serialized file handle to refer to an arbitrary file on the system. In the absence of a security manager, any operations that use the file handle will be carried out using the attacker-supplied file path and file name.

Noncompliant Code Example

This noncompliant code example declares a serializable File object in the class Ser:

```
final class Ser implements Serializable {
  File f;
  public Ser() throws FileNotFoundException {
    f = new File("c:\\filepath\\filename");
  }
}
```

The serialized form of the object exposes the file path, which can be altered. When the object is deserialized, the operations are performed using the altered path, which can cause the wrong file to be read or modified.

Compliant Solution (Not Implementing Serializable)

This compliant solution shows a `final` class `Ser` that does not implement `java.io.Serializable`. Consequently, the `File` object cannot be serialized.

```
final class Ser {
  File f;
  public Ser() throws FileNotFoundException {
    f = new File("c:\\filepath\\filename");
  }
}
```

Compliant Solution (Object Marked Transient)

This compliant solution declares the `File` object `transient`. The file path is not serialized with the rest of the class, and is consequently not exposed to attackers.

```
final class Ser implements Serializable {
  transient File f;
  public Ser() throws FileNotFoundException {
    f = new File("c:\\filepath\\filename");
  }
}
```

Applicability

Deserializing direct handles to system resources can allow the modification of the resources being referred to.

Bibliography

[Long 2012]   ENV01-J. Place all security-sensitive code in a single JAR and sign
                   and seal it

[Oracle 2013c]   Java Platform Standard Edition 7 Documentation

■ 47. Prefer using iterators over enumerations

According to the Java API Interface `Enumeration<E>` documentation [API 2013],

> An object that implements the `Enumeration` interface generates a series of elements, one at a time. Successive calls to the `nextElement` method return successive elements of the series.

As an example, the following code uses an `Enumeration` to display the contents of a `Vector`:

```
for (Enumeration e = vector.elements(); e.hasMoreElements();) {
  System.out.println(e.nextElement());
}
```

The Java API [API 2013] recommends, "New implementations should consider using `Iterator` in preference to `Enumeration`." Iterators are superior to enumerations because they use simpler method names, and, unlike enumerations, iterators have well-defined semantics when elements in a collection are removed while iterating over the collection. Consequently, iterators rather than enumerators should be preferred when examining iterable collections.

Noncompliant Code Example

This noncompliant code example implements a `BankOperations` class with a `removeAccounts()` method used to terminate all the accounts of a particular account holder, as identified by the name. Names can be repeated in the vector if a person has more than one account. The `remove()` method attempts to iterate through all the vector entries, comparing each entry with the name "Harry."

```
class BankOperations {
  private static void removeAccounts(Vector v, String name) {
    Enumeration e = v.elements();

    while (e.hasMoreElements()) {
      String s = (String) e.nextElement();
      if (s.equals(name)) {
        v.remove(name); // Second Harry is not removed
```

```
    }
  }

  // Display current account holders
  System.out.println("The names are:");
  e = v.elements();
  while (e.hasMoreElements()) {
    // Prints Dick, Harry, Tom
    System.out.println(e.nextElement());
  }
}

public static void main(String args[]) {
  // List contains a sorted array of account holder names
  // Repeats are admissible
  List list = new ArrayList(Arrays.asList(
    new String[] {"Dick", "Harry", "Harry", "Tom"}));
  Vector v = new Vector(list);
  removeAccount(v, "Harry");
}
}
```

Upon encountering the first "Harry," it successfully removes the entry, and the size of the vector diminishes to three. However, the index of the Enumeration remains unchanged, causing the program to perform the next (now final) comparison with "Tom." Consequently, the second "Harry" remains in the vector unscathed, having shifted to the second position in the vector.

Compliant Solution

According to the Java API Interface Iterator<E> documentation [API 2013],

> Iterator takes the place of Enumeration in the Java collections framework. Iterators differ from enumerations in two ways:
>
> ■ Iterators allow the caller to remove elements from the underlying collection during the iteration with well-defined semantics.
> ■ Method names have been improved.

This compliant solution remedies the problem described in the noncompliant code example and demonstrates the advantages of using an Iterator over an Enumeration:

```
class BankOperations {
  private static void removeAccounts(Vector v, String name) {
    Iterator i = v.iterator();

    while (i.hasNext()) {
      String s = (String) i.next();
      if (s.equals(name)) {
        i.remove(); // Correctly removes all instances
                    // of the name Harry
      }
    }

    // Display current account holders
    System.out.println("The names are:");
    i = v.iterator();
    while (i.hasNext()) {
      System.out.println(i.next()); // Prints Dick, Tom only
    }
  }

  public static void main(String args[]) {
    List list = new ArrayList(Arrays.asList(
      new String[] {"Dick", "Harry", "Harry", "Tom"}));
    Vector v = new Vector(list);
    remove(v, "Harry");
  }
}
```

Applicability

Using Enumeration when performing remove operations on an iterable Collection may cause unexpected program behavior.

Bibliography

[API 2013]   Interface Enumeration<E>

                  Interface Iterator<E>

[Daconta 2003]   Item 21, "Use Iteration over Enumeration"

■ 48. Do not use direct buffers for short-lived, infrequently used objects

The new I/O (NIO) classes in `java.nio` allow the creation and use of direct buffers. These buffers tremendously increase throughput for repeated I/O activities. However, their creation and reclamation is more expensive than the creation and reclamation of heap-based non-direct buffers because direct buffers are managed using OS-specific native code. This added management cost makes direct buffers a poor choice for single-use or infrequently used cases. Direct buffers are also outside the scope of Java's garbage collector; consequently, injudicious use of direct buffers can cause memory leaks. Finally, frequent allocation of large direct buffers can cause an `OutOfMemoryError`.

Noncompliant Code Example

This noncompliant code example uses both a short-lived local object, `rarelyUsed-Buffer`, and a long-lived, heavily used object, `heavilyUsedBuffer`. Both are allocated in non-heap memory; neither is garbage collected.

```
ByteBuffer rarelyUsedBuffer = ByteBuffer.allocateDirect(8192);
// Use rarelyUsedBuffer once

ByteBuffer heavilyUsedBuffer = ByteBuffer.allocateDirect(8192);
// Use heavilyUsedBuffer many times
```

Compliant Solution

This compliant solution uses an indirect buffer to allocate the short-lived, infrequently used object. The heavily used buffer appropriately continues to use a non-heap, non-garbage-collected direct buffer.

```
ByteBuffer rarelyUsedBuffer = ByteBuffer.allocate(8192);
// Use rarelyUsedBuffer once

ByteBuffer heavilyUsedBuffer = ByteBuffer.allocateDirect(8192);
// Use heavilyUsedBuffer many times
```

Applicability

Direct buffers are beyond the scope of Java's garbage collector and can cause memory leaks if they are used injudiciously. In general, direct buffers should be allocated only when their use provides a significant gain in performance.

Bibliography

[API 2013]   Class ByteBuffer

■ 49. Remove short-lived objects from long-lived container objects

Always remove short-lived objects from long-lived container objects when the task is over. For example, objects attached to a java.nio.channels.SelectionKey object must be removed when they are no longer needed. Doing so reduces the likelihood of memory leaks. Similarly, use of array-based data structures such as ArrayList can introduce a requirement to indicate the absence of an entry by explicitly setting ArrayList's individual array element to null.

This guideline specifically addresses objects referred to from containers. For an example where nulling out objects does not aid garbage collection, see Guideline 75, "Do not attempt to help the garbage collector by setting local reference variables to null."

Noncompliant Code Example (Removing Short-Lived Objects)

In this noncompliant code example, a long-lived ArrayList contains references to both long- and short-lived elements. The programmer marks elements that have become irrelevant by setting a "dead" flag in the object.

```
class DataElement {
  private boolean dead = false;
  // Other fields

  public boolean isDead() { return dead; }
  public void killMe() { dead = true; }
}

// ... Elsewhere

List<DataElement> longLivedList = new ArrayList<DataElement>();

// Processing that renders an element irrelevant

// Kill the element that is now irrelevant
longLivedList.get(someIndex).killMe();
```

The garbage collector cannot collect the dead DataElement object until it becomes unreferenced. Note that all methods that operate on objects of class DataElement must also check whether the instance in hand is dead.

Compliant Solution (Set Reference to null)

In this compliant solution, rather than use a dead flag, the programmer assigns null to ArrayList elements that have become irrelevant:

```
class DataElement {
   // Dead flag removed
   // Other fields
}

// Elsewhere
List<DataElement> longLivedList = new ArrayList<DataElement>();

// Processing that renders an element irrelevant

// Set the reference to the irrelevant DataElement to null
longLivedList.set(someIndex, null);
```

Note that all code that operates on the longLivedList must now check for list entries that are null.

Compliant Solution (Use Null Object Pattern)

This compliant solution avoids the problems associated with intentionally null references by using a singleton sentinel object. This technique is known as the *Null Object pattern* (also known as the *Sentinel pattern*).

```
class DataElement {
  public static final DataElement NULL = createSentinel();
    // Dead flag removed
    // Other fields

  private static final DataElement createSentinel() {
    // Allocate a sentinel object, setting all its fields
    // to carefully chosen "do nothing" values
  }
}

// Elsewhere
List<DataElement> longLivedList = new ArrayList<DataElement>();
```

```
// Processing that renders an element irrelevant
// Set the reference to the irrelevant DataElement to
// the NULL object
longLivedList.set(someIndex, DataElement.NULL);
```

When feasible, programmers should choose this design pattern over the explicit null reference values, as described in Guideline 41, "Return an empty array or collection instead of a null value for methods that return an array or collection."

When using this pattern, the null object must be a singleton and must be final. It may be either public or private, depending on the overall design of the DataElement class. The state of the null object should be immutable after creation; immutability can be enforced either by using final fields or by explicit code in the methods of the DataElement class. See Chapter 8, "Behavioral Patterns, the Null Object," of *Patterns in Java, Volume 1, Second Edition* [Grand 2002], for additional information on this design pattern, and also *The CERT® Oracle® Secure Coding Standard for Java™* [Long 2012], "ERR08-J. Do not catch NullPointerException or any of its ancestors."

Applicability

Leaving short-lived objects in long-lived container objects may consume memory that cannot be recovered by the garbage collector, leading to memory exhaustion and possible denial of service attacks.

Bibliography

[Grand 2002]   Chapter 8, "Behavioral Patterns, the Null Object"

[Long 2012]   ERR08-J. Do not catch NullPointerException or any of its ancestors

Chapter 4

Program Understandability

Program understandability is the ease with which the program can be understood—that is, the ability to determine what a program does and how it works by reading its source code and accompanying documentation [Grubb 2003]. Understandable code is easier to maintain because software maintainers are less likely to introduce defects into code that is clear and comprehensible. Understandability helps in manual analysis of source code because it allows the auditor to more easily spot defects and vulnerabilities.

Some guidelines in this chapter are stylistic in nature; they will help a Java programmer to write clearer, more readable code. Failure to follow these guidelines could result in obscure code and design defects.

■ 50. Be careful using visually misleading identifiers and literals

Use visually distinct identifiers that are unlikely to be misread during development and review of code. Depending on the fonts used, certain characters are visually similar or even identical and can be misinterpreted. Consider the examples in Table 4–1.

The Java Language Specification (JLS) mandates that program source code be written using the Unicode character encoding [Unicode 2013]. Some distinct Unicode characters share identical glyph representation when displayed in many common fonts. For example, the Greek and Coptic characters (Unicode Range 0370–03FF) are frequently indistinguishable from the Greek-character subset of the Mathematical Alphanumeric Symbols (Unicode Range 1D400–1D7FF).

Table 4–1. Misleading characters

Intended Character	Could Be Mistaken for This Character, and Vice Versa
0 (zero)	O (capital *o*)
	D (capital *d*)
1 (one)	I (capital *i*)
	l (lowercase *L*)
2 (two)	Z (capital *z*)
5 (five)	S (capital *s*)
8 (eight)	B (capital *b*)
n (lowercase *N*)	h (lowercase *H*)
rn (lowercase *R*, lowercase *N*)	m (lowercase *M*)

Avoid defining identifiers that include Unicode characters with overloaded glyphs. One straightforward approach is to use only ASCII or Latin-1 characters in identifiers. Note that the ASCII character set is a subset of Unicode.

Do not use multiple identifiers that vary only by one or more visually similar characters. Also, make the initial portions of long identifiers distinct to aid recognition. According to the JLS, §3.10.1, "Integer Literals" [JLS 2013],

> An integer literal is of type `long` if it is suffixed with an ASCII letter L or l (ell); otherwise, it is of type `int`. The suffix L is preferred because the letter l (ell) is often hard to distinguish from the digit 1 (one).

Consequently, use L, not l, to clarify programmer intent when indicating that an integer literal is of type `long`.

Integer literals with leading zeros, in actuality, denote octal values not decimal values. According to §3.10.1, "Integer Literals," of the JLS [JLS 2013],

> An octal numeral consists of an ASCII digit 0 followed by one or more of the ASCII digits 0 through 7 interspersed with underscores, and can represent a positive, zero, or negative integer.

This misinterpretation may result in programming errors and is more likely to occur while declaring multiple constants and trying to enhance the formatting with zero padding.

Noncompliant Code Example

This noncompliant code example has two variables, `stem` and `stern`, within the same scope that can be easily confused and accidentally interchanged:

```
int stem;  // Position near the front of the boat
/* ... */
int stern; // Position near the back of the boat
```

Compliant Solution

This compliant solution eliminates the confusion by assigning visually distinct identifiers to the variables:

```
int bow;   // Position near the front of the boat
/* ... */
int stern; // Position near the back of the boat
```

Noncompliant Code Example

This noncompliant code example prints the result of adding an `int` and a `long` value, even though it may appear that two integers (11111) are being added:

```
public class Visual {
  public static void main(String[] args) {
    System.out.println(11111 + 11111);
  }
}
```

Compliant Solution

This compliant solution uses an uppercase L (`long`) instead of lowercase l to disambiguate the visual appearance of the second integer. Its behavior is the same as that of the noncompliant code example, but the programmer's intent is clear:

```
public class Visual {
  public static void main(String[] args) {
    System.out.println(11111 + 1111L);
  }
}
```

Noncompliant Code Example

This noncompliant code example mixes decimal values and octal values while storing them in an array:

```
int[] array = new int[3];

void exampleFunction() {
  array[0] = 2719;
  array[1] = 4435;
  array[2] = 0042;
  // ...
}
```

It appears that the third element in array is intended to hold the decimal value 42. However, the decimal value 34 (corresponding to the octal value 42) gets assigned.

Compliant Solution

When integer literals are intended to represent a decimal value, avoid padding with leading zeros. Use another technique instead, such as padding with whitespace, to preserve digit alignment.

```
int[] array = new int[3];

void exampleFunction() {
  array[0] = 2719;
  array[1] = 4435;
  array[2] =   42;
  // ...
}
```

Applicability

Failing to use visually distinct identifiers could result in the use of the wrong identifier and lead to unexpected program behavior.

Heuristic detection of identifiers with visually similar names is straightforward. Confusing a lowercase letter *l* with a digit *1* when indicating that an integer denotation is a long value can result in incorrect computations. Automated detection is trivial.

Mixing decimal and octal values can result in improper initialization or assignment.

Detection of integer literals that have a leading zero is trivial. However, determining whether the programmer intended to use an octal literal or a decimal literal is infeasible. Accordingly, sound automated detection is also infeasible. Heuristic checks may be useful.

Bibliography

[Bloch 2005]	Puzzle 4, "It's Elementary"
[JLS 2013]	§3.10.1, "Integer Literals"
[Seacord 2009]	DCL02-C. Use visually distinct identifiers
[Unicode 2013]	

■ 51. Avoid ambiguous overloading of variable arity methods

The *variable arity (varargs)* feature was introduced in JDK v1.5.0 to support methods that accept a variable number of arguments.

According to the Java SE 6 Documentation [Oracle 2011b],

> As an API designer, you should use [variable arity methods] sparingly, only when the benefit is truly compelling. Generally speaking, you should not overload a varargs method, or it will be difficult for programmers to figure out which overloading gets called.

Noncompliant Code Example

In this noncompliant code example, overloading variable arity methods makes it unclear which definition of displayBooleans() is invoked:

```
class Varargs {
  private static void displayBooleans(boolean... bool) {
    System.out.print("Number of arguments: "
                     + bool.length + ", Contents: ");

    for (boolean b : bool) {
      System.out.print("[" + b + "]");
    }
  }
  private static void displayBooleans(boolean bool1,
                                      boolean bool2) {
    System.out.println("Overloaded method invoked");
  }
  public static void main(String[] args) {
    displayBooleans(true, false);
  }
}
```

When run, this program outputs

```
Overloaded method invoked
```

because the nonvariable arity definition is more specific and consequently a better fit for the provided arguments. However, this complexity is best avoided.

Compliant Solution

To avoid overloading variable arity methods, use distinct method names to ensure that the intended method is invoked, as shown in this compliant solution:

```java
class Varargs {
  private static void displayManyBooleans(boolean... bool) {
    System.out.print("Number of arguments: "
                        + bool.length + ", Contents: ");

    for (boolean b : bool) {
      System.out.print("[" + b + "]");
    }
  }
  private static void displayTwoBooleans(boolean bool1,
                                         boolean bool2) {
    System.out.println("Overloaded method invoked");
    System.out.println("Contents: ["
                        + bool1 + "], [" + bool2 + "]");
  }
  public static void main(String[] args) {
    displayManyBooleans(true, false);
  }
}
```

Applicability

Injudicious use of overloaded variable arity methods may create ambiguity and diminish code readability.

It may be desirable to violate this rule for performance reasons. One such reason would be to avoid the cost of creating an array instance and initializing it on every invocation of a method [Bloch 2008].

```java
public void foo() { }
public void foo(int a1) { }
public void foo(int a1, int a2, int... rest) { }
```

When overloading variable arity methods, it is important to avoid any ambiguity regarding which method should be invoked. The preceding code sample avoids the possibility of incorrect method selection by using unambiguous method signatures.

Automated detection is straightforward.

Bibliography

[Bloch 2008]	Item 42, "Use Varargs Judiciously"
[Steinberg 2008]	Using the Varargs Language Feature
[Oracle 2011b]	Varargs

■ 52. Avoid in-band error indicators

An in-band error indicator is a value returned by a method that indicates either a legitimate return value or an illegitimate value that denotes an error. Some common examples of in-band error indicators include

- A valid object or a null reference.

- An integer indicating a positive value, or –1 to indicate that an error occurred.

- An array of valid objects or a null reference indicating the absence of valid objects. (This topic is further addressed in Guideline 41, "Return an empty array or collection instead of a null value for methods that return an array or collection.")

In-band error indicators require the caller to check for the error; however, this checking is often overlooked. Failure to check for such error conditions not only violates *The CERT® Oracle® Secure Coding Standard for Java™* [Long 2012], "EXP00-J. Do not ignore values returned by methods," but also has the unfortunate effect of propagating invalid values that may subsequently be treated as valid in later computations.

Avoid the use of in-band error indicators. They are much less common in Java's core library than in some other programming languages; nevertheless, they are used in the `read(byte[] b, int off, int len)` and `read(char[] cbuf, int off, int len)` families of methods in `java.io`.

In Java, the best way to indicate an exceptional situation is by throwing an exception rather than by returning an error code. Exceptions are propagated across scopes and cannot be ignored as easily as error codes can. When using exceptions, the error-detection and error-handling code is kept separate from the main flow of control.

Noncompliant Code Example

This noncompliant code example attempts to read into an array of characters and to add an extra character into the buffer immediately after the characters that are read.

```
static final int MAX = 21;
static final int MAX_READ = MAX - 1;
static final char TERMINATOR = '\\';
int read;
char [] chBuff = new char[MAX];
BufferedReader buffRdr;

// Set up buffRdr

read = buffRdr.read(chBuff, 0, MAX_READ);
chBuff[read] = TERMINATOR;
```

However, if the input buffer is initially at end-of-file, the `read()` method will return –1, and the attempt to place the terminator character will throw an `Array-IndexOutOfBoundsException`.

Compliant Solution (Wrapping)

This compliant solution defines a `readSafe()` method that wraps the original `read()` method and throws an exception if end-of-file is detected:

```
public static int readSafe(BufferedReader buffer, char[] cbuf,
                           int off, int len) throws IOException {
  int read = buffer.read(cbuf, off, len);
  if (read == -1) {
    throw new EOFException();
  } else {
    return read;
  }
}

// ...

BufferedReader buffRdr;

// Set up buffRdr
```

```
try {
  read = readSafe(buffRdr, chBuff, 0, MAX_READ);
  chBuff[read] = TERMINATOR;
} catch (EOFException eof) {
  chBuff[0] = TERMINATOR;
}
```

Applicability

Using in-band error indicators may result in programmers either failing to check status codes or using incorrect return values, leading to unexpected behavior.

Given the comparatively rare occurrence of in-band error indicators in Java, it may be possible to compile a list of all standard library methods that use them and to automatically detect their use. However, detecting the safe use of in-band error indicators is not feasible in the general case.

Returning an object that might be null on failure or a valid object on success is a common example of an in-band error indicator. Although better method designs are often available, returning an object that may be null can be acceptable under some circumstances. See Guideline 26, "Always provide feedback about the resulting value of a method," for an example.

Bibliography

[API 2013]	Class Reader
[JLS 2013]	Chapter 11, "Exceptions"
[Long 2012]	EXP00-J. Do not ignore values returned by methods

■ 53. Do not perform assignments in conditional expressions

Using the assignment operator in conditional expressions frequently indicates programmer error and can result in unexpected behavior. The assignment operator should not be used in the following contexts:

- `if` (controlling expression)
- `while` (controlling expression)
- `do ... while` (controlling expression)
- `for` (second operand)

- `switch` (controlling expression)
- `?:` (first operand)
- `&&` (either operand)
- `||` (either operand)
- `?:` (second or third operands) where the ternary expression is used in any of these contexts

Noncompliant Code Example

In this noncompliant code example, the controlling expression in the `if` statement is an assignment expression.

```
public void f(boolean a, boolean b) {
  if (a = b) {
    /* ... */
  }
}
```

Although the programmer's intent could have been to assign b to a and test the value of the result, this usage frequently occurs when the programmer mistakenly uses the assignment operator = rather than the equality operator ==.

Compliant Solution

The conditional block shown in this compliant solution only executes when a is equal to b.

```
public void f(boolean a, boolean b) {
  if (a == b) {
    /* ... */
  }
}
```

Unintended assignment of b to a cannot occur.

Compliant Solution

When the assignment is intentional, this compliant solution clarifies the programmer's intent:

```
public void f(boolean a, boolean b) {
  if ((a = b) == true) {
```

```
    /* ... */
  }
}
```

Compliant Solution

It is clearer to express the logic as an explicit assignment followed by the if condition:

```
public void f(boolean a, boolean b) {
  a = b;
  if (a) {
    /* ... */
  }
}
```

Noncompliant Code Example

In this noncompliant code example, an assignment expression appears as an operand of the && operator:

```
public void f(boolean a, boolean b, boolean flag) {
  while ( (a = b) && flag ) {
    /* ... */
  }
}
```

Because && is not a comparison operator, assignment is an illegal operand. Again, this is frequently a case of the programmer mistakenly using the assignment operator = instead of the equals operator ==.

Compliant Solution

When the assignment of b to a is unintentional, this conditional block is now executed only when a is equal to b and flag is true:

```
public void f(boolean a, boolean b, boolean flag) {
  while ( (a == b) && flag ) {
    /* ... */
  }
}
```

Applicability

The use of the assignment operator in controlling conditional expressions frequently indicates programmer error and can result in unexpected behavior.

As an exception to this guideline, it is permitted to use the assignment operator in conditional expressions when the assignment is not the controlling expression (that is, the assignment is a subexpression), as shown in the following compliant solution.

```
public void assignNocontrol(BufferedReader reader)
    throws IOException {
  String line;
  while ((line = reader.readLine()) != null) {
    // ... Work with line
  }
}
```

Bibliography

[Hatton 1995]   §2.7.2, "Errors of Omission and Addition"

■ 54. Use braces for the body of an `if`, `for`, or `while` statement

Use opening and closing braces for `if`, `for`, and `while` statements even when the body contains only a single statement. Braces improve the uniformity and readability of code.

More important, it is easy to forget to add braces when inserting additional statements into a body containing only a single statement, because the conventional program indentation gives strong (but misleading) guidance to the structure.

Noncompliant Code Example

This noncompliant code example authenticates a user with an `if` statement that lacks braces.

```
int login;

if (invalid_login())
  login = 0;
else
  login = 1;
```

This program behaves as expected. However, a maintainer might subsequently add a debug statement or other logic but forget to add opening and closing braces:

```
int login;

if (invalid_login())
  login = 0;
else
  // Debug line added below
  System.out.println("Login is valid\n");
  // The next line is always executed
  login = 1;
```

The code's indentation disguises the functionality of the program, potentially leading to a security vulnerability.

Compliant Solution

This compliant solution uses opening and closing braces even though the `if` and `else` bodies of the `if` statement are single statements:

```
int login;

if (invalid_login()) {
  login = 0;
} else {
  login = 1;
}
```

Noncompliant Code Example

This noncompliant code example nests an `if` statement within another `if` statement, without braces around the `if` and `else` bodies:

```
int privileges;

if (invalid_login())
  if (allow_guests())
    privileges = GUEST;
else
  privileges = ADMINISTRATOR;
```

The indentation might lead the programmer to believe users are granted administrator privileges only when their login is valid. However, the `else` statement actually binds to the inner `if` statement:

```c
int privileges;

if (invalid_login())
  if (allow_guests())
    privileges = GUEST;
  else
    privileges = ADMINISTRATOR;
```

Consequently, this defect allows unauthorized users to obtain administrator privileges.

Compliant Solution

This compliant solution uses braces to eliminate the ambiguity, consequently ensuring that privileges are correctly assigned:

```c
int privileges;

if (invalid_login()) {
  if (allow_guests()) {
    privileges = GUEST;
  }
} else {
  privileges = ADMINISTRATOR;
}
```

Applicability

Failure to enclose the bodies of `if`, `for`, or `while` statements in braces makes code error prone and increases maintenance costs.

Bibliography

[GNU 2013]   §5.3, "Clean Use of C Constructs"

▪ 55. Do not place a semicolon immediately following an `if`, `for`, or `while` condition

Do not use a semicolon after an `if`, `for`, or `while` condition because it typically indicates programmer error and can result in unexpected behavior.

Noncompliant Code Example

In this noncompliant code example, a semicolon is used immediately following an if condition.

```
if (a == b); {
  /* ... */
}
```

The statements in the apparent body of the if statement are always evaluated, regardless of the result of the condition expression.

Compliant Solution

This compliant solution eliminates the semicolon and ensures that the body of the if statement is executed only when the condition expression is true:

```
if (a == b) {
  /* ... */
}
```

Applicability

Placing a semicolon immediately following an if, for, or while condition may result in unexpected behavior.

Bibliography

[Hatton 1995]   §2.7.2, "Errors of Omission and Addition"

■ 56. Finish every set of statements associated with a case label with a break statement

A switch block comprises several case labels and an optional but highly recommended default label. Statements that follow each case label must end with a break statement, which is responsible for transferring the control to the end of the switch block. When omitted, the statements in the subsequent case label are executed. Because the break statement is optional, omitting it produces no compiler warnings. When this behavior is unintentional, it can cause unexpected control flow.

Noncompliant Code Example

In this noncompliant code example, the case where the card is 11 lacks a break statement. As a result, execution continues with the statements for card = 12.

```
int card = 11;

switch (card) {
  /* ... */
  case 11:
    System.out.println("Jack");
  case 12:
    System.out.println("Queen");
    break;
  case 13:
    System.out.println("King");
    break;
  default:
    System.out.println("Invalid Card");
    break;
}
```

Compliant Solution

This compliant solution terminates each case with a break statement.

```
int card = 11;

switch (card) {
  /* ... */
  case 11:
    System.out.println("Jack");
    break;
  case 12:
    System.out.println("Queen");
    break;
  case 13:
    System.out.println("King");
    break;
  default:
    System.out.println("Invalid Card");
    break;
}
```

Applicability

Failure to include break statements can cause unexpected control flow.

The break statement at the end of the final case in a switch statement may be omitted. By convention, this is the default label. The break statement serves to transfer control to the end of the switch block. Fall-through behavior also causes control to arrive at the end of the switch block. Consequently, control transfers to the statements following the switch block without regard to the presence or absence of the break statement. Nevertheless, the final case in a switch statement should end with a break statement in accordance with good programming style [Allen 2000].

Exceptionally, when multiple cases require execution of identical code, break statements may be omitted from all cases except the last one. Similarly, when processing for one case is a proper prefix of processing for one or more other cases, the break statement may be omitted from the prefix case. This should be clearly indicated with a comment. For example:

```
int card = 11;
int value;

// Cases 11,12,13 fall through to the same case
switch (card) {
  // Processing for this case requires a prefix
  // of the actions for the following three
  case 10:
    do_something(card);
    // Intentional fall-through
    // These three cases are treated identically
  case 11:        // Break not required
  case 12:        // Break not required
  case 13:
    value = 10;
    break;        // Break required
  default:
    // Handle error condition
}
```

Also, when a case ends with a return or throw statement or nonreturning method such as System.exit(), the break statement may be omitted.

Bibliography

[JLS 2013]   §14.11, "The switch Statement"

■ 57. Avoid inadvertent wrapping of loop counters

Unless coded properly, a while or for loop may execute forever, or until the counter wraps around and reaches its final value. (See *The CERT® Oracle® Secure Coding Standard for Java™* [Long 2012], "NUM00-J. Detect or prevent integer overflow.") This problem may result from incrementing or decrementing a loop counter by more than one and then testing for equality to a specified value to terminate the loop. In this case, it is possible that the loop counter will leapfrog the specified value and execute either forever, or until the counter wraps around and reaches its final value. This problem may also be caused by naïve testing against limits; for example, looping while a counter is less than or equal to `Integer.MAX_VALUE` or greater than or equal to `Integer.MIN_VALUE`.

Noncompliant Code Example

This noncompliant code example appears to iterate five times.

```
for (i = 1; i != 10; i += 2) {
  // ...
}
```

However, the loop never terminates. Successive values of i are 1, 3, 5, 7, 9, 11, and so on; the comparison with 10 never evaluates to `true`. The value reaches the maximum representable positive number (`Integer.MAX_VALUE`), then wraps to the second lowest negative number (`Integer.MIN_VALUE + 1`). It then works its way up to –1, then 1, and proceeds as described earlier.

Noncompliant Code Example

This noncompliant code example terminates but performs many more iterations than expected:

```
for (i = 1; i != 10; i += 5) {
  // ...
}
```

Successive values of i are 1, 6, and 11, skipping 10. The value of i then wraps from near the maximum positive value to near the lowest negative value and works its way up toward 0. It then assumes 2, 7, and 12, skipping 10 again. After the value wraps from the high positive to the low negative side three more times, it finally reaches 0, 5, and 10, terminating the loop.

Compliant Solution

One solution is to simply ensure the loop termination condition is reached before the counter inadvertently wraps.

```
for (i = 1; i == 11; i += 2) {
  // ...
}
```

This solution can be fragile when one or more of the conditions affecting the iteration must be changed. A better solution is to use a numerical comparison operator (that is, <, <=, >, or >=) to terminate the loop.

```
for (i = 1; i <= 10; i += 2) {
  // ...
}
```

This latter solution can be more robust in the event of changes to the iteration conditions. However, this approach should never replace careful consideration regarding the intended and actual number of iterations.

Noncompliant Code Example

A loop expression that tests whether a counter is less than or equal to Integer.MAX_VALUE or greater or equal to Integer.MIN_VALUE will never terminate because the expression will always evaluate to true. For example, the following loop will never terminate because i can never be greater than Integer.MAX_VALUE:

```
for (i = 1; i <= Integer.MAX_VALUE; i++) {
  // ...
}
```

Compliant Solution

The loop in this compliant solution terminates when i is equal to Integer.MAX_VALUE:

```
for (i = 1; i < Integer.MAX_VALUE; i++) {
  // ...
}
```

If the loop is meant to iterate for every value of i greater than 0, including Integer.MAX_VALUE, it can be implemented as follows:

```
i = 0;
do {
  i++
  // ...
} while (i != Integer.MAX_VALUE);
```

Noncompliant Code Example

This noncompliant code example initializes the loop counter i to 0 and then increments it by two on each iteration, basically enumerating all the even, positive values.

The loop is expected to terminate when i is greater than `Integer.MAX_VALUE - 1`, an even value. In this case, the loop fails to terminate because the counter wraps around before becoming greater than `Integer.MAX_VALUE - 1`.

```
for (i = 0; i <= Integer.MAX_VALUE - 1; i += 2) {
  // ...
}
```

Compliant Solution

The loop in this compliant solution terminates when the counter i is greater than `Integer.MAX_VALUE` minus the step value as the loop-terminating condition.

```
for (i = 0; i <= Integer.MAX_VALUE - 2; i += 2) {
  // ...
}
```

Applicability

Incorrect termination of loops may result in infinite loops, poor performance, incorrect results, and other problems. If any of the conditions used to terminate a loop can be influenced by an attacker, these errors can be exploited to cause a denial of service or other attack.

Bibliography

[JLS 2013]   §15.20.1, "Numerical Comparison Operators <, <=, >, and >="

[Long 2012]   NUM00-J. Detect or prevent integer overflow

■ 58. Use parentheses for precedence of operation

Programmers frequently make errors regarding the precedence of operators because of the unintuitive low precedence levels of &, |, ^, <<, and >>. Avoid mistakes regarding precedence through the suitable use of parentheses, which also improves code readability. The precedence of operations by the order of the subclauses is listed in the Java™ Tutorials [Tutorials 2013].

Although it advises against depending on parentheses for specifying evaluation order, *The CERT® Oracle® Secure Coding Standard for Java™* [Long 2012], "EXP05-J. Do not write more than once to the same variable within an expression," applies only to expressions that contain side effects.

Noncompliant Code Example

The intent of the expression in this noncompliant code example is to add the variable OFFSET to the result of the bitwise logical AND between x and MASK.

```
public static final int MASK = 1337;
public static final int OFFSET = -1337;

public static int computeCode(int x) {
  return x & MASK + OFFSET;
}
```

According to the operator precedence guidelines, the expression is parsed as

```
x & (MASK + OFFSET)
```

This expression is evaluated as follows, resulting in the value 0:

```
x & (1337 - 1337)
```

Compliant Solution

This compliant solution uses parentheses to ensure that the expression is evaluated as intended:

```
public static final int MASK = 1337;
public static final int OFFSET = -1337;

public static int computeCode(int x) {
  return (x & MASK) + OFFSET;
}
```

Noncompliant Code Example

In this noncompliant code example, the intent is to append either "0" or "1" to the string "value=".

```
public class PrintValue {
  public static void main(String[] args) {
    String s = null;
    // Prints "1"
    System.out.println("value=" + s == null ? 0 : 1);
  }
}
```

However, the precedence rules result in the expression to be printed being parsed as ("value=" + s) == null ? 0 : 1.

Compliant Solution

This compliant solution uses parentheses to ensure that the expression evaluates as intended.

```java
public class PrintValue {
  public static void main(String[] args) {
    String s = null;
    // Prints "value=0" as expected
    System.out.println("value=" + (s == null ? 0 : 1));
  }
}
```

Applicability

Mistakes concerning precedence rules can cause an expression to be evaluated in an unintended way, which can result in unexpected and abnormal program behavior.

Parentheses may be omitted from mathematical expressions that follow the algebraic precedence rules. For example, consider the following expression:

x + y * z

By mathematical convention, multiplication is performed before addition; parentheses are redundant in this case:

x + (y * z)

Detection of all expressions using low-precedence operators without parentheses is straightforward. Determining the correctness of such uses is infeasible in the general case, although heuristic warnings could be useful.

Bibliography

[ESA 2005]	Rule 65, Use parentheses to explicitly indicate the order of execution of numerical operators
[Long 2012]	EXP05-J. Do not write more than once to the same variable within an expression
[Tutorials 2013]	Expressions, Statements, and Blocks

■ 59. Do not make assumptions about file creation

Although creating a file is usually accomplished with a single method call, this single action raises multiple security-related questions. What should be done if the file cannot be created? What should be done if the file already exists? What should be the file's initial attributes, such as permissions?

Java provides several generations of file-handling facilities. The original input/output facilities, which included basic file handling, are in the package java.io. More comprehensive facilities were included in JDK 1.4 with the New I/O package java.nio (see New I/O APIs [Oracle 2010b]). Still more comprehensive facilities were included in JDK 1.7 with the New I/O 2 package java.nio.file. Both packages introduced a number of methods to support finer-grained control over file creation.

The CERT® Oracle® Secure Coding Standard for Java™ [Long 2012], "FIO01-J. Create files with appropriate access permissions," explains how to specify the permissions of a newly created file.

Noncompliant Code Example

This noncompliant code example tries to open a file for writing:

```
public void createFile(String filename)
   throws FileNotFoundException{
  OutputStream out = new FileOutputStream(filename);
 // Work with file
}
```

If the file exists before being opened, its former contents will be overwritten with the contents provided by the program.

Noncompliant Code Example (TOCTOU)

This noncompliant code example tries to avoid altering an existing file by creating an empty file using java.io.File.createNewFile(). If a file with the given name already exists, then createNewFile() will return false without destroying the named file's contents.

```
public void createFile(String filename)
   throws FileNotFoundException{
  OutputStream out = new FileOutputStream(filename, true);
  if (!new File(filename).createNewFile()) {
```

```
    // File cannot be created...handle error
  } else {
    out = new FileOutputStream(filename);
    // Work with file
  }
}
```

Unfortunately, this solution is subject to a TOCTOU (time-of-check, time-of-use) race condition. It is possible for an attacker to modify the file system after the empty file is created but before the file is opened, such that the file that is opened is distinct from the file that was created.

Compliant Solution (Files)

This compliant solution uses the `java.nio.file.Files.newOutputStream()` method to atomically create the file, and throw an exception if the file already exists:

```
public void createFile(String filename)
    throws FileNotFoundException{
  try (OutputStream out = new BufferedOutputStream(
        Files.newOutputStream(Paths.get(filename),
                              StandardOpenOption.CREATE_NEW))) {
    // Work with out
  } catch (IOException x) {
    // File not writable...Handle error
  }
}
```

Applicability

The ability to determine whether an existing file has been opened or a new file has been created provides greater assurance that only the intended file is opened or overwritten and that other files remain unaffected.

Bibliography

[API 2013]	Class `java.io.File`
	Class `java.nio.file.Files`
[Long 2012]	FIO01-J. Create files with appropriate access permissions
[Oracle 2010b]	New I/O APIs

■ 60. Convert integers to floating-point for floating-point operations

Incautious use of integer arithmetic to calculate a value for assignment to a floating-point variable can result in loss of information. For example, integer arithmetic always produces integral results, discarding information about any possible fractional remainder. Furthermore, there can be loss of precision when converting integers to floating-point values. See *The CERT® Oracle® Secure Coding Standard for Java™* [Long 2012], "NUM13-J. Avoid loss of precision when converting primitive integers to floating-point," for additional information. Correct programming of expressions that combine integer and floating-point values requires careful consideration.

Operations that could suffer from integer overflow or loss of a fractional remainder should be performed on floating-point values, rather than integral values.

Noncompliant Code Example

In this noncompliant code example, the division and multiplication operations are performed on integral values; the results of these operations are then converted to floating-point.

```
short a = 533;
int b = 6789;
long c = 4664382371590123456L;

float d = a / 7;    // d is 76.0 (truncated)
double e = b / 30;  // e is 226.0 (truncated)
double f = c * 2;   // f is -9.1179793305293046E18
                    // because of integer overflow
```

The results of the integral operations are truncated to the nearest integer and can also overflow. As a result, the floating-point variables d, e, and f are initialized incorrectly because the truncation and overflow take place before the conversion to floating-point.

Note that the calculation for c also violates "NUM00-J. Detect or prevent integer overflow" [Long 2012].

Compliant Solution (Floating-Point Literal)

The following compliant solution performs the multiplication and division operations on floating-point values, avoiding both the truncation and the overflow seen in the noncompliant code example. In every operation, at least one of the operands is of a floating-point type, forcing floating-point multiplication and division, and avoiding truncation and overflow:

```
short a = 533;
int b = 6789;
long c = 4664382371590123456L;

float d = a / 7.0f;       // d is 76.14286
double e = b / 30.;       // e is 226.3
double f = (double)c * 2; // f is 9.328764743180247E18
```

Another compliant solution is to eliminate the truncation and overflow errors by storing the integers in the floating-point variables before performing the arithmetic operations:

```
short a = 533;
int b = 6789;
long c = 4664382371590123456L;

float d = a;
double e = b;
double f = c;

d /= 7;   // d is 76.14286
e /= 30; // e is 226.3
f *= 2;   // f is 9.328764743180247E18
```

As in the previous compliant solution, this practice ensures that at least one of the operands of each operation is a floating-point number. Consequently, the operations are performed on floating-point values.

In both compliant solutions, the original value of c cannot be represented exactly as a double. The representation of type double has only 48 mantissa bits, but a precise representation of the value of c would require 56 mantissa bits. Consequently, the value of c is rounded to the nearest value that can be represented by type double, and the computed value of f (9.328764743180247E18) differs from the exact mathematical result (9328564743180246912). This loss of precision is one of the many reasons correct programming of expressions that mix integer and floating-point operations or values requires careful consideration. See "NUM13-J. Avoid loss of precision when converting primitive integers to floating-point" [Long 2012], for more information about integer-to-floating-point conversion. Even with this loss of precision, however, the computed value of f is far more accurate than that produced in the noncompliant code example.

Noncompliant Code Example

This noncompliant code example attempts to compute the whole number greater than the ratio of two integers. The result of the computation is 1.0 rather than the intended 2.0.

```
int a = 60070;
int b = 57750;

double value = Math.ceil(a/b);
```

As a consequence of Java's numeric promotion rules, the division operation performed is an *integer* division whose result is truncated to 1. This result is then promoted to double before being passed to the Math.ceil() method.

Compliant Solution

This compliant solution casts one of the operands to double before the division is performed.

```
int a = 60070;
int b = 57750;

double value = Math.ceil(a/((double) b));
```

As a result of the cast, the other operand is automatically promoted to double. The division operation becomes a double divide, and value is assigned the correct result of 2.0. As in previous compliant solutions, this practice ensures that at least one of the operands of each operation is a floating-point number.

Applicability

Improper conversions between integers and floating-point values can yield unexpected results, especially from precision loss. In some cases, these unexpected results can involve overflow or other exceptional conditions.

It is acceptable to perform operations using a mix of integer and floating-point values when deliberately exploiting the properties of integer arithmetic before conversion to floating-point. For example, use of integer arithmetic eliminates the need to use the floor() method. Any such code *must* be clearly documented to help future maintainers understand that this behavior is intentional.

Bibliography

[JLS 2013]   §5.1.2, "Widening Primitive Conversion"

[Long 2012]   NUM13-J. Avoid loss of precision when converting primitive integers
                    to floating-point

                    NUM00-J. Detect or prevent integer overflow

■ 61. Ensure that the `clone()` method calls `super.clone()`

Cloning a subclass of a nonfinal class which defines a `clone()` method that fails to
call `super.clone()` will produce an object of the wrong class.

The Java API [API 2013] for the `clone()` method says:

> By convention, the returned object should be obtained by calling `super.clone`. If a
> class and all of its superclasses (except `Object`) obey this convention, it will be the
> case that `x.clone().getClass() == x.getClass()`.

Noncompliant Code Example

In this noncompliant code example, the `clone()` method in the class `Base` fails to
call `super.clone()`:

```java
class Base implements Cloneable {
  public Object clone() throws CloneNotSupportedException {
    return new Base();
  }
  protected void doLogic() {
    System.out.println("Superclass doLogic");
  }
}

class Derived extends Base {
  public Object clone() throws CloneNotSupportedException {
    return super.clone();
  }
  protected void doLogic() {
    System.out.println("Subclass doLogic");
  }
  public static void main(String[] args) {
    Derived dev = new Derived();
    try {
      Base devClone = (Base)dev.clone(); // Has type Base
                                         // instead of Derived
```

```
    devClone.doLogic();  // Prints "Superclass doLogic"
                         // instead of "Subclass doLogic"
  } catch (CloneNotSupportedException e) { /* ... */ }
  }
}
```

Consequently, the object devClone ends up being of type Base instead of Derived, and the doLogic() method is incorrectly applied.

Compliant Solution

This compliant solution correctly calls `super.clone()` in the Base class's `clone()` method.

```
class Base implements Cloneable {
  public Object clone() throws CloneNotSupportedException {
    return super.clone();
  }
  protected void doLogic() {
    System.out.println("Superclass doLogic");
  }
}

class Derived extends Base {
  public Object clone() throws CloneNotSupportedException {
    return super.clone();
  }
  protected void doLogic() {
    System.out.println("Subclass doLogic");
  }
  public static void main(String[] args) {
    Derived dev = new Derived();
    try {
      // Has type Derived, as expected
      Base devClone = (Base)dev.clone();
      devClone.doLogic();  // Prints "Subclass doLogic"
                           // as expected
    } catch (CloneNotSupportedException e) { /* ... */ }
  }
}
```

Applicability

Failing to call `super.clone()` may cause a cloned object to have the wrong type.

Bibliography

[API 2013]   Class Object

■ 62. Use comments consistently and in a readable fashion

Mixing the use of traditional or block comments (starting with /* and ending with */) and end-of-line comments (from // to the end of the line) can lead to misleading and confusing code, which may result in errors.

Noncompliant Code Example

The following noncompliant code examples show mixed comments that may be misunderstood.

```
// */                    /* Comment, not syntax error */

f = g/**//h;             /* Equivalent to f = g / h; */

/*//*/ 1();              /* Equivalent to 1(); */

m = n//**/o
+ p;                     /* Equivalent to m = n + p; */

a = b //*divisor:*/c
+ d;                     /* Equivalent to a = b + d; */
```

Compliant Solution

Use a consistent style of commenting.

```
// Nice simple comment

int i; // Counter
```

Noncompliant Code Example

There are other misuses of comments that should be avoided. This noncompliant code example uses the character sequence /* to begin a comment, but neglects to use the delimiter */ to end the comment. Consequently, the call to the security-critical method is not executed. A reviewer examining this page could incorrectly assume that the code is executed.

```
/* Comment with end comment marker unintentionally omitted
security_critical_method();
/* Some other comment */
```

Using an editor that provides syntax highlighting or that formats the code to identify issues such as missing end comment delimiters can help detect accidental omissions.

Because missing end delimiters are error prone and often viewed as a mistake, this approach is not recommended for commenting out code.

Compliant Solution

This compliant solution demonstrates the recommended way to mark code as "dead." It also takes advantage of the compiler's ability to remove unreachable (dead) code. The code inside the if block must be syntactically correct. If other parts of the program later change in a way that would cause syntax errors, the unexecuted code must be brought up to date to correct the problem. Then, if it is needed again in the future, the programmer need only remove the surrounding if statement and the NOTREACHED comment.

The NOTREACHED comment could tell some compilers and static analysis tools not to complain about this unreachable code. It also serves as documentation.

```
if (false) {  /* Use of critical security method no
               * longer necessary, for now */
  /* NOTREACHED */
  security_critical_method();
  /* Some other comment */
}
```

This is an example of an exceptional situation described in Guideline 63, "Detect and remove superfluous code and values."

Applicability

Confusion over which instructions are executed and which are not can result in serious programming errors and vulnerabilities, including denial of service, abnormal program termination, and data integrity violation. This problem is mitigated by the use of interactive development environments (IDEs) and editors that use fonts, colors, or other mechanisms to differentiate between comments and code. However, the problem can still manifest, for example, when reviewing source code printed on a black-and-white printer.

Nested block comments and inconsistent use of comments can be detected by suitable static analysis tools.

Bibliography

[JLS 2013]   §3.7, "Comments"

■ 63. Detect and remove superfluous code and values

Superfluous code and values may occur in the form of dead code, code that has no effect, and unused values in program logic.

Code that is never executed is known as *dead code*. Typically, the presence of dead code indicates that a logic error has occurred as a result of changes to a program or to the program's environment. Dead code is often optimized out of a program during compilation. However, to improve readability and ensure that logic errors are resolved, dead code should be identified, understood, and removed.

Code that is executed but fails to perform any action, or that has an unintended effect, most likely results from a coding error and can cause unexpected behavior. Statements or expressions that have no effect should be identified and removed from code. Most modern compilers can warn about code that has no effect.

The presence of unused values in code may indicate significant logic errors. To prevent such errors, unused values should be identified and removed from code.

Noncompliant Code Example (Dead Code)

This noncompliant code example demonstrates how dead code can be introduced into a program [Fortify 2013]:

```
public int func(boolean condition) {
  int x = 0;
  if (condition) {
    x = foo();
    /* Process x */
    return x;
  }
  /* ... */
  if (x != 0) {
    /* This code is never executed */
  }
  return x;
}
```

The condition in the second if statement, (x != 0), will never evaluate to true because the only path where x can be assigned a nonzero value ends with a return statement.

Compliant Solution

Remediation of dead code requires the programmer to determine not only why the code is never executed, but also whether the code should have been executed, and then to resolve that situation appropriately. This compliant solution assumes that the dead code should have executed, and consequently the body of the first conditional statement no longer ends with a return.

```
int func(boolean condition) {
  int x = 0;
  if (condition) {
    x = foo();
    /* Process x */
  }
  /* ... */
  if (x != 0) {
    /* This code is now executed */
  }
  return 0;
}
```

Noncompliant Code Example (Dead Code)

In this example, the length() function is used to limit the number of times the function string_loop() iterates. The condition of the if statement inside the loop evaluates to true when the current index is the length of str. However, because i is always strictly less than str.length(), that can never happen.

```
public int string_loop(String str) {
  for (int i=0; i < str.length(); i++) {
    /* ... */
    if (i == str.length()) {
      /* This code is never executed */
    }
  }
  return 0;
}
```

Compliant Solution

Proper remediation of the dead code depends on the intent of the programmer. Assuming the intent is to do something special with the last character in str, the conditional statement is adjusted to check whether i refers to the index of the last character in str.

```
public int string_loop(String str) {
  for (int i=0; i < str.length(); i++) {
    /* ... */
    if (i == str.length()-1) {
      /* This code is now executed */
    }
  }
  return 0;
}
```

Noncompliant Code Example (Code with No Effect)

In this noncompliant code example, the comparison of s to t has no effect:

```
String s;
String t;

// ...

s.equals(t);
```

This error is probably the result of the programmer intending to do something with the comparison, but failing to complete the code.

Compliant Solution

In this compliant solution, the result of the comparison is printed out:

```
String s;
String t;

// ...

if (s.equals(t)) {
  System.out.println("Strings equal");
} else {
  System.out.println("Strings unequal");
}
```

Noncompliant Code Example (Unused Values)

In this example, p2 is assigned the value returned by bar(), but that value is never used:

```
int p1 = foo();
int p2 = bar();

if (baz()) {
  return p1;
} else {
  p2 = p1;
}
return p2;
```

Compliant Solution

This example can be corrected in many different ways depending on the intent of the programmer. In this compliant solution, p2 is found to be extraneous. The calls to bar() and baz() could also be removed if they do not produce any side effects.

```
int p1 = foo();

bar(); /* Removable if bar() lacks side effects */
baz(); /* Removable if baz() lacks side effects */

return p1;
```

Applicability

The presence of dead code may indicate logic errors that can lead to unintended program behavior. The ways in which dead code can be introduced into a program and the effort required to remove it can be complex. As a result, resolving dead code can be an in-depth process requiring significant analysis.

In exceptional situations, dead code may make software resilient to future changes. An example is the presence of a default case in a switch statement even though all possible switch labels are specified (see Guideline 64, "Strive for logical completeness," for an illustration of this example).

It is also permissible to temporarily retain dead code that may be needed later. Such cases should be clearly indicated with an appropriate comment.

The presence of code that has no effect can indicate logic errors that may result in unexpected behavior and vulnerabilities. Unused values in code may indicate significant logic errors.

Code and values that have no effect can be detected by suitable static analysis.

Bibliography

[Fortify 2013]   Code Quality: Dead Code

[Coverity 2007]   Coverity Prevent™ User's Manual (3.3.0)

■ 64. Strive for logical completeness

Software vulnerabilities can result when a programmer fails to consider all possible data states.

Noncompliant Code Example (if Chain)

This noncompliant code example fails to test for conditions in which a is neither b nor c. This may be the correct behavior in this case, but failure to account for all the values of a can result in logic errors if a unexpectedly assumes a different value.

```
if (a == b) {
  /* ... */
}
else if (a == c) {
  /* ... */
}
```

Compliant Solution (if Chain)

This compliant solution explicitly checks for the unexpected condition and handles it appropriately:

```
if (a == b) {
  /* ... */
}
else if (a == c) {
  /* ... */
}
else {
   /* Handle error condition */
}
```

Noncompliant Code Example (switch)

Even though x is supposed to represent a bit (0 or 1) in this noncompliant code example, some previous error may have allowed x to assume a different value.

Detecting and dealing with that inconsistent state sooner rather than later makes the error easier to find.

```
switch (x) {
  case 0: foo(); break;
  case 1: bar(); break;
}
```

Compliant Solution (`switch`)

This compliant solution provides the `default` label to handle all possible values of type `int`:

```
switch (x) {
  case 0: foo(); break;
  case 1: bar(); break;
  default: /* Handle error */ break;
}
```

Noncompliant Code Example (Zune 30)

This noncompliant code example is adapted from C code that appeared in the Zune 30 media player, causing many players to lock up on December 30, 2008, at midnight PST. It contains incomplete logic that causes a denial of service when converting dates.

```
final static int ORIGIN_YEAR = 1980;
/* Number of days since January 1, 1980 */
public void convertDays(long days){
  int year = ORIGIN_YEAR;
  /* ... */
  while (days > 365) {
    if (IsLeapYear(year)) {
      if (days > 366) {
        days -= 366;
        year += 1;
      }
    } else {
        days -= 365;
        year += 1;
    }
  }
}
```

The original `ConvertDays()` C function in the real-time clock (RTC) routines for the MC13783 PMIC RTC takes the number of days since January 1, 1980, and computes the correct year and number of days since January 1 of the correct year.

The flaw in the code occurs when `days` has the value 366 because the loop never terminates. This bug manifested itself on the 366th day of 2008, which was the first leap year in which this code was active.

Compliant Solution (Zune 30)

This proposed rewrite is provided by "A Lesson on Infinite Loops" by Bryant Zadegan [Zadegan 2009]. The loop is guaranteed to exit, as `days` decreases for each iteration of the loop, unless the `while` condition fails, in which case the loop terminates.

```
final static int ORIGIN_YEAR = 1980;
/* Number of days since January 1, 1980 */
public void convertDays(long days){
  int year = ORIGIN_YEAR;
  /* ... */
  int daysThisYear = (IsLeapYear(year) ? 366 : 365);
  while (days > daysThisYear) {
    days -= daysThisYear;
    year += 1;
    daysThisYear = (IsLeapYear(year) ? 366 : 365);
  }
}
```

This compliant solution is for illustrative purposes and may differ from the solution implemented by Microsoft.

Applicability

Failing to take into account all possibilities within a logic statement can lead to a corrupted running state, potentially resulting in unintentional information disclosure or abnormal program termination.

Bibliography

[Hatton 1995]   §2.7.2, "Errors of Omission and Addition"

[Viega 2005]   §5.2.17, "Failure to Account for Default Case in Switch"

[Zadegan 2009]   A Lesson on Infinite Loops

■ 65. Avoid ambiguous or confusing uses of overloading

Method and constructor overloading allows declaration of methods or constructors with the same name but with different parameter lists. The compiler inspects each call to an overloaded method or constructor and uses the declared types of the method parameters to decide which method to invoke. In some cases, however, confusion may arise because of the presence of relatively new language features such as autoboxing and generics.

Furthermore, methods or constructors with the same parameter types that differ only in their declaration order are typically not flagged by Java compilers. Errors can result when a developer fails to consult the documentation at each use of a method or constructor. A related pitfall is to associate different semantics with each of the overloaded methods or constructors. Defining different semantics sometimes necessitates different orderings of the same method parameters, creating a vicious circle. Consider, for example, an overloaded getDistance() method in which one overloaded method returns the distance traveled from the source while another (with reordered parameters) returns the remaining distance to the destination. Implementers may fail to realize the difference unless they consult the documentation at each use.

Noncompliant Code Example (Constructor)

Constructors cannot be overridden and can only be overloaded. This noncompliant code example shows the class Con with three overloaded constructors:

```
class Con {
  public Con(int i, String s) {
    // Initialization Sequence #1
  }
  public Con(String s, int i) {
    // Initialization Sequence #2
  }
  public Con(Integer i, String s) {
    // Initialization Sequence #3
  }
}
```

Failure to exercise caution while passing arguments to these constructors can create confusion because calls to these constructors contain the same number of similarly typed actual parameters. Overloading must also be avoided when the overloaded constructors or methods provide distinct semantics for formal parameters of the same types, differing solely in their declaration order.

Compliant Solution (Constructor)

This compliant solution avoids overloading by declaring public static factory methods that have distinct names in place of the public class constructors:

```
public static Con createCon1(int i, String s) {
  /* Initialization Sequence #1 */
}
public static Con createCon2(String s, int i) {
  /* Initialization Sequence #2 */
}
public static Con createCon3(Integer i, String s) {
  /* Initialization Sequence #3 */
}
```

Noncompliant Code Example (Method)

In this noncompliant code example, the OverLoader class holds a HashMap instance and has overloaded getData() methods. One getData() method chooses the record to return on the basis of its key value in the map; the other chooses on the basis of the actual mapped value.

```
class OverLoader extends HashMap<Integer,Integer> {
  HashMap<Integer,Integer> hm;
  public OverLoader() {
    hm = new HashMap<Integer, Integer>();
    // SSN records
    hm.put(1, 111990000);
    hm.put(2, 222990000);
    hm.put(3, 333990000);
  }

  public String getData(Integer i) { // Overloading sequence #1
    String s = get(i).toString(); // Get a particular record
    return (s.substring(0, 3) + "-" + s.substring(3, 5) + "-" +
            s.substring(5, 9));
  }

  public Integer getData(int i) { // Overloading sequence #2
    return hm.get(i); // Get record at position 'i'
  }
```

```
    // Checks whether the ssn exists
    @Override public Integer get(Object data) {
      // SecurityManagerCheck()

      for (Map.Entry<Integer, Integer> entry : hm.entrySet()) {
        if (entry.getValue().equals(data)) {
          return entry.getValue();  // Exists
        }
      }
      return null;
    }

    public static void main(String[] args) {
      OverLoader bo = new OverLoader();
      // Get record at index '3'
      System.out.println(bo.getData(3));
      // Get record containing data '111990000'
      System.out.println(bo.getData((Integer)111990000));
    }
}
```

For purposes of overload resolution, the signatures of the `getData()` methods differ only in the static type of their formal parameters. The `OverLoader` class inherits from `java.util.HashMap` and overrides its `get()` method to provide the checking functionality. This implementation can be extremely confusing to the client who expects both `getData()` methods to behave in a similar fashion and not depend on whether an index of the record or the value to be retrieved is specified.

Although the client programmer might eventually deduce such behavior, other cases, such as with the `List` interface, may go unnoticed, as Joshua Bloch [Bloch 2008] describes:

> The `List<E>` interface has two overloadings of the remove method: `remove(E)` and `remove(int)`. Prior to release 1.5 when it was "generified," the `List` interface had a `remove(Object)` method in place of `remove(E)`, and the corresponding parameter types, `Object` and `int`, were radically different. But in the presence of generics and autoboxing, the two parameter types are no longer radically different.

Consequently, a programmer may fail to realize that the wrong element has been removed from the list.

A further problem is that in the presence of autoboxing, adding a new overloaded method definition can break previously working client code. This can happen when a new overloaded method with a more specific type is added to an API whose methods used less specific types in earlier versions. For example, if an earlier version of the `OverLoader` class provided only the `getData(Integer)` method, the client could correctly invoke this method by passing a parameter of type `int`; the result would be selected on the basis of its value because the `int` parameter would be autoboxed to `Integer`. Subsequently, when the `getData(int)` method is added, the compiler resolves all calls whose parameter is of type `int` to invoke the new `getData(int)` method, thereby changing their semantics and potentially breaking previously correct code. The compiler is entirely correct in such cases; the actual problem is an incompatible change to the API.

Compliant Solution (Method)

Naming the two related methods differently eliminates both the overloading and the confusion:

```java
public Integer getDataByIndex(int i) {
  // No longer overloaded
}

public String getDataByValue(Integer i) {
  // No longer overloaded
}
```

Applicability

Ambiguous or confusing uses of overloading can lead to unexpected results.

Bibliography

[API 2013]   Interface `Collection<E>`

[Bloch 2008]   Item 41, "Use Overloading Judiciously"

Chapter 5

Programmer Misconceptions

The guidelines in this chapter address areas where developers often make unwarranted assumptions about Java language and library behaviors, or where ambiguities can easily be introduced. Failure to follow these guidelines can result in programs that produce counterintuitive results.

This chapter contains guidelines that address

1. Misconceptions about Java APIs and language features
2. Assumptions and ambiguity-laced programs
3. Situations in which the programmer wanted to do one thing but ended up doing another

■ 66. Do not assume that declaring a reference volatile guarantees safe publication of the members of the referenced object

According to the Java Language Specification (JLS), §8.3.1.4, "`volatile` Fields" [JLS 2013],

> A field may be declared `volatile`, in which case the Java Memory Model ensures that all threads see a consistent value for the variable (§17.4).

This safe publication guarantee applies only to primitive fields and object references. Programmers commonly use imprecise terminology and speak about "member objects." For the purposes of this visibility guarantee, the actual member is the object reference; the objects referred to (aka, *referents*) by volatile object references are beyond the scope of this safe publication guarantee. Consequently, declaring an object reference to be volatile is insufficient to guarantee that changes to the members of the referent are published to other threads. A thread may fail to observe a recent write from another thread to a member field of such an object referent.

Furthermore, when the referent is mutable and lacks thread-safety, other threads might see a partially constructed object or an object in a (temporarily) inconsistent state [Goetz 2007]. However, when the referent is immutable, declaring the reference volatile suffices to guarantee safe publication of the members of the referent. Programmers cannot use the volatile keyword to guarantee safe publication of mutable objects. Use of the volatile keyword can only guarantee safe publication of primitive fields, object references, or fields of immutable object referents.

Confusing a volatile object with the volatility of its member objects is a similar error to the one described in Guideline 73, "Never confuse the immutability of a reference with that of the referenced object."

Noncompliant Code Example (Arrays)

This noncompliant code example declares a volatile reference to an array object:

```java
final class Foo {
  private volatile int[] arr = new int[20];

  public int getFirst() {
    return arr[0];
  }

  public void setFirst(int n) {
    arr[0] = n;
  }

  // ...
}
```

Values assigned to an array element by one thread—for example, by calling setFirst()—might not be visible to another thread calling getFirst(), because the volatile keyword guarantees safe publication only for the array reference; it makes no guarantee regarding the actual data contained within the array.

This problem arises when the thread that calls `setFirst()` and the thread that calls `getFirst()` lack a *happens-before relationship*. A happens-before relationship exists between a thread that *writes* to a volatile variable and a thread that *subsequently reads* it. However, `setFirst()` and `getFirst()` each read from a volatile variable—the volatile reference to the array. Neither method writes to the volatile variable.

Compliant Solution (`AtomicIntegerArray`)

To ensure that the writes to array elements are atomic and that the resulting values are visible to other threads, this compliant solution uses the `AtomicIntegerArray` class defined in `java.util.concurrent.atomic`:

```
final class Foo {
  private final AtomicIntegerArray atomicArray =
    new AtomicIntegerArray(20);

  public int getFirst() {
    return atomicArray.get(0);
  }

  public void setFirst(int n) {
    atomicArray.set(0, 10);
  }

  // ...
}
```

`AtomicIntegerArray` guarantees a happens-before relationship between a thread that calls `atomicArray.set()` and a thread that subsequently calls `atomicArray.get()`.

Compliant Solution (Synchronization)

To ensure visibility, accessor methods must synchronize access while performing operations on nonvolatile elements of an array, whether the array is referred to by a volatile or a nonvolatile reference. Note that the code is thread-safe, even though the array reference is not volatile.

```
final class Foo {
  private int[] arr = new int[20];

  public synchronized int getFirst() {
    return arr[0];
  }
```

```
public synchronized void setFirst(int n) {
  arr[0] = n;
}
}
```

Synchronization establishes a happens-before relationship between threads that synchronize on the same lock. In this case, the thread that calls `setFirst()` and the thread that subsequently calls `getFirst()` on the same object instance both synchronize on that instance, so safe publication is guaranteed.

Noncompliant Code Example (Mutable Object)

This noncompliant code example declares the `Map` instance field volatile. The instance of the `Map` object is mutable because of its `put()` method.

```
final class Foo {
  private volatile Map<String, String> map;

  public Foo() {
    map = new HashMap<String, String>();
    // Load some useful values into map
  }

  public String get(String s) {
    return map.get(s);
  }

  public void put(String key, String value) {
    // Validate the values before inserting
    if (!value.matches("[\\w]*")) {
      throw new IllegalArgumentException();
    }
    map.put(key, value);
  }
}
```

Interleaved calls to `get()` and `put()` may result in the retrieval of internally inconsistent values from the `Map` object because `put()` modifies its state. Declaring the object reference volatile is insufficient to eliminate this data race.

Noncompliant Code Example (Volatile-Read, Synchronized-Write)

This noncompliant code example attempts to use the volatile-read, synchronized-write technique described in Java Theory and Practice [Goetz 2007]. The `map` field is declared volatile to synchronize its reads and writes. The `put()` method is also synchronized to ensure it is executed atomically.

```
final class Foo {
  private volatile Map<String, String> map;

  public Foo() {
    map = new HashMap<String, String>();
    // Load some useful values into map
  }
  public String get(String s) {
    return map.get(s);
  }
  public synchronized void put(String key, String value) {
    // Validate the values before inserting
    if (!value.matches("[\\w]*")) {
      throw new IllegalArgumentException();
    }
    map.put(key, value);
  }
}
```

The volatile-read, synchronized-write technique uses synchronization to preserve atomicity of compound operations, such as increment, and provides faster access times for atomic reads. However, it fails for mutable objects because the safe publication guarantee provided by `volatile` extends only to the field itself (the primitive value or object reference); the referent is excluded from the guarantee, as are the referent's members. In effect, a write and a subsequent read of the map lack a happens-before relationship.

This technique is also discussed in *The CERT® Oracle® Secure Coding Standard for Java™* [Long 2012], "VNA02-J. Ensure that compound operations on shared variables are atomic."

Compliant Solution (Synchronized)

This compliant solution uses method synchronization to guarantee visibility:

```
final class Foo {
  private final Map<String, String> map;
  public Foo() {
    map = new HashMap<String, String>();
    // Load some useful values into map
  }
  public synchronized String get(String s) {
```

```
    return map.get(s);
  }
  public synchronized void put(String key, String value) {
    // Validate the values before inserting
    if (!value.matches("[\\w]*")) {
      throw new IllegalArgumentException();
    }
    map.put(key, value);
  }
}
```

It is unnecessary to declare the map field volatile because the accessor methods are synchronized. The field is declared final to prevent publication of its reference when the referent is in a partially initialized state (see "TSM03-J. Do not publish partially initialized objects," for more information [Long 2012]).

Noncompliant Code Example (Mutable Subobject)

In this noncompliant code example, the volatile format field stores a reference to a mutable object, java.text.DateFormat:

```
final class DateHandler {
  private static volatile DateFormat format =
    DateFormat.getDateInstance(DateFormat.MEDIUM);

  public static java.util.Date parse(String str)
      throws ParseException {
    return format.parse(str);
  }
}
```

Because DateFormat is not thread-safe [API 2013], the value for Date returned by the parse() method may not correspond to the str argument.

Compliant Solution (Instance per Call/Defensive Copying)

This compliant solution creates and returns a new DateFormat instance for each invocation of the parse() method [API 2013]:

```
final class DateHandler {
  public static java.util.Date parse(String str)
      throws ParseException {
```

```
    return DateFormat.getDateInstance(
        DateFormat.MEDIUM).parse(str);
  }
}
```

Compliant Solution (Synchronization)

This compliant solution makes DateHandler thread-safe by synchronizing statements within the parse() method [API 2013]:

```
final class DateHandler {
  private static DateFormat format =
    DateFormat.getDateInstance(DateFormat.MEDIUM);

  public static java.util.Date parse(String str)
      throws ParseException {
    synchronized (format) {
      return format.parse(str);
    }
  }
}
```

Compliant Solution (ThreadLocal Storage)

This compliant solution uses a ThreadLocal object to create a separate DateFormat instance per thread:

```
final class DateHandler {
  private static final ThreadLocal<DateFormat> format =
    new ThreadLocal<DateFormat>() {
    @Override protected DateFormat initialValue() {
      return DateFormat.getDateInstance(DateFormat.MEDIUM);
    }
  };
  // ...
}
```

Applicability

Incorrectly assuming that declaring a field volatile guarantees safe publication of a referenced object's members can cause threads to observe stale or inconsistent values.

Technically, strict immutability of the referent is a stronger condition than is fundamentally required for safe publication. When it can be determined that a referent is thread-safe by design, the field that holds its reference may be declared volatile. However, this approach to using `volatile` decreases maintainability and should be avoided.

Bibliography

[API 2013]	Class `DateFormat`
[Goetz 2007]	Pattern 2, "One-Time Safe Publication"
[JLS 2013]	§8.3.1.4, "`volatile` Fields"
[Long 2012]	OBJ05-J. Defensively copy private mutable class members before returning their references
	TSM03-J. Do not publish partially initialized objects
	VNA02-J. Ensure that compound operations on shared variables are atomic
[Miller 2009]	"Mutable Statics"

■ 67. Do not assume that the `sleep()`, `yield()`, or `getState()` methods provide synchronization semantics

According to the JLS, §17.3, "Sleep and Yield" [JLS 2013],

> It is important to note that neither `Thread.sleep` nor `Thread.yield` have any synchronization semantics. In particular, the compiler does not have to flush writes cached in registers out to shared memory before a call to `Thread.sleep` or `Thread.yield`, nor does the compiler have to reload values cached in registers after a call to `Thread.sleep` or `Thread.yield`.

Code that bases its concurrency safety on thread suspension or yields to processes that

- Flush cached registers,
- Reload any values,
- Or provide any happens-before relationships when execution resumes.

is incorrect and is consequently disallowed. Programs must ensure that communication between threads has proper synchronization, happens-before, and safe publication semantics.

Noncompliant Code Example (`sleep()`)

This noncompliant code attempts to use the nonvolatile primitive Boolean member done as a flag to terminate execution of a thread. A separate thread sets done to true by calling the shutdown() method.

```java
final class ControlledStop implements Runnable {
  private boolean done = false;

  @Override public void run() {
    while (!done) {
      try {
        Thread.sleep(1000);
      } catch (InterruptedException e) {
        // Reset interrupted status
        Thread.currentThread().interrupt();      }
    }
  }

  public void shutdown() {
    this.done = true;
  }
}
```

The compiler, in this case, is free to read the field this.done once and to reuse the cached value in each execution of the loop. Consequently, the while loop might never terminate, even when another thread calls the shutdown() method to change the value of this.done [JLS 2013]. This error could have resulted from the programmer incorrectly assuming that the call to Thread.sleep() causes cached values to be reloaded.

Compliant Solution (Volatile Flag)

This compliant solution declares the flag field volatile to ensure that updates to its value are made visible across multiple threads:

```java
final class ControlledStop implements Runnable {
  private volatile boolean done = false;

  @Override public void run() {
    //...
  }

  // ...
}
```

The `volatile` keyword establishes a happens-before relationship between this thread and any other thread that sets `done`.

Compliant Solution (`Thread.interrupt()`)

A better solution for methods that call `sleep()` is to use thread interruption, which causes the sleeping thread to wake immediately and handle the interruption.

```
final class ControlledStop implements Runnable {

  @Override public void run() {
    // Record current thread so others can interrupt it
    myThread = currentThread();
    while (!Thread.interrupted()) {
      try {
        Thread.sleep(1000);
      } catch (InterruptedException e) {
        Thread.currentThread().interrupt();
      }
    }
  }

  public void shutdown(Thread th) {
    th.interrupt();
  }
}
```

Note that the interrupting thread must know which thread to interrupt; logic for tracking this relationship has been omitted from this solution.

Noncompliant Code Example (`Thread.getState()`)

This noncompliant code example contains a `doSomething()` method that starts a thread. The thread supports interruption by checking a flag and waits until notified. The `stop()` method checks to see whether the thread is blocked on the wait; if so, it sets the flag to true and notifies the thread so that the thread can terminate.

```
public class Waiter {
  private Thread thread;
  private boolean flag;
  private final Object lock = new Object();
```

```
public void doSomething() {
  thread = new Thread(new Runnable() {
    @Override public void run() {
      synchronized (lock) {
        while (!flag) {
          try {
            lock.wait();
            // ...
          } catch (InterruptedException e) {
            // Forward to handler
          }
        }
      }
    }
  });
  thread.start();
}

public boolean stop() {
  if (thread != null) {
    if (thread.getState() == Thread.State.WAITING) {
      synchronized (lock) {
        flag = true;
        lock.notifyAll();
      }
      return true;
    }
  }
  return false;
}
```

Unfortunately, the stop() method incorrectly uses the Thread.getState() method to check whether the thread is blocked and has not terminated before delivering the notification. Using the Thread.getState() method for synchronization control, such as checking whether a thread is blocked on a wait, is inappropriate. Java Virtual Machines (JVMs) are permitted to implement blocking using spin-waiting; consequently, a thread can be blocked without entering the WAITING or TIMED_WAITING state [Goetz 2006]. Because the thread may never enter the WAITING state, the stop() method might fail to terminate the thread.

If doSomething() and stop() are called from different threads, the stop() method could fail to see the initialized thread, even though doSomething() was called earlier, unless there is a happens-before relationship between the two calls. If the two methods are invoked by the same thread, they automatically have a happens-before relationship and consequently cannot encounter this problem.

Compliant Solution

This compliant solution removes the check for determining whether the thread is in the WAITING state. This check is unnecessary because invoking notifyAll() affects only threads that are blocked on an invocation of wait():

```
public class Waiter {
  // . . .
  private Thread thread;
  private volatile boolean flag;
  private final Object lock = new Object();

  public boolean stop() {
    if (thread != null) {
      synchronized (lock) {
        flag = true;
        lock.notifyAll();
      }
      return true;
    }
    return false;
  }
}
```

Applicability

Relying on the Thread class's sleep(), yield(), and getState() methods for synchronization control can cause unexpected behavior.

Bibliography

[Goetz 2006]

[JLS 2013]   §17.3, "Sleep and Yield"

■ 68. Do not assume that the remainder operator always returns a nonnegative result for integral operands

The JLS, §15.17.3, "Remainder Operator %" [JLS 2013], states,

> The remainder operation for operands that are integers after binary numeric promotion (§5.6.2) produces a result value such that (a/b)*b+(a%b) is equal to a. This identity holds even in the special case that the dividend is the negative integer of

largest possible magnitude for its type and the divisor is -1 (the remainder is 0). It follows from this rule that the result of the remainder operation can be negative only if the dividend is negative, and can be positive only if the dividend is positive; moreover, the magnitude of the result is always less than the magnitude of the divisor.

The result of the remainder operator has the same sign as the dividend (the first operand in the expression):

```
5 % 3 produces 2
5 % (-3) produces 2
(-5) % 3 produces -2
(-5) % (-3) produces -2
```

As a result, code that depends on the remainder operation to always return a positive result is erroneous.

Noncompliant Code Example

This noncompliant code example uses the integer hashKey as an index into the hash array:

```
private int SIZE = 16;
public int[] hash = new int[SIZE];

public int lookup(int hashKey) {
  return hash[hashKey % SIZE];
}
```

A negative hash key produces a negative result from the remainder operator, causing the lookup() method to throw a java.lang.ArrayIndexOutOfBoundsException.

Compliant Solution

This compliant solution calls the imod() method which always returns a positive remainder:

```
// Method imod() gives nonnegative result
private int SIZE = 16;
public int[] hash = new int[SIZE];
```

```
private int imod(int i, int j) {
  int temp = i % j;
  // Unary minus will succeed without overflow
  // because temp cannot be Integer.MIN_VALUE
  return (temp < 0) ? -temp : temp;
}

public int lookup(int hashKey) {
  return hash[imod(hashKey, SIZE)];
}
```

Applicability

Incorrectly assuming a positive remainder from a remainder operation can result in erroneous code.

Bibliography

[JLS 2013]   §15.17.3, "Remainder Operator %"

■ 69. Do not confuse abstract object equality with reference equality

Java defines the equality operators == and != for testing reference equality, but uses the equals() method defined in Object and its subclasses for testing abstract object equality. Naïve programmers often confuse the intent of the == operation with that of the Object.equals() method. This confusion is frequently evident in the context of processing String objects.

As a general rule, use the Object.equals() method to check whether two objects have equivalent contents, and use the equality operators == and != to test whether two references specifically refer to *the same object*. This latter test is referred to as *referential equality*. For classes that require overriding the default equals() implementation, care must be taken to also override the hashCode() method (see *The CERT® Oracle® Secure Coding Standard for Java™* [Long 2012], "MET09-J. Classes that define an equals() method must also define a hashCode() method").

Numeric boxed types (for example, Byte, Character, Short, Integer, Long, Float, and Double) should also be compared using Object.equals(), rather than the == operator. While reference equality may appear to work for Integer values between the range –128 and 127, it may fail if either of the operands in the comparison are outside that range. Numeric relational operators other than equality (such as

<, <=, >, and >=) can be safely used to compare boxed primitive types (see "EXP03-J. Do not use the equality operators when comparing values of boxed primitives" [Long 2012], for more information).

Noncompliant Code Example

This noncompliant code example declares two distinct `String` objects that contain the same value:

```
public class StringComparison {
  public static void main(String[] args) {
    String str1 = new String("one");
    String str2 = new String("one");
    System.out.println(str1 == str2); // Prints "false"
  }
}
```

The reference equality operator `==` evaluates to `true` only when the values it compares refer to the same underlying object. The references in this example are unequal because they refer to distinct objects.

Compliant Solution (`Object.equals()`)

This compliant solution uses the `Object.equals()` method when comparing string values:

```
public class StringComparison {
  public static void main(String[] args) {
    String str1 = new String("one");
    String str2 = new String("one");
    System.out.println(str1.equals(str2)); // Prints "true"
  }
}
```

Compliant Solution (`String.intern()`)

Reference equality behaves like abstract object equality when it is used to compare two strings that are results of the `String.intern()` method. This compliant solution uses `String.intern()` and can perform fast string comparisons when only one copy of the string one is required in memory.

```
public class StringComparison {
  public static void main(String[] args) {
    String str1 = new String("one");
    String str2 = new String("one");

    str1 = str1.intern();
    str2 = str2.intern();

    System.out.println(str1 == str2); // Prints "true"
  }
}
```

Use of `String.intern()` should be reserved for cases in which the tokenization of strings either yields an important performance enhancement or dramatically simplifies code. Examples include programs engaged in natural language processing and compiler-like tools that tokenize program input. For most other programs, performance and readability are often improved by the use of code that applies the `Object.equals()` approach and that lacks any dependence on reference equality.

The JLS provides few guarantees about the implementation of `String.intern()`. For example,

- The cost of `String.intern()` grows as the number of intern strings grows. Performance should be no worse than $O(n \log n)$, but the JLS lacks a specific performance guarantee.

- In early Java Virtual Machine (JVM) implementations, interned strings became immortal: they were exempt from garbage collection. This can be problematic when large numbers of strings are interned. More recent implementations can garbage-collect the storage occupied by interned strings that are no longer referenced. However, the JLS lacks any specification of this behavior.

- In JVM implementations prior to Java 1.7, interned strings are allocated in the `permgen` storage region, which is typically much smaller than the rest of the heap. Consequently, interning large numbers of strings can lead to an out-of-memory condition. In many Java 1.7 implementations, interned strings are allocated on the heap, relieving this restriction. Once again, the details of allocation are unspecified by the *JLS*; consequently, implementations may vary.

String interning may also be used in programs that accept repetitively occurring strings. Its use boosts the performance of comparisons and minimizes memory consumption.

When canonicalization of objects is required, it may be wiser to use a custom canonicalizer built on top of `ConcurrentHashMap`; see Joshua Bloch's *Effective Java™, Second Edition*, Item 69 [Bloch 2008] for details.

Applicability

Confusing reference equality and object equality can lead to unexpected results.

Using reference equality in place of object equality is permitted only when the defining classes guarantee the existence of *at most one* object instance for each possible object value. The use of static factory methods, rather than public constructors, facilitates instance control; this is a key enabling technique. Another technique is to use an `enum` type.

Use reference equality to determine whether two references point to the same object.

Bibliography

[Bloch 2008]	Item 69, "Prefer Concurrency Utilities to wait and notify"
[FindBugs 2008]	ES, "Comparison of String Objects Using == or !="
[JLS 2013]	§3.10.5, "String Literals"
	§5.6.2, "Binary Numeric Promotion"
[Long 2012]	EXP03-J. Do not use the equality operators when comparing values of boxed primitives
	MET09-J. Classes that define an `equals()` method must also define a `hashCode()` method

■ 70. Understand the differences between bitwise and logical operators

The conditional AND and OR operators (`&&` and `||`, respectively) exhibit short-circuit behavior. That is, the second operand is evaluated only when the result of the conditional operator cannot be deduced solely by evaluating the first operand. Consequently, when the result of the conditional operator *can* be deduced solely from the result of the first operand, the second operand will remain unevaluated; its side effects, if any, will never occur.

The bitwise AND and OR operators (`&` and `|`) lack short-circuit behavior. Similar to most Java operators, they evaluate both operands. They return the same Boolean results as `&&` and `||` respectively, but can have different overall effects depending on the presence or absence of side effects in the second operand.

Consequently, either the & or the && operator can be used when performing Boolean logic. However, there are times when the short-circuiting behavior is preferred and other times when the short-circuiting behavior causes subtle bugs.

Noncompliant Code Example (Improper &)

This noncompliant code example, derived from Flanagan [Flanagan 2005], has two variables with unknown values. The code must validate its data, and then check whether array[i] is a valid index.

```
int array[]; // May be null
int i;       // May be an invalid index for array
if (array != null & i >= 0 &
    i < array.length & array[i] >= 0) {
  // Use array
} else {
  // Handle error
}
```

This code can fail as a result of the same errors it is trying to prevent. When array is NULL or i is not a valid index, the reference to array and array[i] will cause either a NullPointerException or an ArrayIndexOutOfBoundsException to be thrown. The exception occurs because the & operator fails to prevent evaluation of its right operand, even when evaluation of its left operand proves that the right operand is inconsequential.

Compliant Solution (Use &&)

This compliant solution mitigates the problem by using &&, which causes the evaluation of the conditional expression to terminate immediately if any of the conditions fail, thereby preventing a runtime exception:

```
int array[]; // May be null
int i;       // May be an invalid index for array
if (array != null && i >= 0 &&
    i < array.length && array[i] >= 0) {
  // Handle array
} else {
  // Handle error
}
```

Compliant Solution (Nested if Statements)

This compliant solution uses multiple if statements to achieve the proper effect.

```
int array[]; // May be null
int i;       // May be a valid index for array
if (array != null) {
  if (i >= 0 && i < array.length) {
    if (array[i] >= 0) {
      // Use array
    } else {
      // Handle error
    }
  } else {
    // Handle error
  }
} else {
  // Handle error
}
```

Although correct, this solution is more verbose and could be more difficult to maintain. Nevertheless, this solution is preferable when the error-handling code for each potential failure condition is different.

Noncompliant Code Example (Improper &&)

This noncompliant code example demonstrates code that compares two arrays for ranges of members that match. Here i1 and i2 are valid array indices in array1 and array2, respectively. Variables end1 and end2 are the indices of the ends of the matching ranges in the two arrays.

```
if (end1 >= 0 & i2 >= 0) {
  int begin1 = i1;
  int begin2 = i2;
  while (++i1 < array1.length &&
         ++i2 < array2.length &&
         array1[i1] == array2[i2]) {
    // Arrays match so far
  }
  int end1 = i1;
  int end2 = i2;
  assert end1 - begin1 == end2 - begin2;
}
```

The problem with this code is that when the first condition in the `while` loop fails, the second condition does not execute. That is, once `i1` has reached `array1.length`, the loop terminates after `i1` is incremented. Consequently, the apparent range over `array1` is larger than the apparent range over `array2`, causing the final assertion to fail.

Compliant Solution (Use &)

This compliant solution mitigates the problem by judiciously using &, which guarantees that both `i1` and `i2` are incremented, regardless of the outcome of the first condition:

```
public void exampleFuntion() {
  while (++i1 < array1.length &      // Not &&
         ++i2 < array2.length &&
         array1[i1] == array2[i2]){
    // Do something
  }
}
```

Applicability

Failure to understand the behavior of the bitwise and conditional operators can cause unintended program behavior.

Bibliography

[Flanagan 2005]	§2.5.6., "Boolean Operators"
[JLS 2013]	§15.23, "Conditional-And Operator &&"
	§15.24, "Conditional-Or Operator ||"

■ 71. Understand how escape characters are interpreted when strings are loaded

Many classes allow inclusion of escape sequences in character and string literals. Examples include `java.util.regex.Pattern` as well as classes that support XML- and SQL-based actions by passing string arguments to methods. According to the JLS, §3.10.6, "Escape Sequences for Character and String Literals" [JLS 2013],

> The character and string escape sequences allow for the representation of some nongraphic characters as well as the single quote, double quote, and backslash characters in character literals (§3.10.4) and string literals (§3.10.5).

Correct use of escape sequences in string literals requires understanding how the escape sequences are interpreted by the Java compiler, as well as how they are interpreted by any subsequent processor, such as an SQL engine. SQL statements may require escape sequences (for example, sequences containing \t, \n, \r) in certain cases, such as when storing raw text in a database. When representing SQL statements in Java string literals, each escape sequence must be preceded by an extra backslash for correct interpretation.

As another example, consider the `Pattern` class used in performing regular expression-related tasks. A string literal used for pattern matching is compiled into an instance of the `Pattern` type. When the pattern to be matched contains a sequence of characters identical to one of the Java escape sequences—"\" and "n", for example—the Java compiler treats that portion of the string as a Java escape sequence and transforms the sequence into an actual newline character. To insert a newline escape sequence, rather than a literal newline character, the programmer must precede the "\n" sequence with an additional backslash to prevent the Java compiler from replacing it with a newline character. The string constructed from the resulting sequence,

```
\\n
```

consequently contains the correct two-character sequence \n and correctly denotes the escape sequence for newline in the pattern.

In general, for a particular escape character of the form \X, the equivalent Java representation is

```
\\X
```

Noncompliant Code Example (String Literal)

This noncompliant code example defines a method, `splitWords()`, that finds matches between the string literal (`WORDS`) and the input sequence. It is expected that `WORDS` would hold the escape sequence for matching a word boundary. However, the Java compiler treats the "\b" literal as a Java escape sequence, and the string `WORDS` silently compiles to a regular expression that checks for a single backspace character.

```
public class Splitter {
  // Interpreted as backspace
  // Fails to split on word boundaries
  private final String WORDS = "\b";

  public String[] splitWords(String input){
    Pattern pattern = Pattern.compile(WORDS);
    String[] input_array = pattern.split(input);
    return input_array;
  }
}
```

Compliant Solution (String Literal)

This compliant solution shows the correctly escaped value of the string literal WORDS
that results in a regular expression designed to split on word boundaries:

```
public class Splitter {
  // Interpreted as two chars, '\' and 'b'
  // Correctly splits on word boundaries
  private final String WORDS = "\\b";

  public String[] split(String input){
    Pattern pattern = Pattern.compile(WORDS);
    String[] input_array = pattern.split(input);
    return input_array;
  }
}
```

Noncompliant Code Example (String Property)

This noncompliant code example uses the same method, splitWords(). This time
the WORDS string is loaded from an external properties file.

```
public class Splitter {
  private final String WORDS;

  public Splitter() throws IOException {
    Properties properties = new Properties();
    properties.load(new FileInputStream("splitter.properties"));
    WORDS = properties.getProperty("WORDS");
  }
```

```
public String[] split(String input){
  Pattern pattern = Pattern.compile(WORDS);
  String[] input_array = pattern.split(input);
  return input_array;
  }
}
```

In the properties file, the WORD property is once again incorrectly specified as \b.

WORDS=\b

This is read by the Properties.load() method as a single character b, which causes the split() method to split strings along the letter b. Although the string is interpreted differently than if it were a string literal, as in the previous noncompliant code example, the interpretation is incorrect.

Compliant Solution (String Property)

This compliant solution shows the correctly escaped value of the WORDS property:

WORDS=\\b

Applicability

Incorrect use of escape characters in string inputs can result in misinterpretation and potential corruption of data.

Bibliography

[API 2013]   Class Pattern, "Backslashes, Escapes, and Quoting"

                  Package java.sql

[JLS 2013]   §3.10.6, "Escape Sequences for Character and String Literals"

■ 72. Do not use overloaded methods to differentiate between runtime types

Java supports overloading methods and can distinguish between methods with different signatures. Consequently, with some qualifications, methods within a class can have the same name if they have different parameter lists. In method overloading, the method to be invoked at runtime is determined at compile time. Consequently, the overloaded method associated with the static type of the object is invoked even when the runtime type differs for each invocation.

For program understandability, do not introduce ambiguity while overloading (see Guideline 65, "Avoid ambiguous or confusing uses of overloading"), and use overloaded methods sparingly [Tutorials 2013].

Noncompliant Code Example

This noncompliant code example attempts to use the overloaded display() method to perform different actions depending on whether the method is passed an ArrayList<Integer> or a LinkedList<String>:

```
public class Overloader {
  private static String display(ArrayList<Integer> arrayList) {
    return "ArrayList";
  }

  private static String display(LinkedList<String> linkedList) {
    return "LinkedList";
  }

  private static String display(List<?> list) {
    return "List is not recognized";
  }

  public static void main(String[] args) {
    // Single ArrayList
    System.out.println(display(new ArrayList<Integer>()));
    // Array of lists
    List<?>[] invokeAll = new List<?>[] {
        new ArrayList<Integer>(),
        new LinkedList<String>(),
        new Vector<Integer>()};

    for (List<?> list : invokeAll) {
      System.out.println(display(list));
    }
  }
}
```

At compile time, the type of the object array is List. The expected output is Array-List, ArrayList, LinkedList, and List is not recognized (because java.util.Vector is neither an ArrayList nor a LinkedList). The actual output is ArrayList followed by List is not recognized repeated three times. The cause of this unexpected behavior is that overloaded method invocations are affected *only* by the compile-time type of their arguments: ArrayList for the first invocation and List for the others.

Compliant Solution

This compliant solution uses a single display method and instanceof to distinguish between different types. As expected, the output is ArrayList, ArrayList, LinkedList, List is not recognized:

```java
public class Overloader {
  private static String display(List<?> list) {
    return (
      list instanceof ArrayList ? "Araylist" :
      (list instanceof LinkedList ? "LinkedList" :
      "List is not recognized")
    );
  }

  public static void main(String[] args) {
    // Single ArrayList
    System.out.println(display(new ArrayList<Integer>()));

    List<?>[] invokeAll = new List<?>[] {
        new ArrayList<Integer>(),
        new LinkedList<String>(),
        new Vector<Integer>()};

    for (List<?> list : invokeAll) {
      System.out.println(display(list));
    }
  }
}
```

Applicability

Ambiguous uses of overloading can lead to unexpected results.

Bibliography

[API 2013]	Interface Collection<E>
[Bloch 2008]	Item 41, "Use Overloading Judiciously"
[Tutorials 2013]	Defining Methods

■ 73. Never confuse the immutability of a reference with that of the referenced object

Immutability helps to support security reasoning. It is safe to share immutable objects without risking modification by the recipient [Mettler 2010].

Programmers often incorrectly assume that declaring a field or variable final makes the referenced object immutable. Declaring variables that have a primitive type to be final does prevent changes to their values after initialization (by normal Java processing). However, when the variable has a reference type, the presence of a final clause in the declaration only makes *the reference itself* immutable. The final clause has no effect on the referenced object. Consequently, the fields of the referenced object may be mutable. For example, according to the JLS, §4.12.4, "final Variables" [JLS 2013],

> If a final variable holds a reference to an object, then the state of the object may be changed by operations on the object, but the variable will always refer to the same object.

This also applies to arrays, because arrays are objects; if a final variable holds a reference to an array, then the components of the array may still be changed by operations on the array, but the variable will always refer to the same array.

Similarly, a final method parameter obtains an immutable copy of the *object reference*. Again, this has no effect on the mutability of the referenced data.

Noncompliant Code Example (Mutable Class, final Reference)

In this noncompliant code example, the programmer has declared the reference to the point instance to be final under the incorrect assumption that doing so prevents modification of the *values* of the instance variables x and y. The values of the instance variables can be changed after their initialization because the final clause applies only to the reference to the point instance and not to the referenced object.

```
class Point {
  private int x;
  private int y;

  Point(int x, int y) {
    this.x = x;
    this.y = y;
  }
```

```
  void set_xy(int x, int y) {
    this.x = x;
    this.y = y;
  }

  void print_xy() {
    System.out.println("the value x is: " + this.x);
    System.out.println("the value y is: " + this.y);
  }
}

public class PointCaller {
  public static void main(String[] args) {
    final Point point = new Point(1, 2);
    point.print_xy();

    // Change the value of x, y
    point.set_xy(5, 6);
    point.print_xy();
  }
}
```

Compliant Solution (`final` Fields)

When the values of the x and y instance variables must remain immutable after their initialization, they should be declared `final`. However, this invalidates the `set_xy()` method because it can no longer change the values of x and y:

```
class Point {
  private final int x;
  private final int y;

  Point(int x, int y) {
    this.x = x;
    this.y = y;
  }

  void print_xy() {
    System.out.println("the value x is: " + this.x);
    System.out.println("the value y is: " + this.y);
  }

  // set_xy(int x, int y) no longer possible
```

With this modification, the values of the instance variables become immutable and consequently match the programmer's intended usage model.

Compliant Solution (Provide Copy Functionality)

If the class must remain mutable, another compliant solution is to provide copy functionality. This compliant solution provides a clone() method in the class Point, avoiding the elimination of the setter method:

```java
final public class Point implements Cloneable {
  private int x;
  private int y;

  Point(int x, int y) {
    this.x = x;
    this.y = y;
  }

  void set_xy(int x, int y) {
    this.x = x;
    this.y = y;
  }

  void print_xy() {
    System.out.println("the value x is: "+ this.x);
    System.out.println("the value y is: "+ this.y);
  }

  public Point clone() throws CloneNotSupportedException {
    Point cloned = (Point) super.clone();
    // No need to clone x and y as they are primitives
    return cloned;
  }
}

public class PointCaller {
  public static void main(String[] args)
      throws CloneNotSupportedException {
    Point point = new Point(1, 2); // Is not changed in main()
    point.print_xy();

    // Get the copy of original object
    Point pointCopy = point.clone();
    // pointCopy now holds a unique reference to the
    // newly cloned Point instance

    // Change the value of x,y of the copy
    pointCopy.set_xy(5, 6);

    // Original value remains unchanged
```

```
        point.print_xy();
    }
}
```

The `clone()` method returns a copy of the original object that reflects the state of the original object at the moment of cloning. This new object can be used without exposing the original object. Because the caller holds the only reference to the newly cloned instance, the instance variables cannot be changed without the caller's cooperation. This use of the `clone()` method allows the class to remain securely mutable. (See *The CERT® Oracle® Secure Coding Standard for Java™* [Long 2012], "OBJ04-J. Provide mutable classes with copy functionality to safely allow passing instances to untrusted code.")

The `Point` class is declared `final` to prevent subclasses from overriding the `clone()` method. This enables the class to be suitably used without any inadvertent modifications of the original object.

Noncompliant Code Example (Arrays)

This noncompliant code example uses a `public static final` array, `items`:

```
public static final String[] items = {/* . . . */};
```

Clients can trivially modify the contents of the array, even though declaring the array reference to be `final` prevents modification of the reference itself.

Compliant Solution (Index Getter)

This compliant solution makes the array `private` and provides public methods to get individual items and array size:

```
private static final String[] items = {/* . . . */};

public static final String getItem(int index) {
  return items[index];
}

public static final int getItemCount() {
  return items.length;
}
```

Providing direct access to the array objects themselves is safe because `String` is immutable.

Compliant Solution (Clone the Array)

This compliant solution defines a `private` array and a `public` method that returns a copy of the array:

```
private static final String[] items = {/* . . . */};

public static final String[] getItems() {
  return items.clone();
}
```

Because a copy of the array is returned, the original array values cannot be modified by a client. Note that a manual deep copy could be required when dealing with arrays of objects. This generally happens when the objects do not export a `clone()` method. Refer to "OBJ06-J. Defensively copy mutable inputs and mutable internal components" [Long 2012], for more information.

As before, this method provides direct access to the array objects themselves, but this is safe because `String` is immutable. If the array contained mutable objects, the `getItems()` method could return an array of cloned objects instead.

Compliant Solution (Unmodifiable Wrappers)

This compliant solution declares a `private` array from which a `public` immutable list is constructed:

```
private static final String[] items = {/* . . . */};

public static final List<String> itemsList =
  Collections.unmodifiableList(Arrays.asList(items));
```

Neither the original array values nor the `public` list can be modified by a client. For more details about unmodifiable wrappers, refer to Guideline 3, "Provide sensitive mutable classes with unmodifiable wrappers." This solution can also be used when the array contains mutable objects.

Applicability

Incorrectly assuming that `final` references cause the contents of the referenced object to remain mutable can result in an attacker modifying an object believed to be immutable.

Bibliography

[Bloch 2008]	Item 13, "Minimize the Accessibility of Classes and Members"
[Core Java 2003]	Chapter 6, "Interfaces and Inner Classes"
[JLS 2013]	§4.12.4, "final Variables"
	§6.6, "Access Control"
[Long 2012]	OBJ04-J. Provide mutable classes with copy functionality to safely allow passing instances to untrusted code
	OBJ06-J. Defensively copy mutable inputs and mutable internal components
[Mettler 2010]	"Class Properties for Security Review in an Object-Capability Subset of Java"

■ 74. Use the serialization methods writeUnshared() and readUnshared() with care

When objects are serialized using the writeObject() method, each object is written to the output stream only once. Invoking the writeObject() method on the same object a second time places a back-reference to the previously serialized instance in the stream. Correspondingly, the readObject() method produces at most one instance for each object present in the input stream that was previously written by writeObject().

According to the Java API [API 2013], the writeUnshared() method

> writes an "unshared" object to the ObjectOutputStream. This method is identical to writeObject, except that it always writes the given object as a new, unique object in the stream (as opposed to a back-reference pointing to a previously serialized instance).

Similarly, the readUnshared() method

> reads an "unshared" object from the ObjectInputStream. This method is identical to readObject, except that it prevents subsequent calls to readObject and readUnshared from returning additional references to the deserialized instance obtained via this call.

Consequently, the writeUnshared() and readUnshared() methods are unsuitable for round-trip serialization of data structures that contain reference cycles.

Consider the following code example:

```
public class Person {
  private String name;

  Person() {
    // Do nothing - needed for serialization
  }

  Person(String theName) {
    name = theName;
  }

  // Other details not relevant to this example
}

public class Student extends Person implements Serializable {
  private Professor tutor;

  Student() {
    // Do nothing - needed for serialization
  }

  Student(String theName, Professor theTutor) {
    super(theName);
    tutor = theTutor;
  }

  public Professor getTutor() {
    return tutor;
  }
}

public class Professor extends Person implements Serializable {
  private List<Student> tutees = new ArrayList<Student>();

  Professor() {
    // Do nothing - needed for serialization
  }

  Professor(String theName) {
    super(theName);
  }
```

```
    public List<Student> getTutees () {
      return tutees;
    }

    /**
     * checkTutees checks that all the tutees
     * have this Professor as their tutor
     */
    public boolean checkTutees () {
      boolean result = true;
      for (Student stu: tutees) {
        if (stu.getTutor() != this) {
          result = false;
          break;
        }
      }
      return result;
    }
  }

  // ...

  Professor jane = new Professor("Jane");
  Student able = new Student("Able", jane);
  Student baker = new Student("Baker", jane);
  Student charlie = new Student("Charlie", jane);
  jane.getTutees().add(able);
  jane.getTutees().add(baker);
  jane.getTutees().add(charlie);
  System.out.println("checkTutees returns: " + jane.checkTutees());
  // Prints "checkTutees returns: true"
```

Professor and Student are types that extend the basic type Person. A student (that is, an object of type Student) has a tutor of type Professor. A professor (that is, an object of type Professor) has a list (actually, an ArrayList) of tutees (of type Student). The method checkTutees() checks whether all of the tutees of this professor have this professor as their tutor, returning true if that is the case and false otherwise.

Suppose that Professor Jane has three students, Able, Baker, and Charlie, all of whom have Professor Jane as their tutor. Issues can arise if the writeUnshared() and readUnshared() methods are used with these classes, as demonstrated in the following noncompliant code example.

Noncompliant Code Example

This noncompliant code example attempts to serialize data using writeUnshared().

```
String filename = "serial";
try (ObjectOutputStream oos = new ObjectOutputStream(new
        FileOutputStream(filename))) {
  // Serializing using writeUnshared
  oos.writeUnshared(jane);
} catch (Throwable e) {
  // Handle error
}

// Deserializing using readUnshared
try (ObjectInputStream ois = new ObjectInputStream(new
        FileInputStream(filename))){
  Professor jane2 = (Professor)ois.readUnshared();
  System.out.println("checkTutees returns: " +
                        jane2.checkTutees());
} catch (Throwable e) {
  // Handle error
}
```

However, when the data is deserialized using readUnshared(), the checkTu-tees() method no longer returns true because the tutor objects of the three students are different from the original Professor object.

Compliant Solution

This compliant solution uses the writeObject() and readObject() methods to ensure that the tutor object referred to by the three students has a one-to-one mapping with the original Professor object. The checkTutees() method correctly returns true.

```
String filename = "serial";
try (ObjectOutputStream oos = new ObjectOutputStream(new
        FileOutputStream(filename))) {
  // Serializing using writeUnshared
  oos.writeObject(jane);
} catch (Throwable e) {
  // Handle error
}
```

```
// Deserializing using readUnshared
try (ObjectInputStream ois = new ObjectInputStream(new
        FileInputStream(filename))) {
Professor jane2 = (Professor)ois.readObject();
System.out.println("checkTutees returns: " +
                        jane2.checkTutees());
} catch (Throwable e) {
  // Handle error
}
```

Applicability

Using the writeUnshared() and readUnshared() methods may produce unexpected results when used for the round-trip serialization of data structures containing reference cycles.

Bibliography

[API 2013]   Class ObjectOutputStream

                            Class ObjectInputStream

■ 75. Do not attempt to help the garbage collector by setting local reference variables to null

Setting local reference variables to null to "help the garbage collector" is unnecessary. It adds clutter to the code and can make maintenance difficult. Java just-in-time compilers (JITs) can perform an equivalent liveness analysis and most implementations do so.

A related bad practice is the use of a finalizer to null out references. See *The CERT® Oracle® Secure Coding Standard for Java™* [Long 2012], "MET12-J. Do not use finalizers," for additional details.

This guideline applies specifically to local variables. For a case where explicitly erasing objects is useful, see Guideline 49, "Remove short-lived objects from long-lived container objects."

Noncompliant Code Example

In this noncompliant code example, buffer is a local variable that holds a reference to a temporary array. The programmer attempts to help the garbage collector by assigning null to the buffer array when it is no longer needed.

```
{ // Local scope
  int[] buffer = new int[100];
  doSomething(buffer);
  buffer = null;
}
```

Compliant Solution

Program logic occasionally requires tight control over the lifetime of an object refer-enced from a local variable. In the unusual cases where such control is necessary, use a lexical block to limit the scope of the variable, because the garbage collector can collect the object immediately when it goes out of scope [Bloch 2008].

This compliant solution uses a lexical block to control the lifetime of the buffer object:

```
{ // Limit the scope of buffer
  int[] buffer = new int[100];
  doSomething(buffer);
}
```

Applicability

It is unnecessary to set local reference variables to null when they are no longer needed in a mistaken attempt to help the garbage collector reclaim the associated memory.

Bibliography

[Bloch 2008]   Item 6, "Eliminate Obsolete Object References"
[Long 2012]   MET12-J. Do not use finalizers

Appendix  A

Android

This appendix describes the applicability of the guidelines in this book to developing Java apps for the Android platform.

Guideline	Applicability
1. Limit the lifetime of sensitive data	Applicable[1]
2. Do not store unencrypted sensitive information on the client side	Applicable
3. Provide sensitive mutable classes with unmodifiable wrappers	Unknown
4. Ensure that security-sensitive methods are called with validated arguments	Applicable in principle[2]
5. Prevent arbitrary file upload	Applicable in principle
6. Properly encode or escape output	Applicable in principle
7. Prevent code injection	Applicable in principle[3]
8. Prevent XPath injection	Applicable
9. Prevent LDAP injection	Applicable in principle[4]

1. The noncompliant code example is more difficult to exploit on Dalvik because each app executes in its own Dalvik VM, making the string object more difficult to access from other apps.

2. On Android, `AccessControlContext()` is not available.

3. `ScriptEngineManager` is not included in the Android SDK.

4. Applicable in principle for Android apps that try to implement their own LDAP.

Guideline	Applicability
10. Do not use the `clone()` method to copy untrusted method parameters	Applicable
11. Do not use `Object.equals()` to compare cryptographic keys	Applicable
12. Do not use insecure or weak cryptographic algorithms	Applicable
13. Store passwords using a hash function	Applicable
14. Ensure that `SecureRandom` is properly seeded	Applicable
15. Do not rely methods that can be overridden by untrusted code	Applicable
16. Avoid granting excess privileges	Not applicable[5]
17. Minimize privileged code	Not applicable[6]
18. Do not expose methods that use reduced-security checks to untrusted code	Not applicable
19. Define custom security permissions for fine-grained security	Not applicable
20. Create a secure sandbox using a security manager	Not applicable
21. Do not let untrusted code misuse privileges of callback methods	Unknown
22. Minimize the scope of variables	Applicable
23. Minimize the scope of the `@SuppressWarnings` annotation	Applicable
24. Minimize the accessibility of classes and their members	Applicable
25. Document thread-safety and use annotations where applicable	Applicable
26. Always provide feedback about the resulting value of a method	Applicable
27. Identify files using multiple file attributes	Applicable in principle[7]
28. Do not attach significance to the ordinal associated with an enum	Applicable
29. Be aware of numeric promotion behavior	Applicable
30. Enable compile-time type checking of variable arity parameter types	Applicable
31. Do not apply public final to constants whose value might change in later releases	Applicable

5. Android doesn't use `AccessController`.

6. Android doesn't use `AccessController`.

7. On Android, `openFileOutput()` and `openFileInput()` are preferred for file I/O.

Guideline	Applicability
32. Avoid cyclic dependencies between packages	Applicable
33. Prefer user-defined exceptions over more general exception types	Applicable
34. Try to gracefully recover from system errors	Applicable
35. Carefully design interfaces before releasing them	Applicable
36. Write garbage collection–friendly code	Applicable
37. Do not shadow or obscure identifiers in subscopes	Applicable
38. Do not declare more than one variable per declaration	Applicable
39. Use meaningful symbolic constants to represent literal values in program logic	Applicable
40. Properly encode relationships in constant definitions	Applicable
41. Return an empty array or collection instead of a null value for methods that return an array or collection	Applicable
42. Use exceptions only for exceptional conditions	Applicable
43. Use a `try`-with-resources statement to safely handle closeable resources	Not applicable[8]
44. Do not use assertions to verify the absence of runtime errors	Applicable in principle[9]
45. Use the same type for the second and third operands in conditional expressions	Applicable
46. Do not serialize direct handles to system resources	Applicable
47. Prefer using iterators over enumerations	Applicable
48. Do not use direct buffers for short-lived, infrequently used objects	Applicable
49. Remove short-lived objects from long-lived container objects	Applicable
50. Be careful using visually misleading identifiers and literals	Applicable
51. Avoid ambiguous overloading of variable arity methods	Applicable
52. Avoid in-band error indicators	Applicable
53. Do not perform assignments in conditional expressions	Applicable
54. Use braces for the body of an `if`, `for`, or `while` statement	Applicable
55. Do not place a semicolon immediately following an `if`, `for`, or `while` condition	Applicable

---

8. The Android SDK currently does not support Java7, so `try`-with-resources is not available on Android.

9. On Android, `assert()` is ignored by default.

Guideline	Applicability
56. Finish every set of statements associated with a `case` label with a `break` statement	Applicable
57. Avoid inadvertent wrapping of loop counters	Applicable
58. Use parentheses for precedence of operation	Applicable
59. Do not make assumptions about file creation	Applicable in principle[10]
60. Convert integers to floating-point for floating-point operations	Applicable
61. Ensure that the `clone()` method calls `super.clone()`	Applicable
62. Use comments consistently and in a readable fashion	Applicable
63. Detect and remove superfluous code and values	Applicable
64. Strive for logical completeness	Applicable
65. Avoid ambiguous or confusing uses of overloading	Applicable
66. Do not assume that declaring a reference volatile guarantees safe publication of the members of the referenced object	Applicable
67. Do not assume that the `sleep()`, `yield()`, or `getState()` methods provide synchronization semantics	Applicable
68. Do not assume that the remainder operator always returns a nonnegative result for integral operands	Applicable
69. Do not confuse abstract object equality with reference equality	Applicable
70. Understand the differences between bitwise and logical operators	Applicable
71. Understand how escape characters are interpreted when strings are loaded	Applicable
72. Do not use overloaded methods to differentiate between runtime types	Applicable
73. Never confuse the immutability of a reference with that of the referenced object	Applicable
74. Use the serialization methods `writeUnshared()` and `readUnshared()` with care	Applicable
75. Do not attempt to help the garbage collector by setting local reference variables to `null`	Applicable

---

10. On Android, `java.nio.file` is not available.

Glossary

atomicity When applied to an operation on primitive data, indicates that other threads that might access the data might see the data as it exists before the operation occurs or after the operation has completed, but may never see an intermediate value of the data.

canonicalization Reducing the input to its equivalent simplest known form.

class variable "A *class variable* is a field declared using the keyword `static` within a class declaration, or with or without the keyword `static` within an interface declaration. A class variable is created when its class or interface is prepared and is initialized to a default value. The class variable effectively ceases to exist when its class or interface is unloaded" [JLS 2013, §4.12.3, "Kinds of Variables"].

condition predicate An expression constructed from the state variables of a class that must be true for a thread to continue execution. The thread pauses execution, via `Object.wait()`, `Thread.sleep()`, or some other mechanism, and is resumed later, presumably when the requirement is true and when it is notified [Goetz 2006].

controlling expression The top-level expression in the conditional expression of an `if`, `while`, `do... while`, or `switch` statement.

data race "When a program contains two conflicting accesses that are not ordered by a happens-before relationship, it is said to contain a *data race*" [JLS 2013, §17.4.5, "Happens-before Order"].

happens-before order "Two actions can be ordered by a happens-before relationship. If one action happens-before another, then the first is visible to and ordered before the second. . . . It should be noted that the presence of a happens-before relationship between two actions does not necessarily imply that they have to take place in that order in an implementation. If the reordering produces results consistent with a legal execution, it is not illegal. . . . More specifically, if two actions share a happens-before relationship, they do not necessarily have to appear to have happened in that order to any code with which they do not share a happens-before relationship. Writes in one thread that are in a data race with reads in another thread may, for example, appear to occur out of order to those reads" [JLS 2013, §17.4.5, "Happens-before Order"].

heap memory "Memory that can be shared between threads is called shared memory or heap memory. All instance fields, static fields and array elements are stored in heap memory. . . . Local variables, formal method parameters or exception handler parameters are never shared between threads and are unaffected by the memory model" [JLS 2013, §17.4.1, "Shared Variables"].

hide One class field hides a field in a superclass if they have the same identifier. The hidden field is not accessible from the class. Likewise, a class method hides a method in a superclass if they have the same identifier, but incompatible signatures. The hidden method is not accessible from the class. See the JLS, §8.4.8.2, "Hiding (by Class Methods)" [JLS 2013] for the formal definition. Contrast with override.

immutable When applied to an object, immutable means that its state cannot be changed after being initialized. An object is immutable if

- Its state cannot be modified after construction;
- All its fields are final; and
- It is properly constructed (the `this` reference does not escape during construction) [Goetz 2006].

It is technically possible to have an immutable object without all fields being `final`. `String` is such a class but this relies on delicate reasoning about benign data races that requires a deep understanding of the Java Memory Model.

liveness Every operation or method invocation executes to completion without interruptions, even if it goes against safety.

memory model "The rules that determine how memory accesses are ordered and when they are guaranteed to be visible are known as the memory model of the Java programming language" [Arnold 2006]. "A memory model describes, given a program and an execution trace of that program, whether the execution trace is a legal execution of the program" [JLS 2013, §17.4, "Memory Model"].

normalization Lossy conversion of the data to its simplest known (and anticipated) form. "When implementations keep strings in a normalized form, they can be assured that equivalent strings have a unique binary representation" [Davis 2008].

obscure One scoped identifier obscures another identifier in a containing scope if the two identifiers are the same but the obscuring identifier does not shadow the obscured identifier. This can happen if the obscuring identifier is a variable and the obscured identifier is a type, for example. See the JLS, §6.4.2, "Obscuring" [JLS 2013], for more information.

override One class method overrides a method in a superclass if they have compatible signatures. The overridden method is still accessible from the class via the `super` keyword. See the JLS, §8.4.8.1, "Overriding (by Instance Methods)" [JLS 2013], for the formal definition. Contrast with hide.

publishing objects "Publishing an object means making it available to code outside of its current scope, such as by storing a reference to it where other code can find it, returning it from a nonprivate method, or passing it to a method in another class" [Goetz 2006].

race condition "General races cause nondeterministic execution and are failures in programs intended to be deterministic" [Netzer 1992]. "A race condition occurs when the correctness of a computation depends on the relative timing or interleaving of multiple threads by the runtime" [Goetz 2006].

safe publication "To publish an object safely, both the reference to the object and the [state of the object] must be made visible to other threads at the same time. A properly constructed object can be safely published by:

- Initializing an object reference from a static initializer;
- Storing a reference to it into a volatile field or AtomicReference;
- Storing a reference to it into a final field of a properly constructed object; or
- Storing a reference to it into a field that is properly guarded by a lock" [Goetz 2006, §3.5 "Safe Publication"].

safety Its main goal is to ensure that all objects maintain consistent states in a multithreaded environment [Lea 2000].

sanitization Validating input and transforming it to a representation that conforms to the input requirements of a complex subsystem. For example, a database may require all invalid characters to be escaped or eliminated before their storage. Input sanitization is the elimination of unwanted characters from the input by means of removing, replacing, encoding, or escaping the characters.

security flaw A software defect that poses a potential security risk [Seacord 2013].

sensitive code Any code that performs operations that would be forbidden to untrusted code. Also, any code that accesses *sensitive data*. For example, code whose correct operation requires enhanced privileges is typically considered to be sensitive.

sensitive data Any data that must be kept secure. Consequences of this security requirement include the following:

- Untrusted code is forbidden to access sensitive data
- Trusted code is forbidden to leak sensitive data to untrusted code

Examples of sensitive data include passwords and personally identifiable information.

shadow One scoped identifier shadows another identifier in a containing scope if the two identifiers are the same, and they both reference variables. They may also both reference methods or types. The shadowed identifier is not accessible in the scope of the shadowing identifier. See the JLS, §6.4.1, "Shadowing" [JLS 2013], for more information. Contrast with obscure.

synchronization "The Java programming language provides multiple mechanisms for communicating between threads. The most basic of these methods is *synchronization*, which is implemented using monitors. Each object in Java is associated with a monitor, which a thread can lock or unlock. Only one thread at a time may hold a lock on a monitor. Any other threads attempting to lock that monitor are blocked until they can obtain a lock on that monitor" [JLS 2013, §17.1, "Synchronization"].

thread-safe An object is thread-safe if it can be shared by multiple threads without the possibility of any data races. "A thread-safe object performs synchronization internally, so multiple threads can freely access it through its public interface without further synchronization" [Goetz 2006]. Immutable classes are thread-safe by definition. Mutable classes may also be thread-safe if they are properly synchronized.

trusted code Code that is loaded by the primordial class loader regardless of whether or not it constitutes the Java API. In this text, this meaning is extended to include code that is obtained from a known entity and given permissions that untrusted code lacks. By this definition, untrusted and trusted code can coexist in the namespace of a single class loader (not necessarily the primordial class loader). In such cases, the security policy must make this distinction clear by assigning appropriate privileges to trusted code while denying the same from untrusted code.

untrusted code   Code of unknown origin that can potentially cause some harm when executed. Untrusted code may not always be malicious, but it is usually hard to determine automatically. Consequently, untrusted code should be run in a sandboxed environment.

volatile   "A write to a volatile field happens-before every subsequent read of that field" [JLS 2013, §17.4.5, "Happens-before Order"]. "Operations on the master copies of volatile variables on behalf of a thread are performed by the main memory in exactly the order that the thread requested" [JVMSpec 1999]. Accesses to a `volatile` variable are sequentially consistent, which also means that the operations are exempt from compiler optimizations. Declaring a variable `volatile` ensures that all threads see the most up-to-date value of the variable if any thread modifies it. Volatile guarantees atomic reads and writes of primitive values, but it does not guarantee the atomicity of composite operations such as variable incrementation (read-modify-write sequence).

vulnerability   "A set of conditions that allows an attacker to violate an explicit or implicit security policy" [Seacord 2013].

References

[**Allen 2000**] Vermeulen, Allan, Scott W. Ambler, Greg Bumgardner, Eldon Metz, Trevor Misfeldt, Jim Shur, and Patrick Thompson. *The Elements of Java™ Style*. New York, NY: Cambridge University Press (2000).

[**Apache 2013**] Apache Tika: A Content Analysis Toolkit. The Apache Software Foundation (2013). http://tika.apache.org/index.html

[**API 2006**] Java™ Platform, Standard Edition 6 API Specification. Oracle (2006/2011). http://docs.oracle.com/javase/6/docs/api/

[**API 2013**] Java™ Platform, Standard Edition 7 API Specification. Oracle (2013). http://docs.oracle.com/javase/7/docs/api/index.html

[**Arnold 2006**] Arnold, Ken, James Gosling, and David Holmes. *The Java™ Programming Language, Fourth Edition*. Boston, MA: Addison-Wesley (2006).

[**Bloch 2001**] Bloch, Joshua. *Effective Java™: Programming Language Guide*. Boston, MA: Addison-Wesley (2001).

[**Bloch 2005**] Bloch, Joshua, and Neal Gafter. *Java™ Puzzlers: Traps, Pitfalls, and Corner Cases*. Boston, MA: Addison-Wesley (2005).

[**Bloch 2008**] Bloch, Joshua. *Effective Java™: Programming Language Guide, Second Edition*. Boston, MA: Addison-Wesley (2008).

[**Campione 1996**] Campione, Mary, and Kathy Walrath. *The Java™ Tutorial: Object-Oriented Programming for the Internet*. Reading, MA: Addison-Wesley (1996).

[**Chan 1998**] Chan, Patrick, Rosanna Lee, and Douglas Kramer. *The Java™ Class Libraries: Supplement for the Java™ 2 Platform, Volume 1, Second Edition*. Upper Saddle River, NJ: Prentice Hall (1998).

[**Conventions 2009**] Code Conventions for the Java Programming Language. Oracle (2009). www.oracle.com/technetwork/java/codeconv-138413.html

[**Coomes 2007**] Coomes, John, Peter Kessler, and Tony Printezis. "Garbage Collection–Friendly Programming." JavaOne Conference (2007). http://docs .huihoo.com/javaone/2007/java-se/TS-2906.pdf

[**Core Java 2003**] Horstmann, Cay S., and Gary Cornell. *Core Java™ 2, Volume I: Fundamentals, Seventh Edition*. Upper Saddle River, NJ: Prentice Hall (2003).

[**Coverity 2007**] Coverity Prevent™ User's Manual (3.3.0). Coverity (2007).

[**Daconta 2003**] Daconta, Michael C., Kevin T. Smith, Donald Avondolio, and W. Clay Richardson. *More Java Pitfalls: 50 New Time-Saving Solutions and Workarounds*. Indianapolis, IN: Wiley (2003).

[**Davis 2008**] Unicode Standard Annex #15: Unicode Normalization Forms, ed. Mark Davis and Ken Whistler. Unicode (2008). http://unicode.org/reports/tr15/

[**ESA 2005**] *Java Coding Standards*. ESA Board for Software Standardisation and Control (BSSC) (2005). http://software.ucv.ro/~eganea/SoftE/JavaCodingStandards.pdf

[**FindBugs 2008**] FindBugs Bug Descriptions (2008/2011). http://findbugs .sourceforge.net/bugDescriptions.html

[**Flanagan 2005**] Flanagan, David. *Java™ in a Nutshell, Fifth Edition*. Sebastopol, CA: O'Reilly (2005).

[**Fortify 2013**] A Taxonomy of Coding Errors That Affect Security, "Java/JSP." Fortify Software (2013). www.hpenterprisesecurity.com/vulncat/en/vulncat/index.html

[**GNU 2013**] GNU Coding Standards, §5.3, "Clean Use of C Constructs." Richard Stallman and other GNU Project volunteers (2013). www.gnu.org/prep/standards/ standards.html#Syntactic-Conventions

[**Goetz 2004**] Goetz, Brian. Java Theory and Practice: Garbage Collection and Performance: Hints, Tips, and Myths about Writing Garbage Collection-Friendly Classes. IBM developerWorks (2004). www.ibm.com/developerworks/java/library/ j-jtp01274/index.html

[Goetz 2006] Goetz, Brian, Tim Peierls, Joshua Bloch, Joseph Bowbeer, David Holmes, and Doug Lea. *Java Concurrency in Practice*. Boston, MA: Addison-Wesley (2006).

[Goetz 2007] Goetz, Brian. Java Theory and Practice: Managing Volatility: Guidelines for Using Volatile Variables. IBM developerWorks (2007). www.ibm .com/developerworks/java/library/j-jtp06197/index.html

[Gong 2003] Gong, Li, Gary Ellison, and Mary Dageforde. *Inside Java™ 2 Platform Security: Architecture, API Design, and Implementation, Second Edition*. Boston, MA: Addison-Wesley (2003).

[Goodliffe 2007] Goodliffe, Pete. *Code Craft: The Practice of Writing Excellent Code*. San Francisco, CA: No Starch Press, (2007).

[Grand 2002] Grand, Mark. *Patterns in Java™, Volume 1: A Catalog of Reusable Design Patterns Illustrated with UML, Second Edition*. Indianapolis, IN: Wiley (2002).

[Grubb 2003] Grubb, Penny, and Armstrong A. Takang. *Software Maintenance: Concepts and Practice, Second Edition*. River Edge, NJ: World Scientific (2003).

[Guillardoy 2012] Guillardoy, Esteban. Java 0Day Analysis (CVE-2012-4681). (2012). http://immunityproducts.blogspot.com.ar/2012/08/java-0day-analysis-cve-2012-4681.html

[Hatton 1995] Hatton, Les. *Safer C: Developing Software for High-integrity and Safety-critical Systems*. New York, NY: McGraw-Hill, (1995).

[Hawtin 2006] Hawtin, Thomas. [drlvm][kernel_classes] ThreadLocal Vulnerability. MarkMail (2006). http://markmail.org/message/4scermxmn5oqhyi

[Havelund 2009] Havelund, Klaus, and Al Niessner. JPL Coding Standard, Version 1.1. California Institute of Technology (2009). http://lars-lab.jpl.nasa.gov/ JPL_Coding_Standard_Java.pdf

[Hirondelle 2013] Passwords Never Clear in Text. Hirondelle Systems (2013). www.javapractices.com/topic/TopicAction.do?Id=216

[ISO/IEC 9126-1:2001] *Software Engineering—Product Quality, Part 1, Quality Model* (ISO/IEC 9126-1:2001). Geneva, Switzerland: International Organization for Standardization (2001).

[ISO/IEC/IEEE 24765:2010] *Software Engineering—Product Quality, Part 1, Quality Model* (ISO/IEC/IEEE 24765:2010). Geneva, Switzerland: International Organization for Standardization (2010).

[JLS 2013] Gosling, James, Bill Joy, Guy Steele, Gilad Bracha, and Alex Buckley. The Java Language Specification: Java SE 7 Edition. Oracle America, Inc. (2013). http://docs.oracle.com/javase/specs/jls/se7/html/index.html

[JVMSpec 1999] The Java™ Virtual Machine Specification, Second Edition. Sun Microsystems, Inc. (1999). http://docs.oracle.com/javase/specs/

[Kalinovsky 2004] Kalinovsky, Alex. Covert Java™: Techniques for Decompiling, Patching, and Reverse Engineering. Indianapolis, IN: SAMS (2004).

[Knoernschild 2002] Knoernschild, Kirk. Java™ Design: Objects, UML, and Process. Boston, MA: Addison-Wesley (2002).

[Lea 2000] Lea, Doug. Concurrent Programming in Java™: Design Principles and Patterns, Second Edition. Boston, MA: Addison-Wesley (2000).

[Lo 2005] Lo, Chia-Tien Dan, Witawas Srisa-an, and J. Morris Chang. "Security Issues in Garbage Collection." STSC Crosstalk (2005). www.eng.auburn .edu/users/hamilton/security/papers/STSC%20CrossTalk%20-%20Security%20 Issues%20in%20Garbage%20Collection%20-%20Oct%a02005.pdf

[Long 2012] Long, Fred, Dhruv Mohindra, Robert C. Seacord, Dean F. Sutherland, and David Svoboda. The CERT® Oracle® Secure Coding Standard for Java™. Boston, MA: Addison-Wesley (2012).

[Manion 2013] Manion, Art. "Anatomy of Java Exploits," CERT/CC Blog (2013). www.cert.org/blogs/certcc/2013/01/anatomy_of_java_exploits.html

[McGraw 1999] McGraw, Gary, and Ed Felten. Securing Java: Getting Down to Business with Mobile Code, Second Edition. New York, NY: Wiley (1999).

[Mettler 2010] Mettler, Adrian, and David Wagner. "Class Properties for Security Review in an Object-Capability Subset of Java." Proceedings of the 5th ACM SIGPLAN Workshop on Programming Languages and Analysis for Security (PLAS '10). New York, NY: ACM (2010). DOI: 10.1145/1814217.1814224. http://dl.acm.org/ citation.cfm?doid=1814217.1814224

[Miller 2009] Miller, Alex. Java™ Platform Concurrency Gotchas. JavaOne Conference (2009).

[Netzer 1992] Netzer, Robert H. B., and Barton P. Miller. "What Are Race Conditions? Some Issues and Formalization." ACM Letters on Programming Languages and Systems 1(1):74–88 (1992). http://dl.acm.org/citation .cfm?id=130616.130623

[Oaks 2001] Oaks, Scott. Java™ Security. Sebastopol, CA: O'Reilly (2001).

[**Oracle 2010a**] Java SE 6 HotSpot™ Virtual Machine Garbage Collection Tuning. Oracle (2010). www.oracle.com/technetwork/java/javase/gc-tuning-6-140523.html

[**Oracle 2010b**] New I/O APIs. Oracle (2010). http://docs.oracle.com/javase/1.5.0/docs/guide/nio/

[**Oracle 2011a**] Java™ PKI Programmer's Guide. Oracle (2011). http://docs.oracle.com/javase/6/docs/technotes/guides/security/certpath/CertPathProgGuide.html

[**Oracle 2011b**] Java SE 6 Documentation. Oracle (2011). http://docs.oracle.com/javase/6/docs/index.html

[**Oracle 2011c**] Package javax.servlet.http. Oracle (2011). http://docs.oracle.com/javaee/6/api/javax/servlet/http/package-summary.html

[**Oracle 2011d**] Permissions in the Java™ SE 6 Development Kit (JDK). Oracle (2011). http://docs.oracle.com/javase/6/docs/technotes/guides/security/permissions.html

[**Oracle 2013a**] API for Privileged Blocks. Oracle (2013). http://download.java.net/jdk8/docs/technotes/guides/security/doprivileged.html

[**Oracle 2013b**] "Reading ASCII Passwords from an InputStream Example," Java™ Cryptography Architecture (JCA) Reference Guide. Oracle (2013). http://docs.oracle.com/javase/7/docs/technotes/guides/security/crypto/CryptoSpec.html#ReadPassword

[**Oracle 2013c**] Java Platform Standard Edition 7 Documentation. Oracle (2013). http://docs.oracle.com/javase/7/docs/

[**Oracle 2013d**] Oracle Security Alert for CVE-2013-0422. Oracle (2013). www.oracle.com/technetwork/topics/security/alert-cve-2013-0422-1896849.html

[**OWASP 2009**] Session Fixation in Java. OWASP (2009). https://www.owasp.org/index.php/Session_Fixation_in_Java

[**OWASP 2011**] Cross-site Scripting (XSS). OWASP (2011). www.owasp.org/index.php/Cross-site_Scripting_%28XSS%29

[**OWASP 2012**] "Why Add Salt?" Hashing Java. OWASP (2012). www.owasp.org/index.php/Hashing_Java

[**OWASP 2013**] OWASP Guide Project. The Open Web Application Security Project (OWASP) (2013). www.owasp.org/index.php/OWASP_Guide_Project

[**Paar 2010**] Paar, Christof, and Jan Pelzl. *Understanding Cryptography: A Textbook for Students and Practitioners*. Heidelberg, NY: Springer (2010).

[**Pistoia 2004**] Pistoia, Marco, Nataraj Nagaratnam, Larry Koved, and Anthony Nadalin. *Enterprise Java™ Security: Building Secure J2EE™ Applications*. Boston, MA: Addison-Wesley (2004).

[**Policy 2010**] Default Policy Implementation and Policy File Syntax, Document revision 1.6. Oracle (2010). http://docs.oracle.com/javase/1.4.2/docs/guide/ security/PolicyFiles.html

[**SCG 2010**] Secure Coding Guidelines for the Java Programming Language, Version 4.0. Oracle (2010). www.oracle.com/technetwork/java/seccodeguide-139067.html

[**Seacord 2009**] Seacord, Robert C. *The CERT® C Secure Coding Standard*. Boston, MA: Addison-Wesley (2009).

[**Seacord 2012**] Seacord, Robert C., Will Dormann, James McCurley, Philip Miller, Robert Stoddard, David Svoboda, and Jefferson Welch. *Source Code Analysis Laboratory (SCALe)* (CMU/SEI-2012-TN-013). Pittsburgh, PA: Carnegie Mellon University (2012). www.sei.cmu.edu/library/abstracts/reports/12tn013.cfm

[**Seacord 2013**] Seacord, Robert C. *Secure Coding in C and C++, Second Edition*. Boston, MA: Addison-Wesley (2013). See www.cert.org/books/secure-coding for news and errata.

[**SecuritySpec 2010**] Java Security Architecture. Oracle (2010). http://docs .oracle.com/javase/1.5.0/docs/guide/security/spec/security-specTOC.fm.html

[**Sen 2007**] Sen, Robi. Avoid the Dangers of XPath Injection. IBM developerWorks (2007). www.ibm.com/developerworks/xml/library/x-xpathinjection/index.html

[**Sethi 2009**] Sethi, Amit. Proper Use of Java's SecureRandom. Cigital Justice League Blog (2009). www.cigital.com/justice-league-blog/2009/08/14/proper-use-of-javas-securerandom/

[**Steinberg 2008**] Steinberg, Daniel H. Using the Varargs Language Feature. Java Developer Connection Tech Tips (2008). www.java-tips.org/java-se-tips/java.lang/ using-the-varargs-language-feature.html

[**Sterbenz 2006**] Sterbenz, Andreas, and Charlie Lai. Secure Coding Antipatterns: Avoiding Vulnerabilities. JavaOne Conference (2006). https://confluence.ucdavis .edu/confluence/download/attachments/16218/ts-1238.pdf?version=1&modificatio ndate=1180213302000

[**Sutherland 2010**] Sutherland, Dean F., and William L. Scherlis. "Composable Thread Coloring." In *Proceedings of the 15th ACM SIGPLAN Symposium on Principles and Practice of Parallel Programming (PPoPP '10)*. New York, NY: ACM (2010). http://dl.acm.org/citation.cfm?doid=1693453.1693485

[**Tutorials 2013**] The Java™ Tutorials. Oracle (2013). http://docs.oracle.com/javase/tutorial/index.html

[**Unicode 2013**] Unicode 6.2.0. Mountain View, CA: The Unicode Consortium (2013). www.unicode.org/versions/Unicode6.2.0/

[**Viega 2005**] Viega, John. *CLASP Reference Guide, Volume 1.1*. Secure Software, 2005.

[**W3C 2003**] The World Wide Web Security FAQ. World Wide Web Consortium (W3C) (2003). www.w3.org/Security/Faq/wwwsf2.html

[**Ware 2008**] Ware, Michael S. *Writing Secure Java Code: A Taxonomy of Heuristics and an Evaluation of Static Analysis Tools*. James Madison University (2008). http://mikeware.us/thesis/

[**Zadegan 2009**] Zadegan, Bryant. A Lesson on Infinite Loops. winJade.net (2009). http://winjade.net/2009/01/lesson-on-infinite-loops/

Index

Testing conformance to the CERT® secure coding standards

Software developers are often faced with the challenge of reconciling code quality with time and budget constraints. Ensuring that code conforms to the CERT® secure coding standards represents a significant investment that may be difficult to justify.

Let us help to ease the burden. Using our Source Code Analysis Laboratory (SCALe), we can test your source code for conformance to CERT secure coding standards. This process offers you a variety of benefits:

- You don't have to dedicate time and resources to analyzing the code yourself.
- If your software system passes conformance testing, you will be authorized to promote that version with the CERT Conformance Tested seal.
- Your conforming system will be listed in our online registry of certificates.
- You and your customers can feel confident in the quality of your code.

For more information about our work, visit the secure coding area of the CERT website:

www.cert.org/secure-coding

CERT is a registered mark owned by Carnegie Mellon University.

Addison
Wesley

Software Engineering Institute | Carnegie Mellon

SEI SERIES · A CERT® BOOK

THE CERT®
ORACLE® SECURE
CODING STANDARD
FOR JAVA™

FRED LONG | DHRUV MOHINDRA | ROBERT C. SEACORD
DEAN F. SUTHERLAND | DAVID SVOBODA

ISBN-13: 978-0-321-80395-5

"In the Java world, security is not viewed as an add-on feature. It is a pervasive way of thinking. Those who forget to think in a secure mind-set end up in trouble. But just because the facilities are there doesn't mean that security is assured automatically. A set of standard practices has evolved over the years. *The CERT® Oracle® Secure Coding Standard for Java™* is a compendium of these practices. These are not theoretical research papers or product marketing blurbs. This is all serious, mission-critical, battle-tested, enterprise-scale stuff."

—**James A. Gosling**, Father of the Java Programming Language

Books | eBooks | Video | Software
For more information and sample content,
visit informit.com/title/9780321803955

Available in print and eBook formats at informit.com
and other retail stores

ALWAYS LEARNING

PEARSON

75 RECOMMENDATIONS FOR
RELIABLE AND SECURE PROGRAMS

"A must-read for all Java developers."
— MARY ANN DAVIDSON, CSO, Oracle

JAVA
CODING
GUIDELINES

FRED LONG | DHRUV MOHINDRA | ROBERT C. SEACORD
DEAN F. SUTHERLAND | DAVID SVOBODA

Foreword by JAMES A. GOSLING, Father of the Java Programming Language

Safari
Books Online

FREE
Online Edition

Your purchase of *Java*™ *Coding Guidelines* includes access to a free online edition for 45 days through the **Safari Books Online** subscription service. Nearly every Addison-Wesley Professional book is available online through **Safari Books Online**, along with thousands of books and videos from publishers such as Cisco Press, Exam Cram, IBM Press, O'Reilly Media, Prentice Hall, Que, Sams, and VMware Press.

Safari Books Online is a digital library providing searchable, on-demand access to thousands of technology, digital media, and professional development books and videos from leading publishers. With one monthly or yearly subscription price, you get unlimited access to learning tools and information on topics including mobile app and software development, tips and tricks on using your favorite gadgets, networking, project management, graphic design, and much more.

Activate your FREE Online Edition at
informit.com/safarifree

STEP 1:   Enter the coupon code: WMABXAA.

STEP 2:   New Safari users, complete the brief registration form.
Safari subscribers, just log in.

If you have difficulty registering on Safari or accessing the online edition,
please e-mail customer-service@safaribooksonline.com